To John, who made it all possible

The Houses on the Green

Eileen Simkiss

ISBN: 978-1-897-66601-2

THE HOUSES ON THE GREEN

1820

Although Ardwick had been a distant village only forty years earlier, it was now joined to the town by continuous streets.

The Hall was still in existence but Ardwick was becoming a delightful suburb with elegant houses and an expanded Green with a lake in its centre which all contributed to its charm. Beyond the Green, there were few roads and few houses.

A stone had been placed at the corner of the Green, indicating that the distance into the town was exactly one mile. From this vantage point, mansions with gardens and hedge and tree bordered fields could be seen. To the south lay meadows and cultivated land divided by a long, winding country lane traversed by a brook with a narrow bridge.

Of the families in the area, thirty four were employed purely in agriculture, a figure which would not represent any great reduction from the numbers in earlier years. For some time before and for some years to come, the greater part of Ardwick's rapidly increasing population would find employment on the other side of the river in the ever expanding regions of trade and industry. However, at this time, local industry was restricted to a couple of dye works, which contaminated the previously clear water in the river and the brook, a brewery and a pin and paper factory. All these places of employment were within easy walking distance of the Green in the days when walking was the most usual method of transportation for the working man.

At the junction, where the milestone had been placed, there was, and still is, a small, roughly triangular piece of land. Bounded on one side by the major road to London, which had previously been a Roman road and on the other, by the road leading to the next village, the land was intersected by a country lane, forming the third side of the triangle.

At the point of the triangle nearest to the Green, there were three large residences surrounded by trees and gardens. Well away from the more affluent abodes, were three terraces of cottages for farm workers, each built around a pump. The smoke from these small, scattered communities was the only signs of man's habitation within the fields and meadows in contrast to the quiet majesty of the hills which encircled the landscape.

By 1883, the surrounding countryside had been almost completely obliterated by factories and a huge, sprawling railways goods yard and the view of the hills obscured by large buildings and smoke from factory chimneys. The Green itself was, however, still in existence although the lake had disappeared.

On the triangular piece of land, back to back dwellings for over six hundred families had been built.

Chapter 1

1954

William Whitehead was close to despair. Elbows on the table and head in hands, he tried to make some sense of his most recent meeting with George Turner at the Town Hall. The application to have his properties excluded from the compulsory purchase order seemed to have stalled completely. The red tape and bureaucracy surrounding the whole clearance scheme was complex and intimidating. No matter how many forms he completed and how many requests he made, he felt as though he was banging his head against a brick wall.

Just now, he felt that it was perhaps pointless to try and fight the system. The easy option would be to take the compensation. It would set him up nicely for the rest of his life. He could buy a small bungalow with a garden, somewhere a little further out of the city. There'd be no financial worries, no building maintenance and no roof repairs to deal with. He'd have time to do a bit more gardening, go out on more manoeuvres with the TA and generally take it easy. He rubbed his hand tiredly across his eyes.

Pretty as the picture he'd mentally just painted appeared, he knew it had no basis in reality. He sat up straight in his chair and pulled back his shoulders.

I won't give up. I'll fight them to the bitter end. They can't ride roughshod over William Whitehead. Surely the private individual has some rights, even in this day and age.

He looked around his comfortable home. There were some nice pieces; a couple of them inherited and a dresser he'd bought at auction after the war. He'd lived here a long time and would hate to leave. He was concerned too about his tenants.

"It must be getting to me at last," he muttered.

He had done as much as he could for the moment. The paperwork was all complete, pending a meeting of the Planning Committee within the next couple of months. He'd been advised unofficially that it would be extremely unlikely that a definite decision would be reached at that stage and it would be probably be several weeks before a final ruling was made. Even then, there was the possibility of an appeal and that could take several months more.

It was difficult to come to terms with the uncertainty, of not only his own future, but the future of the other tenants in the row.

He constantly walked the tightrope of trying to keep their spirits up while trying not to raise false hopes. It seemed pointless to let them know what had happened at the Town Hall today as he could see neither progress nor setback. Better leave it as it stood. They all knew the Planning Committee would be meeting soon, time enough to worry them further when the date was set and a formal decision reached.

A knock at the front door roused him from thought and as he went down the narrow hallway, he realised just how long he'd been sitting there. This was surely Mikey, who'd said he'd come at three o'clock. William flung the door open with a grand gesture, holding up his pocket watch. He looked at Mikey, then looked at the watch.

"Half a minute early, I see. Not good enough, young Mikey, perhaps I ought to close the door for another thirty seconds."

"Oh Uncle William, you're always telling me how important it is to be p.p.p.punctual."

He stumbled a little over the unaccustomed word.

"I'm here now and you know I'm dying to get that carpet from Mrs Gresty's. It's going to look smashing in my front room. It's red, with big coloured flowers round the edge and ever so thick."

William winced slightly at the description. He knew Mikey loved bright colours and was a bit of a magpie. He'd had to dissuade him several times from taking into his house every bit of old furniture that came his way, pointing out that there would soon be no room to move. But something so brightly coloured was irresistible to Mikey and William was prepared to give in gracefully for an item so obviously useful. A thick carpet of whatever colour would certainly keep the sitting room warmer during the winter months and William hoped wryly that Mikey would still be around in the winter to enjoy it.

"All right, my lad. Let's go next door and see how you're doing."

"Well, Uncle William, I've already rolled up the old carpet. I just need a hand to get it into the yard so the bin men can take it on Monday. I've already had a word and they said it's no trouble. They're already shifting so much rubbish from 'round here anyway."

"Well done. Let's have a look, shall we?"

They went up the short path to number three and through the front door, which Mikey had left ajar. The old carpet was neatly rolled and had been pulled into the kitchen at the back. Mikey had obviously swept the floor where the carpet had been and cleaned the surrounding area. William could see the brush and shovel and a bucket of water in the kitchen.

"You've done a grand job here, Mikey. We'll just lug this old carpet out and you can empty that bucket, just to be on the safe side. We don't want mucky water all over your new carpet, do we? Come on now, didn't you say Mrs Gresty would be waiting for us?"

"I said we'd be there between three and half past so I'm sure she'll be in."

There were few people around at this time of day and some of the houses were already boarded up and looking rather sad.

Mikey knocked politely on the door of an end terraced. Mrs Gresty gestured them into the front room. There were boxes everywhere, on top of sideboard and chairs, every surface had its own box and there were more piled on top of each other in the corners. Mrs Gresty looked hot and harassed. She tucked wisps of hair back up into the scarf she wore tied in a turban around her head and pulled her apron straight.

"Whatever will you think, Mr Whitehead, catching me in this state but I'm sure you understand, with the move an' all. The men'll be here at eight in the morning so I have to finish packing up tonight. These removal firms must be making a mint of money with so many families moving house. I'll be sorry to leave this place, I must say. I brought my family up here but we've no choice. They've given us a first floor flat out in Wythenshawe. I know it's all new and there's a lovely bathroom and trees and everything planted all around but you know, I'll miss this old place."

Mr Whitehead smiled sympathetically and Mrs Gresty continued in a rush,

"There's a row of new shops been built nearby and we'll only be a few minutes' walk from Wythenshawe Park. The flat's right near the bus stop and there's plenty of buses into town so Jim can get to work easy enough. 'Course we'll have the extra to find for the fares and he's not getting any younger. He'll have to leave home earlier in the morning and get home later at night and the new shops are all very well but you can bet that they'll be dearer than shopping at the market.

We won't know anybody either. Not like round here, where we've known most people for years. You know, my grandma lived in the next street and my own mother lived next to her and my kids ran in and out of their houses as though they were their own. I can't see

3

that kind of thing happening out at the new place. Still, it's all in the name of progress, I suppose"

"I suppose you're right," murmured William, giving her the opportunity to get it off her chest.

"You know, I'm glad the kids are all married. I wouldn't like to move out there into the back of beyond with a couple of teenagers on my hands. There's nothing for them to do out there and we wouldn't have the spare cash for them to be going into town every five minutes like they can from here. As it is, they live so far away from the new place we'll hardly see them. I can't expect them to go traipsing all that way very often with the kiddies, it'll cost a fortune."

She was becoming more and more agitated.

"And another thing, the rooms in the flat are ever so pokey, that's how Mikey comes to get this carpet. I've only had it a couple of years and there's no wear on it at all. It just won't fit anywhere, it's a crying shame, really. Still, I know it's going to a good home and Mikey will look after it, won't you love?"

"Course I will, Mrs Gresty. I'll take real good care of it."

"Well, Mr Whitehead. I suppose I'd better let you get on. Heaven knows, I've enough to do and Jim is hoping to get off work a bit earlier tonight to give me a lift. He rolled the carpet up first thing this morning, before we started stacking all these boxes and we'll have a bit more room when it's gone."

Mr Whitehead turned to Mrs Gresty and put out his hand. She wiped the dust off on her apron and shook his hand firmly. This kind of physical contact was not usual, even between neighbours, but under the circumstances it somehow seemed appropriate. Everything was different now and there was no other physical gesture William could make and keep within the proprieties of the neighbourhood.

"I can only wish you all the best, Mrs Gresty. Thank you so much for your kindness. We're going to miss you both and I hope you settle into this new place without too much trouble. You know that if you're ever down this way you'll be welcome to call in for a cuppa."

William could see that Mrs Gresty was on the verge of tears and he had to clear his own throat to speak. Best get on with it. There was no point in upsetting her, or himself, for that matter, and he gave Mikey a dig in the ribs.

"Come on then. Let's get cracking and let Mrs Gresty get on with her packing."

They bent and hoisted the carpet onto their shoulders. Mikey was obviously upset at the goodbyes and could only bob his head towards Mrs Gresty and mumble his thanks before he was marched out the front door by the speed of the moving carpet over Uncle William's right shoulder.

***

Judy was weary and worn from yet another fruitless search.

She'd found the address on the crumpled slip of paper only after walking up and down the narrow, cheerless streets of Lower Ardwick and asking directions. Misdirected twice, by the time she knocked on the peeling front door, she was already disheartened. Truth to tell, she didn't much fancy the look of the house. The front door opened straight onto the street and through the smeared windows, she could see that the net curtains at the bay window were yellowed and nicotine stained.

Some of the other houses in the street looked quite inviting, with crisp, clean curtains and smartly painted steps. However, the step upon which she was standing hadn't seen a coat of paint or a scrubbing brush for quite a while. She braced herself for disappointment as she heard shuffling steps coming down the lobby towards the front door. The door opened just a crack and she could see a pair of small, suspicious eyes sunken into a great doughy face.

"Well, what do you want?" said a voice sharply from behind the shabby door.

"Mrs Brown? I've... I've come about the rooms," she said haltingly, "Are they still free?"

The door opened just a little wider and Judy could see into the dark, squalid hallway, no more promising than the outside of the house.

"Come in, love," said the rather scruffy woman who'd opened the door in a slightly friendlier tone of voice.

"They're up at the top if you want to have a look. It's a long way up, so you'll probably have to carry her," gesturing at the toddler holding Judy's hand.

Judy slowly climbed the stairs. She'd become aware of the unsavoury smells wafting around the stairway, fried food and cigarettes, she thought. Ahead of her, she could see only the swaying of a huge backside in a stained and creased woollen skirt of indeterminate colour and the greasy ties of a large, soiled pinafore but she could hear the woman puffing and creaking up every step.

By the time they reached the top landing, Judy was almost ready to run for it. She may well have done so had she not been slogging up the stairs with a sturdy child in her arms.

"'Ere we are then," said the woman, throwing open a door with a flourish.

"This is it. It's only two rooms really, but it's nice and private, like."

Judy stepped inside and looked around the small, dark bedroom; just one narrow wardrobe and a chest of drawers with half the handles missing. Both had obviously been given a hasty coat of paint in the distant past but this was now badly chipped and the original paintwork was showing through. A double bed covered with a tattered counterpane was pushed against the wall, just about leaving room to move between the window and the bed, no room to swing a cat, really.

She walked back into the other room and looked around. A sagging old sofa was placed in front of a two bar electric fire, a small, rickety looking table and two spindly chairs and one corner was curtained off. She pulled back the greasy curtain to find two gas rings encrusted with burnt-on food, a square, stained sink with a dripping cold water tap and two coin meters, one for gas and one for electricity.

"Well, what do you think, love? Will it suit? It's ever so cheap and near the buses and everythink. 'Course the bathroom and lavvy is one flight down and you have to share with the other tenants. We had it put in the little bedroom a few years ago; saves going in the yard in the cold and the old tin bath in front of the fire."

By this time, Nina had wriggled to be put down and was looking around inquisitively. She climbed up onto the old sofa, knees first and turned to plonk herself down.

"There, look at that. She's made herself at home already. I know there's some as objects, but I don't mind childer mysen. Just don't let her run around on the landing, it echoes through the house some'at shameful."

Judy walked over to look through the window. All she could see was backyard after backyard with a narrow entry between this row and the one facing; dull grey slate roofs and outhouse after outhouse, no trace of anything growing except for a small, stunted tree at the very end of the row. She struggled to subdue the tears she could feel beginning to well in her eyes. She cleared her throat quietly and blinked hard a couple of times before she turned back to the woman.

"Well," she said, rather nervously. "I do have something else to look at this afternoon. Can I let you know?"

"Please yoursen. But don't blame me if it's gone when you come back. There's folk queuing up for digs all over the town. I won't have any trouble letting this and there's not many landladies round 'ere what'd welcome a child. But like I said, please yoursen."

By this time, Judy just wanted to be out of the house. She held out her hand and waited while Nina clambered down off the sofa.

"Come on, sweetheart," she whispered. "We've got to be going now."

She made her way down the stairs as quickly as she could, clutching Nina in her arms. She smiled weakly at Mrs Brown and said,

"I'll let you know as soon as I can," and hurried out of the front door. She could feel the woman's eyes boring into her back as she walked down the street and turned the corner. She stopped briefly and leaned against a gable end to catch her breath. The air in the cheerless streets seemed fresh in comparison with the atmosphere in the house, its odours still lingering in her nostrils.

Taking Nina's hand firmly in hers, she started her journey back towards the bus stop. The strain of the last two years was beginning to show in her face. She was only twenty three but sometimes she felt twice that. Dressed simply but neatly in slacks, a shirt and a hand knitted cardigan, her small, slender form seemed almost boyish until one caught sight of her face. Even though her hair had been pulled back into a severe pony tail, several strands had now escaped to soften the outline of her face with its pointed chin and high cheek bones. She didn't regard herself as pretty. In fact, when she thought about it, which was very seldom, she felt her eyes were her best feature; a light, clear grey set rather wide apart and fringed with dark lashes. She wore no make-up but her skin was clear and her pallor was emphasized by the dark, warm brown of her hair.

They reached a busy road and Judy thought that she could take a short cut to bring them to the bus-stop. They crossed and entered another maze of streets. Judy could see that some of the houses were empty and realised that they must be in a clearance area where houses were due to be demolished. In some rows, windows in several houses had been covered with corrugated iron but in others, all the houses were intact, obviously still occupied.

7

Nina was becoming fractious. She was tired too and was clamouring for the loo and Judy could feel her beginning to drag on her arm. She turned a corner and almost walked into a man carrying one end of a rolled up carpet. He was rather tall but wiry, maybe late forties, with a mass of steel grey hair and piercing blue eyes. Judy smiled at him and caught sight of the other end of the carpet, which was resting on the shoulder of a second man. Probably twenty five years younger, his round, fresh face beamed at her.

"I'm sorry, Miss" he said. "I must have startled you. Are you all right?"

Judy was embarrassed but she knew that Nina wouldn't let up even though she suspected that the nearest public toilet was in the park, five minutes' walk away. She could feel her face reddening but the older man just smiled at her.

Nina began to tug at Judy's hand and jiggle about.

"Mummy, mummy, want to go."

Only momentarily distracted by the novelty of two men with a carpet over their shoulders, she started squirming again, becoming more insistent,

"Mummy, *mummy*"

"Now then, miss, there's no need to worry. I live just at the end of this terrace and the child can gladly use my facilities, as it were."

His voice was gruff but kindly.

The young man at the other end of the carpet grinned furiously and pulled a face at Nina, who giggled and hid her face against Judy's legs.

"Come on, sweetheart. This nice gentleman will let us use his toilet."

It wasn't the first time that Nina had been the reason that Judy, who was usually so shy, was forced to make contact with total strangers. She was such an engaging little madam.

They reached the end of the terrace and stopped outside the house next to the last. The sun had broken through the clouds and everywhere looked much brighter.

"Look here, Mikey, just rest the carpet on the wall for a minute or two while I get these two young ladies sorted out."

He pulled his keys, which were fastened with a thin chain to his belt, from out of his pocket and went up the short path to the front door of the last house in the row. Judy could see that this house was a little larger and a little grander than the other four in the terrace although the whole row looked clean and neat and in a good state of repair.

"Come on in, my dear," said the grey haired gentleman. "Go on up the stairs. It's the first door on the left. I'll just go and help Mikey into the house with his new carpet."

He left the front door open and Judy and Nina made their way up the stairs. Although the bathroom was rather old fashioned, with a wooden box with a chain above the toilet and the bath on cast iron feet, the walls looked as though they had been freshly painted and a clean, striped towel hung on a wooden stand near the hand basin. The hand basin and the bath shined and the lino, which was partially covered by a square of carpet, had been polished to a high gloss.

As Judy came down the stairs with Nina once more in her arms, she couldn't fail to compare this house, with its smell of polish and clean walls and floor, with the hovel she'd just left. They'd just reached the foot of the stairs when William returned.

"You look rather tired, my dear, and I'm sure the child is too heavy for you. I hope you won't be offended if I offer you a cup of tea. I was going to make some anyway for Mikey and me. It's hard work carrying carpets and I hope you'll stay and join us."

After only a slight hesitation, Judy smiled gratefully,

"That would be lovely. I could really use a cup of tea just now."

"Come on through and we'll soon have you fixed up."

Judy put Nina down and they followed, down the carpeted hall and into a room at the back where the furniture shone in the afternoon sun. He gestured towards the settee.

"Do sit down and make yourself at home. It won't take a minute to put the kettle on."

Judy sat down on the large brown settee and pulled Nina onto her lap. She was happy just to sit for a minute and she hugged Nina to her tightly. She didn't usually talk to strangers and lacked confidence in her dealings with people.

She'd had a difficult, lonely time since Nina was born and had never been good at making casual conversation.

She heard the front door open again and footsteps down the hall. Mikey put his head around the door and smiled at her.

"Is the kettle on then?" he asked. "I'm s.s.s.spitting feathers."

Half an hour later found them talking together like old friends. Nina was sitting on Mikey's knee, playing with his fine, fair hair and giggling at the faces and funny noises he made. Judy had realised that

9

Mikey was, in official parlance, slightly educationally sub-normal. His speech was a little slow and he had a slight stammer. Unkind people probably referred to his being 'not quite a full shilling' but he was a kind boy, about twenty four, with an obviously cheerful disposition. He was clearly a favourite with Mr Whitehead, the man at whose table they were now sitting, drinking tea and eating biscuits. He was also a great hit with Nina and was keeping her amused with his antics, leaving Judy and Mr Whitehead free to carry on their conversation.

Judy was now feeling much better and had warmed to Mr Whitehead's old fashioned kindness. He wondered what she was doing in this neck of the woods and she found herself telling him about her disappointing search for lodgings.

"I live only about fifteen minutes from here up on Dickinson Road,' she told him 'but now Nina is getting bigger and more active, it's hard to keep her quiet. The landlady didn't seem to mind so much when she was a baby but now she's running around and chattering, she is constantly looking down her nose and has complained several times about the noise. I really must find somewhere else to live but so many people won't take children. On the other hand, I hate to be constantly "shushing" her. I don't want to break her spirit and so we go out every afternoon, in practically all weathers, so that she's tired enough to fall asleep quickly at night."

To her horror, she found her voice beginning to wobble and her eyes fill with tears. She swallowed a sob.

"I don't know why I'm telling you all this. You've been so kind and it's so long since I was able to talk to anybody, you seem to have caught me with my defences down."

Mr Whitehead leaned across the table and patted her hand.

"Don't you worry, my dear. I expect it's done you the world of good to get it off your chest. It must be hard for you to cope with the little lass all on your own."

She could hear the unspoken question, 'where's her father?' but he didn't ask and she didn't volunteer the information. Nina looked across at her mother and sensed that she was upset. She wriggled her way down from Mikey's knee and came across to her mother, resting her dark curly head on her lap. Judy stroked the child's hair absent-mindedly.

"Well, we really must be going. We still have to find the nearest bus stop and it will soon be rush hour."

"Now then, don't be in such a hurry. Let me make a fresh pot of tea and then I have a proposition which may be of interest to you."

He turned to Mikey.

"Mikey, just you cut along now and see if Miss Hartley's home from work yet. If she is, ask her if she would be kind enough to drop in here for a few minutes. I'll be round after tea to help you lay the carpet and perhaps I'll have some good news for you then."

Mikey rose from his chair and smiling and waving to Nina, went to the door.

"Righto, Uncle William. I'll go and see if she's in and then I'll see you later", he said in his slow way. With a last wave at Nina he left the room.

Mr Whitehead took the cups and saucers into the kitchen to rinse them and to re-fill the kettle and Judy lifted Nina onto her knee. She was beginning to tire now and settled down with her head against her mother's chest, thumb in mouth and Judy felt her breathing begin to deepen. It was always difficult if Nina became tired during the late afternoon. If she let her sleep, she would have to carry her to the bus stop and hope that she would be able to get her into bed without waking her. If she kept her awake, she'd become more and more fractious.

Mr Whitehead had just come back into the sitting room when they heard a brisk tapping at the front door.

"That'll be Miss Hartley," he said, going down the hallway to let her in. Judy could hear the murmur of voices coming toward the sitting room.

"How kind of you to come straight away, Margaret. I wouldn't normally have troubled you so soon after you got home from work but I need your help."

"Well, William," Judy heard a crisp, no-nonsense sort of voice respond, "I'll be only too happy to help, if I can. It's little enough I can do for you as a rule."

Mr Whitehead ushered a small, neat lady into the sitting room. She was probably somewhere in her early forties, smartly dressed in a navy blue suit, the severity of which was broken by a white blouse with a soft bow at the neck. She was wearing neat but sensible navy court shoes with a medium heel and her hair, which had probably been a rich auburn in her youth, was neatly coiled back into a French pleat. Just a touch of palest pink lipstick showed on her lips but her nose was powdered and a little discreet mascara had been applied to the eyelashes around her grey green eyes.

11

"Oh, I didn't realize you had company," she exclaimed as she saw Judy sitting in one of the straight backed chairs with little Nina cuddled against her but she smiled warmly before she turned to Mr Whitehead to ask,

"What can I do for you?"

"Well, Miss Hartley, first things first. Perhaps we could get the little lass settled in a more comfortable position before we start. Why don't you sit here?" he said, gesturing towards one of the chairs placed at the table.

He put a couple of cushions at the end of the big settee, carefully lifted Nina out of her mother's arms and gently laid her on the settee. He took Judy's cardigan, which she'd placed on the back of her chair, and carefully covered her with it so as not to disturb her.

"There," he said, "let's get some fresh tea made and then we can get down to business."

Back in the kitchen at the rear of the house, they could hear him filling the kettle and rattling the cups and saucers. Miss Hartley smiled at Judy, although she looked a little mystified.

"She's a lovely little girl. How old is she?"

"She's two and a bit and although she can be a handful at times, I wouldn't be without her for the world. She's very sweet tempered most of the time but she can get a bit cranky when she's tired."

"I expect that's normal. I can get a bit cross myself when I'm tired," said Miss Hartley, smiling understandingly.

"Have you known Mr Whitehead long?" she asked.

"Quite honestly, I met him only about an hour ago and I'm as puzzled as you are. I can't think what he wants to talk to us both about."

"I expect he has his reasons. I've known him a long time and underneath that stern exterior there's a heart of gold, although he wouldn't be too pleased to hear me say it."

Mr Whitehead came back into the sitting room balancing a tray with a fresh pot of tea and three cups and saucers. Judy was faintly amused by the courtly manner in which he treated Miss Hartley, asking her politely if she would be 'mother.' When all three had fresh cups of tea in front of them, Mr Whitehead leaned forward with his arms on the table.

"It's like this, my dear. The five houses in this row belong to me and I've rented them out for years. Mikey, you already know, lives next door and Miss Hartley here lives next door but one to him and then Mr and Mrs Goldman at the end. As you've probably realised, most of this area, from the Park and between the main roads up to Hyde and Stockport Road has been designated a slum clearance area and the Corporation are currently buying up most of the property under compulsory purchase orders.

Of course, this all takes time and they won't be able to start demolition until all the families have been re-housed. In the meantime, I'm still hoping to have my houses excluded from the purchase order. They're in good repair and have inside toilets and bathrooms and are just on the edge of the clearance area. It's a long, slow job and the officials at the Town Hall are far from easy to deal with."

He stopped briefly to take a sip of his tea while Miss Hartley smiled at him encouragingly. She appeared to have guessed his intentions and nodded at him to carry on.

"To come to the point," he said, "the house between Mikey and Miss Hartley is empty. Poor old Mrs Phelan died about six months ago. She was well into her eighties and we looked after her between us for as long as we could but after she fell and broke her hip, they whipped her off into hospital and, to cut a long story short, she never came out.

She'd lived here with her husband, John, since they married in the early nineteen hundreds. In fact, they were living here when I inherited the houses, and she stayed on after John died in the late forties. There was no family that we could trace. She never mentioned anybody, even when she was very old and rambling a bit. The solicitors advertised for relations but they've given up now. There was very little cash, just the contents of the house, which aren't worth much and which I'm entitled to dispose of now the house has been empty for so long."

He paused again while Judy and Miss Hartley waited for him to continue. By this time, Judy was absolutely fascinated.

"I can't take a tenant on a long let because I'm not sure what will happen with the Town Hall but I reckon we've several months until final decisions are made and before they start demolition, if the worst comes to the worst. Well, my proposal is this; how would you like to move in?"

Judy's heart surged with hope. She contemplated the bliss of a place of her own, the possibility of a bedroom to herself again, her own kitchen and bathroom. No more scurrying along passages and hallways between bathroom and bedroom, trying to keep Nina quiet, no more cooking on a couple of rings in a boxed-off corner;   it seemed to good to be true.

Just a moment, let's not get carried away here. I won't be able to afford it, I know I won't.

She could feel the disappointment seeping into her bones.

Mr Whitehead had mistaken the reason for her hesitation.

"I asked Miss Hartley to come in while I talked to you so that she could vouch for my respectability, as it were. She's been living here since 1942 and you can see that her reputation is above reproach," he said, turning to smile at Miss Hartley.

"Well, I'm sure our respectability speaks for itself and you've already met Mikey, who's a good hearted boy, but maybe you have someone you need to consult before you make a decision," she said enquiringly.

"No, there's no-one but me and Nina. I'd take your offer like a shot but I don't really think I can afford it. I'm struggling a bit for the rent on the rooms we're in now, never mind the rent for a whole house," she admitted honestly.

"Don't be too hasty," said Mr Whitehead. "The house is standing empty. It's completely furnished, even though the stuff is a bit old fashioned, and any rent I receive will be better than the place being empty. Old houses fall into disrepair very quickly if they're left unoccupied for any length of time. You'd be doing me a favour really. It would be an ideal solution for you and the little lass. It possibly wouldn't be permanent, that depends on the Town Hall, but it would give you at least a few months to make other, more suitable arrangements. If the worst should happen, the powers that be would have to offer to re-house you anyway."

Margaret interrupted encouragingly.

"Do consider it.   Things aren't ideal around here at the moment as more people move away but these five are lovely little houses and I'm sure we'd all make you welcome. It would be lovely to have a child around," she said wistfully. "Please think it over."

She stood up to leave, touching Judy briefly on the shoulder.

"I'll leave you and Mr Whitehead to talk over the details. Whatever you decide to do, please feel free to come and see me anytime. I'd love to see the baby when she's awake and we could have a chat and a cup of tea."

She left the room and they heard her brisk footsteps disappearing down the hallway. She let herself out, quietly closing the smartly painted door behind her, and walked down the short path into the street, past Mikey's house and Mrs Phelan's empty house and then up to her own front door.

As she fumbled in the pocket of her jacket for her door key, she was aware of the curtains in the house at the end of the row twitching slightly. Mrs Goldman was at the window again, watching the comings and goings in the street. Even though she knew she would receive no acknowledgement, she smiled and waved at the window, turned the key and went into her own house.

Chapter 2

Friday night again, they seemed to come around faster and faster as the years went by and then before she knew it, it was Monday morning and time for another slog through until Friday night.

Not that she didn't love her job; she knew that Mr Robinson relied on her. He often said that he didn't know how he'd manage without her but over recent months, more and more of the day-to-day running of the office had been falling on her shoulders. Mr Robinson came in a little late a couple of times a week and disappeared more frequently for a longer than usual lunch and then his office door remained closed for most of the afternoon.

On these afternoons he was curt almost to the point of rudeness if she had to disturb him. She had unwittingly fallen into the habit of screening his calls very carefully, not letting anyone disturb him unnecessarily and taking messages wherever possible. Appropriate action could be taken the following morning when Mr Robinson was more likely to be approachable.

She had to admit she was becoming worried. Other people were beginning to notice what was going on. Only yesterday, she'd overhead two of the pool typists in the ladies' on the third floor. Phrases such as 'seems to be losing his grip' and 'Margaret Hartley's holding the whole thing together,' wafted over the door of the toilet cubicle. She was almost tempted to wait in the cubicle until she heard them leave but knew they may stand there gossiping for ages.

She'd smoothed down her hair, flushed the toilet and pulled back the bolt with a firm hand. One of the girls at least had the grace to blush when they saw her emerging. The other one, who'd just finished her make-up, swiftly threw the paraphernalia spread out around the sink into her make-up bag, chucked the whole lot into her bucket bag and made a speedy exit with a sheepish smile. Over her shoulder, she urged her companion to hurry, muttering about old so-and-so being a tartar for time keeping so they'd better get a move on.

Human nature being what it is, people were sure to gossip. Internal politics were, after all, the lifeblood of an organisation which occupied one of the largest office buildings on Mosley Street.

Secrets were hard to keep and scandal was food and drink to most of the staff, particularly the girls in the typing pool and the men in the packing and dispatch department in the basement who were even more avid for the latest news from the upper floors.

If gossip was already being bandied around the typing pool, it was only a matter of time until what now seemed to be common knowledge would filter through to the upper echelons of the organization.

She felt so helpless. Events would now gain their own momentum and her desperate efforts to cover up would obviously not work for much longer. Still, it was Friday night, and there was nothing she could do now. Probably better to enjoy her weekend and see what happened on Monday.

She went straight up the stairs, took off her suit, hanging it carefully outside the wardrobe door, ready for pressing, and tossed the blouse into the linen basket in the corner.

Putting on a pair of old slacks and a loose blouse, she went downstairs to have her tea; cheese on toast, followed by a fruit tart. Then she'd spend an hour or so cleaning her house so that she would only have the washing to do in the morning.

She had her system worked out so that most of Saturday afternoon and evening were free. Sunday morning, she'd lie in bed half an hour longer but would be up and ready for church, leaving the house in good time for the service which started at ten.

***

There had been a time when routine had meant little to her and she had lived each day almost minute by minute, never knowing what the following day would bring. That had all ended with the telegram to tell her that David had been killed in action.

She had painfully put some kind of a life together for herself, relying on a strict timetable and keeping herself eternally busy to get her through the day until that, in itself, had become a way of life. Although many years had passed, the house was still full of memories of the time she'd spent there with David, the laughter and the passion, which she remembered unashamedly.

Perhaps if Judy did move into number five with the baby, that would bring some new life to the row. Judy was too young to look so careworn and perhaps she would welcome some female companionship and some help with Nina. They would have to wait and see. After all, there was nothing settled yet.

17

Now then, down to brass tacks," huffed Mr Whitehead. "What are you paying at the moment and how much notice do you have to give?"

"Twelve shillings a week – and I have to give a week's notice."

Judy was embarrassed to disclose her private affairs to a man who was all but a total stranger and she could feel the wretched blush beginning to rise in her cheeks for the second time that afternoon.

Mr Whitehead's businesslike manner helped to relieve her misgivings and she had to smile when he spluttered,

"How much? It's downright daylight robbery," said Mr Whitehead, smiling grimly. "I'd dearly love to give them a piece of my mind but I don't suppose that would help much."

Nina was still fast asleep, thumb in mouth, with that soft, angelic look particular to sleeping children. Her dark hair was tousled but she was resting comfortably on the big old settee.

"Now, now. Don't say anything else. I'm going to ask Mikey if he'll watch the little one for a few minutes while I show you the house. I won't be more than a minute or two."

Judy sat as though stunned when Mr Whitehead went next door. Was this really possible? What if she did take Mr Whitehead's offer and was able to give Nina some freedom, only to have to go back into rented rooms a few months later. Would that be worse than never having any freedom at all? Was the avoidance of that disappointment worth losing a chance to give her child some semblance of normality? Her thoughts were disjointed and she was undecided what to do. She wished she had someone to talk it over with.

Mr Whitehead returned with Mikey.

"Now look here, we'll just stand these two straight chairs with their backs to the settee so she won't roll off if she turns over. She seems sound asleep and will be safe enough with Mikey for a little while, won't she Mikey?"

"Course she will, Uncle William,' responded Mikey, looking very proud to be left in charge, even if only for a few minutes. 'I'll look after her and I won't move from this chair until you come back."

"I'll just get the keys," said Mr Whitehead, opening a cupboard in which Judy could see several sets of keys hanging on hooks, all neatly labelled.

"Here we are then, the sooner we go, the sooner we'll be back. Come along now."

They went out of the house and up the short path to the house next door but one.

"I haven't been in for a couple of weeks," said Mr Whitehead, "so it might be a little musty. Nothing half an hour with the windows open won't cure."

He opened the door and stepped back so that Judy could enter the house before him. She stepped straight into the front room, which was painted an old fashioned rose colour.

"As you can see," said Mr Whitehead, "the rest of the houses are not as big as mine. They're tiny really but many a large family has been brought up in a house this size. I believe that mine was built as a manager's house, which is why it's a little grander, while the rest of them were just for working men."

Judy looked around. Although the furniture was old, it had been well looked after. A sideboard against the back wall had obviously been regularly polished although it currently showed a fine layer of dust. There was a small, well stuffed sofa and two matching armchairs. In the chimney breast was a fireplace with a black leaded and tiled surround and a mantelpiece with candlesticks. Above the fireplace hung a photo of a couple in a wooden frame. The dark haired, pretty woman in a long, smoothly draped white dress, with flowers in her hair was holding a bouquet of flowers in her right hand while her left hand, with the wedding ring prominently displayed, was delicately balanced on her knee. A large, handsome man, with centre parted hair and a trim little moustache towered next to her, hand protectively placed on her shoulder.

"Is that Mr and Mrs Phelan?"

"Yes, it is and I don't think it's been off that wall since the day she brought it home. Come along now and we'll have a look at the kitchen."

They went through to the back of the house, passing the stairs which ran up between the two rooms.

"Here we are. You see, it's quite habitable."

There was an array of cupboards, a sink and a gas cooker. A tiny fireplace had been built across one corner and there was a heavy wooden table and chairs against the wall under the window. Best of all, an old wooden rocking chair had been placed in front of the

19

fireplace, with a hand crocheted, highly coloured blanket folded across the back.

Against her better judgement, Judy felt her hopes beginning to rise.

"Follow me," and Mr Whitehead led the way up the steep stairs to the first floor. He stepped into the front bedroom. It was furnished very plainly but the wooden furniture had been lovingly cared for and would need little work to bring it back to a full shine. There was a large bed with a polished headboard and the mattress was covered with a dust sheet. A rag rug on either side of the bed would protect bare feet from the linoleum below.

"This way now," said Mr Whitehead and stepped across the tiny landing towards the back of the house.

"As you can see, the back bedroom has been split in two to make a bathroom. Although it's small, it has everything you need and this room would be fine for the little lass.'

Judy looked around. There was just a simple wardrobe and a chest of drawers, both painted white, and a narrow, single bed. She stepped to the window and looked out. There was a fairly large yard to the rear, surrounded by a brick wall, with a gate into the street at the back. Mrs Phelan had obviously had green fingers and had made a little garden. The flower beds showed signs of neglect, with weeds springing up through the plants, but the garden had been lovingly tended and carefully planted and new growth could be seen in the borders. It needed tidying up but Judy could just imagine little Nina out there playing, safe and free.

Mr Whitehead cleared his throat. He was obviously none too happy being in such intimate circumstances with a lady, even if she were young enough to be his daughter.

"Shall we go downstairs?" he asked.

Back down the stairs in the sitting room, he gestured towards a chair. Judy sat down, even though she was now becoming a little anxious about having left Nina with Mikey for so long.

"Well, you must have gathered that my name is William Whitehead but it seems strange that I don't know yours. You've been sitting drinking tea in my house while your little lass made free with my settee and I don't even know your name."

"My name's Judy Minshull," she responded, "and before we go any further, although I was married when Nina was born, I haven't seen her father since she was about three weeks old. He didn't seem able to cope with a baby and when I came back from the shops one day, I found he'd packed his bags and left. He did leave me a note saying he was sorry but I haven't seen him since, although he does send money now and then to help with Nina."

'It's really none of my business and of course I don't want to pry but naturally, I did wonder. However, that's all by the by. Let's get down to business. May I call you Judy?"

Judy nodded, smiling.

"Now then, Judy, this is what I propose. As I said, the house has been empty for some time and it's difficult to let, under the circumstances. If you want it until I manage to clear things up finally with the Town Hall, I would suggest a rent of ten shillings per week, which is a bit less than you're paying now, I know. However, in a way, you'll be doing me a favour because I don't want it standing empty and it might have some influence with the 'powers that be' if the whole row is occupied. I'm prepared to take a chance on you, provided you're prepared to take a chance on me. What do you say?"

Despite her previous misgivings, Judy made a sudden decision.

"Yes. I'd love it. It will give Nina and me a chance of some kind of normal life, for a few months at least. I'm not sure you're being altogether fair to yourself with the rent but who am I to look a gift horse in the mouth."

"Good, that's settled then. If you're not altogether happy with the rent, let's go on the present agreement and then review the situation, say in six months' time. Who know what might happen by then? Let's go and tell Mikey the good news. He has no idea what's going on, poor lad."

Judy took one last, proprietorial look around the front room and pulled the door closed behind her, anxious now to get back to Nina.

As they opened the door of number one, she was surprised to hear voices from the back room. She hurried down the hall and found Mikey, with Nina on his knee, chanting a nursery rhyme, which had Nina chortling and nodding her head. She knew that they spent too much time alone together but she couldn't help a sudden pang to see Nina so happy with someone else, a thought she tried to suppress.

Mikey handed Nina over to Judy with one of his broad beams which became broader and broader as Mr Whitehead explained that Judy and Nina would be moving in next door to him, and very soon at that.

"Well, that's really grand," he said in his slow way. "That's really grand. Could I come and see her sometimes? She's such a little love."

"Of course you can,' said Judy warmly, responding to the kindness in the boy's eyes and his obvious pleasure at their news. "You'll be able to see her often and she's really taken to you. She's usually not very good with strangers."

"Do you really think so?" asked Mikey, pleased at the implied compliment.

"Of course, you'll soon be great pals. You've made such a good start with her."

"Oh, I hope you're right. When are you moving in?" said Mikey, anxious to get on with things.

"Now then, Mikey, we can't rush things. Judy here has to give one week's notice at her present digs and she has to pack up her stuff and move in. Perhaps we could help her with that," broke in Mr Whitehead.

"It's getting late now, my dear. I'm afraid you'll have a long wait at the bus stop at this time of night and the little lass must be getting hungry. Why not wait another half hour or so? I'll make you both a sandwich and then I'll run you home."

"I really don't want to impose you any further. You've already been so kind that I don't know how to thank you."

Mr Whitehead could see that Judy was now struggling with her pride, torn between accepting even more help from him and the probability that the child would become hungry and fractious before she got her home.

"I've got an even better idea. Why don't we send young Mikey here round to the chip shop and then we'll all have tea together."

"Oh yes, let's do that. I'll go round to the chippy, Uncle William. If it's Mrs Johnson that serves me, she always puts in some scratchings. She's very nice, is Mrs Johnson."

Mr Whitehead looked at Judy enquiringly.

"If you're sure it's no bother. I'll have fish, chips and peas and Nina can have some of mine."

She fished out her purse, looking at Mr Whitehead almost defiantly, and gave Mikey some money. Mr Whitehead didn't react.

"Here's ten bob, young Mikey. I'll have the same and you can have whatever you fancy. I'll treat you but I'd cut along now, you know they're always busy on Fridays."

Mikey struggled into his jacket and set off at a gallop down the hall.

"I'll just warm the plates and cut some bread and butter. Perhaps you'd like to take Nina upstairs and wash her hands and face," said Mr Whitehead tactfully, and disappeared into the kitchen.

Fifteen minutes later, they were sitting round the table. Fish and chips it may have been but Judy couldn't remember enjoying a meal more. Although she had Nina perched on her knee, she was managing to tuck in and Mr Whitehead had given Nina a small, patterned tea plate with her own little portion, with instructions that she should eat up so that she could see the picture on the plate. The child must have been famished. She was waving a small fork in one hand and a piece of bread and butter in the other, for once too busy to chatter.

After tea, Mr Whitehead looked at Judy.

"I'll just bring the car round to the front. Mikey will wash up, won't you Mikey? I want to get these two ladies home now. It must be near Nina's bedtime and don't forget, you'll be seeing her again soon."

Mikey jumped up and started to stack the plates.

"Course I will, Uncle William, and I'll be ever so careful. 'Bye bye, my lamb, see you soon," he said, suddenly putting down the stack of plates and flapping his hand at Nina.

"Bye bye" she giggled, flapping back.

"Bye, Mikey," called Judy as she went down the hall. "We'll be seeing you soon, I hope."

They were just disappearing through the front door as Judy heard him mutter,

"I hope so, oh! I hope so."

Mikey waited until he heard the front door close and then a few minutes later, Uncle William's car pulled away. He smiled to himself.

What a smashing day. Work until dinner time, dinner in the canteen and then home to do his jobs before they went to Mrs Gresty's. He'd felt quite important walking through the streets like a delivery man. He'd walked with his shoulders back like Uncle William, keeping in step as well as he could.

Then afterwards, looking after that bonny child. He'd been really proud to be left in charge like that and now here was Uncle William trusting him to clear up and wash the dishes.

He carried the stacked dishes through to the back kitchen, scraped the plates clean and then carefully washed and dried them and put them away. He folded the tea towel in half, just as he'd seen Uncle William do and hung it carefully across the bar on the back of the kitchen door to dry off. It was a good thing he'd had Uncle William to help him sort himself out when his Mam died, otherwise he'd still just be muddling along.

He took a last look around the kitchen, checked the chairs were all neatly placed under the table in the next room and went along the hall to let himself out. Uncle William would surely call when he got home and tell him what was happening. He was dying to know when they'd be moving in and whether Uncle William would let him help. That would be another important job for him. He was good at jobs like that. He could lift and carry as good as anybody, even Uncle William.

Judy stood in the doorway of the house at number one, waiting for Mr Whitehead to bring the car and looking across the street at the houses facing. Nina was jigging up and down and pulling on her hand. She, at least, seemed happy enough and when the great shiny black car pulled round the corner, she was absolutely delighted.

"Car, Mummy, look. Big car."

The car was a big old Wolsey. The chrome glinted in the early evening sun and the black coachwork shone like glass. Mr Whitehead got out, walked around the car and opened the passenger door for Judy and Nina.

"In you get, my dear. Hold tight to the little lass, she seems a bit excited. Now I'll just get on to the Stockport Road and you can tell me where to turn."

Nina sat on her mother's knee, eyes round and shining with the excitement of her first car ride. Judy cuddled her and looked out of the window too, watching Nina point her pudgy little fingers at the things that caught her attention.

She suddenly realised that they were nearly home.

"Right at the next set of traffic lights please, Mr Whitehead. Then it's about two hundred yards down on the left, almost facing the market."

They turned at the lights and Judy said,

"There's the house. That's my landlady on the doorstep talking to the man with the bike. It's the insurance man, he always calls on Fridays."

Mr Whitehead drew the car to a slow but stately halt.

"Just hang on a minute and I'll help you to get Nina out."

He got out of the car and walked in his firm, upright manner around the bonnet of the car to the passenger side. He opened the door and held out his arms for Nina, who surprisingly allowed herself to be lifted and held until her mother got out and closed the door.

Judy could hear her landlady sniffing for emphasis and she couldn't help but overhear her comments.

"Well, here's a turn up for the books. Home in a big car, looks as though she's landed on her feet. Looks a bit of a toff, don't he? Probably got a bob or two, even if he is old enough to be her father."

Judy was so astounded she forgot to be embarrassed and looked at Mr Whitehead, hoping against hope that he hadn't heard. If anything, his back was even straighter and he'd drawn himself up to his full height and fixed the landlady with a steely gaze. She mumbled a bit but her eyes dropped and she looked a little flustered.

He marched up the garden path with the child in his arms and as they neared the step, he turned and said to Judy,

"I'll carry her up the stairs. She's tired and she's much too heavy for you. Which floor did you say it is, perhaps you'd better lead the way?"

Judy stepped forward and had to squeeze past the couple at the front door. Mr Whitehead followed her as she went up to the second floor and unlocked the door.

"Well, this is it. It isn't much but it's home."

The room was light and airy and although the furniture was a little shabby, it was clean and tidy.

"Not for much longer. As I said, it's daylight robbery. Would you like me to have a word with your landlady? I wouldn't mind putting a quiet flea in her ear."

"No thank you. I'll speak to her myself. I'm not very brave but I do try to fend for myself and this is a problem for me to sort out. I'm grateful for your offer but I'll deal with it."

"Just as you like, my dear," said Mr Whitehead, not altogether pleased at being deprived of the opportunity of giving the landlady a piece of his mind but understanding that Judy needed to deal with her own problems.

25

"Well, if you give her notice tonight, you can move into number five next Saturday. Mikey is at home on Saturdays and he'd love to help. It might be a good idea if you came before then though to have a proper look and see if there's anything you need to buy and perhaps get the place cleaned up a bit. You could make a start tomorrow, if you like. Do you have a pushchair for Nina."

He was fairly sure that Judy would decline further offers of help and that she was inclined to be a little touchy if her independence appeared to be threatened.

"I'd love to. Would eleven o'clock be all right then I could do some shopping on my way?"

"That'll be fine. I'd better be on my way now before that old baggage has something else to say. I'll see you in the morning. Good night, Judy. 'Night, 'night, Nina" and he left the room, closing the door quietly behind him.

Judy started to undress Nina.

"What a day we've had, my darling. Who would have thought that something that started so badly could end so well? Let's get you washed and into bed."

She put Nina's little dressing gown on her and watched as the child tried to push her tiny feet into her slippers. She could see it was bedtime. She took the child along the landing to the bathroom and locked the door. The water wasn't very hot, again, and it took a few minutes to clean the bath. Then she ran about four inches of water into the bath and stood Nina in it.

"Won't be long, sweetheart,' she said, wiping her daughter's face and washing the sturdy little body with a soapy cloth"

"There we are, out you come, all clean and shiny like a little wet fish."

She lifted Nina out of the bath and wrapped her in a towel, rubbing her dry and chatting to her. Leaving her perched on the toilet seat still wrapped in the towel, she wiped out the bath yet again.

"Come on, sweetheart. Let's get you into bed."

In less than ten minutes, Nina was tucked up and fast asleep. No complaints about the noise tonight. Nina had been happy to get into the big bed she shared with her mother. She'd dropped off even before the end of the first verse of the lullaby her mother sang her every night.

Judy sat for a few minutes on the side of the bed, watching her child sleep and stroking the little dark head, her thoughts drifting.

Well, I'd better make a move

26

She'd just risen to go back into the other room when she heard a tap on the door.

She wasn't altogether surprised to see Mrs Beacon, her landlady, standing on the landing.

"Won't you come in for a minute, Mrs. Beacon? I wanted to have a word with you anyway but we'll have to be quiet because Nina's just gone to sleep."

Mrs Beacon looked a little shamefaced.

"I didn't mean to upset you love. I'm sure it's all above board and sometimes my mouth does run away with me."

"Not to worry, Mrs Beacon. I was going to give you a week's notice tonight anyway. We'll be leaving next Saturday morning. I've found somewhere else to live where Nina won't be such a bother."

"Oh, she's no bother, really. It's just sometimes the other tenants complain about the noise and apart from an odd little upset like that, you've been a good tenant. You keep the place spotless and the rent's as regular as clockwork too. There's really no need for you to move, you know."

The feeling that Mrs Beacon was backing down and trying to ingratiate herself gave her a bit more courage.

"Well, you know, Mrs Beacon, the noise level certainly works both ways. Those tenants that complain about the noise Nina makes at eight o'clock in the morning and about seven in the evening certainly don't mind how much noise they make when they come in after the pubs close."

She looked Mrs Beacon squarely in the eye. They both knew that Mrs Beacon was partial to a drop or two. She spent most Friday and Saturday nights in the Bull's Head round the corner, returning to the house rowdy and definitely the worse for wear at eleven o'clock or later.

"They probably only complain because they have thick heads themselves. So if you want me to put my notice in writing, I'll do it gladly. Otherwise can we just take it that I'll be moving out about ten o'clock a week tomorrow? I've made other arrangements now anyway."

Mrs Beacon started to turn nasty.

"I see," she sniffed. "If that's the way of it, you'll do what you want, I suppose. Going to live with that chap are you, the one that brought you home?"

"I hardly think that where and with whom we are going to live is any of your business, Mrs Beacon,' she said witheringly. 'Now if

27

you'll excuse me, we've had a busy day and I intend to get an early night."

She opened the door wide so that Mrs Beacon had no alternative than to leave and closed it firmly behind her. She could still hear Mrs Beacon muttering on the landing but now she didn't really care. In fact, she was proud of the way she'd handled herself and could feel her face glowing in self approval.

That told her. I've burned my bridges now so there's no use worrying anymore.

Filling the kettle to the brim, she put it on the gas ring. While the water was heating, she went into the bedroom and got her cotton nightie and old red slippers. She couldn't face the bathroom again tonight and, having stripped down, she sponged herself in much the same as she had Nina, topping up the water in the bowl from the kettle. Dressed in nightie and slippers, she got down a beaker from the shelves above the sink and made herself a mug of cocoa. She sat down in the only comfortable chair in the room, nursing the warm mug in cupped hands and thinking over the events of the day. It all seemed too good to be true but she pushed her misgivings to the back of her mind and started to plan.

She could easily be on the bus by half past ten and back at the little house by eleven o'clock. At least the buses ran frequently along Stockport Road. She finished her cocoa, cleaned her teeth at the sink and then went into the other room to slide into bed with Nina, who was sound asleep. Her last conscious thought as she drifted off was 'number five Tiverton Place' and she fell asleep, one arm around Nina, with a smile on her face.

Chapter 3

Judy woke next morning to find Nina tickling her ear. She turned drowsily to give her a squeeze and they lay there for a moment or two, warm and cosy. Judy lifted her arm to squint at her watch, ten past eight. Nina had slept well. She was beginning to wriggle and mutter now though, obviously hungry.

Judy got out of bed and walked over to the window. It was a little hazy and she thought it may well turn into a 'scorcher' later. She put on her slippers and started to organize breakfast; cereal and milk for Nina and a piece of toast and a cup of tea for her. Nina also managed a piece of toast and then stood quietly while Judy washed her hands and face. Judy dressed her in a pair of clean, but faded dungarees.

"Who knows what you might get into later," she laughed.

Then she got herself washed and dressed. She too, put on her oldest slacks and a clean blouse and then, picking up a jacket for Nina and her cardigan, she put her purse in her pocket, found a shopping bag and then set off down the stairs. She pulled out the trolley which Mrs Beacon allowed her to keep in a cupboard under the stairs, and took it to the front door, where she strapped Nina in.

They set off for the market just across the road where she did most of her shopping. It was cheaper than the local shops and she loved the way the stallholders shouted across at each other, bantering and laughing. She always went early, before the crowds and many of the regulars knew her and Nina by sight, shouting

"Good morning, darlin'" and "Hello, love, how's it going?"

She bought fresh food to last until next market day and, fairly loaded, struggled back across the road, pushing the trolley with one hand and carrying the heavy bag in the other.

"We'll be going out again in a little while, sweetheart. Won't that be nice?"

Nina nodded.

She re-packed the bag with cleaning stuff and carefully wedged the sandwiches on top. She put a couple of spoonfuls of loose tea into a bag and screwed the top tight. She could buy a bottle of milk from the corner shop when she got there.

She was beginning to get excited and couldn't wait to have another look at the house. It didn't seem real. Another week and then she and Nina would have a place of their own.

"Well, let's get going," she said, picking up the bag and Nina's teddy bear and started down the stairs, rather glad not to bump into Mrs Beacon or any of the other tenants.

The conductor had been on the platform when she got on the bus and helped her with her bag and the trolley. She settled herself with Nina on her knee and when he came to collect the fares, he asked

"Where are you getting off love?" and sure enough, he was on the platform waiting to help her off with Nina, the trolley and the heavy bag.

The sun had now really broken through the haze and was shining brightly into the narrow streets which only yesterday had seemed so stark and cheerless. Everything was so much brighter today and Judy looked around, trying to work out how many of the houses still had people living in them. She spotted the 'chippy' and the corner shop, windows packed on one side with faded advertising placards for malt drinks and headache tablets and on the other side with bread and cakes.

"That's handy," she said to Nina, "we can buy our bread and milk here, at least until they pull the place down. As soon as we're settled, we'll come and explore properly. It can only be a few minutes' walk to the park, it always looks lovely when we pass on the bus. We can go for a walk in the afternoon when the weather's fine and stay at home when it rains. You can play to your heart's content and I won't have to worry about you running around and making a noise."

They turned the corner into Tiverton Place and she paused. She could see the whole row from here and it did look splendid. The houses looked like little palaces. All the doors and steps were freshly painted, the windows shining, the paths were brushed and the tiny front gardens were neat and tidy. Perhaps number five didn't look as spick and span as the rest but she'd soon change that. She looked again at number one and could see that it was, indeed, substantially larger than the other houses in the terrace. It had had a garden at the side but this had now been replaced by a wooden garage, also painted black and white like the fronts of the houses.

She pushed the trolley across the road, up the path of number one and knocked smartly with the shiny brass knocker. Mr Whitehead appears, smiling.

"I thought it would be you, my dear. I'll just get the keys and you can make a start."

He returned a couple of minutes later and escorted Judy and Nina up the path of number five. He handed over the keys with a flourish.

"Here you are, you open the door, it's more or less your house now."

Judy picked out the Yale key from the other two on the ring and inserted it ceremoniously into the lock, pushed the door open and stepped inside. This was it, her very own place. Nina, still in the trolley, was kicking her little legs and struggling to get out but for once, Judy didn't notice. She didn't think now about when she might have to leave, she stood in the doorway almost trembling with anticipation; her own place at last.

Mr Whitehead cleared his throat.

"Let's get you properly inside and sorted out and get the little lass unbuckled from this fiendish contraption," he said bending to release Nina.

"Do you want some help or would you rather manage on your own?"

"Mr Whitehead," said Judy firmly, "you've been so kind to us already. I'm sure I can manage and I'm keen to get started. I've brought some cleaning stuff with me and something for our lunch so I'll just go and rummage around the kitchen and if there's something I need that isn't there, I'll bring it with me next time. I can't tell you how much I'm looking forward to it all."

Mr Whitehead, despite his brusque manner, was more perceptive than most people gave him credit for. He realised he had to be careful not to injure Judy's pride and threaten her hard-won independence. She'd been managing on her own, with a baby, for two years and he knew instinctively not to offer too much.

"Right, I'll leave you to it. Although you don't officially take over the house until next Saturday, keep the keys and then you can come and go as you please. No doubt I'll see you later in the week and we can arrange to collect your belongings. Come in a taxi, if you'd prefer, but I'd be happy to collect you and you may need to make more than one journey. Anyway, Mikey is really looking forward to helping out and he can carry any really heavy stuff but it's up to you."

Judy, not wanting to appear prickly but anxious now to be alone with Nina in the house, replied,

"That would be brilliant, Mr Whitehead. I'll knock on your door later in the week and we can arrange a time. There isn't so much to bring. The biggest things are Nina's chair and my old sewing machine and apart from that, there are just a few things from the kitchen and our clothes."

"Bye for now then," and smiling at Nina, who had also parroted the "'bye then", he left the house, gently closing the front door behind him.

***

Mrs Goldman sat back in the hard, straight backed chair in the recess formed by the bay window. Very little happened along the row and in the street that she didn't know about. After all, she spent most of the day, every day, sitting there with her sewing on her knee and her other bits and pieces, scissors, thread and so on, on the small round table next to her.

She had watched the comings and goings up and down the path the day before; Mikey with his carpet and then Mr Whitehead coming and going with that girl with the child and here she was, back again, with a great shopping bag this time. Margaret Hartley's bay had obscured the transaction at the front door of number five but she had seen Mr Whitehead pass the keys over and then disappear quite smartly, leaving the girl in the house.

It could only mean one thing. She must be moving in. Well thank goodness it wasn't next door and she wouldn't have to listen to the racket made by a small child all hours of the day and night. There were enough changes going on around the area at the moment, people leaving all the time and more and more houses being boarded up.

She left the house only on Saturdays when her husband took her to the shops. They shopped very carefully from a list she had prepared and he did all the talking. She had to admire the way he could laugh and joke with the shopkeepers and never seemed to mind when people laughed at his funny accent. He was so clever and worked so hard and yet he never complained and did his best to keep them both cheerful. She sometimes thought that he deserved someone more like himself, someone who could shake off their troubles and laugh with him.

She listened carefully to him when he told her not to take things so much to heart, to try to live more in the present and keep her spirits up and she did try, she really did. She was grateful that he never got impatient with her when things got her down. Heaven knows, things were bad enough and although he constantly reassured her that they were safe, she had an awful foreboding that the worst could still happen. They would have to move from here, where she'd felt comparatively safe, and start again. They would have to make a home somewhere else, where everything was new and strange and she wouldn't even recognise the people passing by her window. She felt a clammy sweat break out on her forehead and down her back as she imagined going into shops she had never even seen before and having to speak in front of total strangers.

Heaven help me, I'll never do it. I can't do it. Jakob will have to do the shopping on his own and then I'm letting him down again. He probably won't say anything but I'll know I'm letting him down.'

She could feel the panic rising and her hands became more and more agitated, fingers plucking at the sewing on her lap. She looked around the room. Everything was in its proper place. All the brass work gleamed, the furniture was highly polished, not a speck of dirt to be seen anywhere. This reassured her a little and she took a deep breath and made an effort to calm her riotous thoughts. She looked at the clock on the mantelpiece. Not really time yet to stop for a 'cuppa' but perhaps it would help her settle down and get back to work. She had several pieces to finish and it was a beautiful day. If she finished early enough, she could spend half an hour in the garden later on when the sun came round the back. She always felt better with the sun on her face and soil under her fingertips. The sight of growing vegetables, planted in neat rows, and the flowers beginning their summer show always made her feel better, no matter how upset she was.

She put down her sewing, stood up decisively, and went into the kitchen to put the kettle on. She would pull herself together and carry out her plan; finish her work, do a little gardening and then it would be time to start cooking for when Jakob came home from work. He worked very hard and deserved a decent meal and a smiling face when he came through the door in the evening and today, at least, she intended to give him both.

***

33

Judy picked up Nina, hugging her tight and kissing her soft, warm cheek.

"This is it darling. This is our own little house. We can close the front door behind us and keep out the world. Come on, let's have a look round."

She walked through to the kitchen for another look and then climbed the stairs.

"Here's the bathroom, chicken. No more sharing. When the bath is cleaned it will stay that way until we use it again. We won't have to clear up anyone else's mess. This will be your bedroom. You'll be sleeping in this bed all on your own and over here, just across the landing, will be Mummy's room. You'll only have to call out and I'll hear you,"

She stood for a moment, still hugging Nina tightly. Nina pulled away slightly and looked intently into her mother's eyes. Then she leaned forward, put both arms around Judy's neck and her cheek next to hers and squeezed. Judy felt a lump rising in her throat and tears springing to her eyes as she squeezed Nina back.

"We'll be happy here, sweetheart. I know we will," she whispered into her daughter's ear, rocking her from side to side and kissing her, tiny kisses all over her little face.

They started down the stairs and Judy thought to herself,

I'll have to get organised here.

She smiled wryly as she realised she'd unconsciously uttered one of Auntie Mary's well worn phrases.

She couldn't think about all that now, after all, she had to get organised.'

She went into the kitchen and put Nina down. If she was going to let her loose in the house, the first thing she would have to do would be to block the stairs. Nina had never had free access to stairs before and might decide to go mountaineering. She brought the two straight chairs from the kitchen and placed them upside down, their legs poking upwards, against the stairs. The first purchase would have to be a safety gate. There was a second hand shop on the way home that sometimes had cots and other baby stuff, she might find one there. She had a little money put by and this was an essential.

"Come on sweetheart, let's have a look what's out the back," she said, fishing the keys out of her pocket.

She unlocked the kitchen door into the yard at the back. It was actually much larger than she'd thought and although, like the house, it needed attention now, she could see that it had been carefully tended.

"It won't take me long to tidy this up, sweetheart, but we'll have to get the house sorted out first."

She looked around. There were one or two rose bushes in one bed, various other unidentifiable plants coming through in the other bed and a climbing plant of some kind against the back wall next to the gate. The narrow flower beds were against the walls, leaving the paved centre of the yard clear and there was a clothes line running from one wall to the other.

Imagine being able to hang out the washing after two years trying to dry their bits and pieces over clothes maiden in front of a gas fire which gobbled shillings.

She realised that the third key on the bunch was for an outhouse which was built against the kitchen wall.

"This must have been the outside loo. Let's just have a quick look what's in here."

The lock was a bit stiff but once opened, the little outhouse yielded a treasure trove; a hoe and a rake, a couple of trowels and, what luck, a small folding table and chairs for the garden.

"Look, Nina, everything we need to turn this little garden back into what it was before Mrs Phelan died."

The bunker next to the outhouse was half full of coal. She wouldn't even have to lay out cash for fuel for a while, especially with summer well on its way.

They went back into the kitchen and Judy thought the best thing would be to start with an inventory of what was there and what she actually needed. She turned the tap, the water was on. She turned on one of the taps of the old fashioned cooker, the gas hissed out. She flicked the switch for the kitchen light, the electricity was on. There was a gas water heater on the wall above the sink and when she turned on the tap, she realised that Mr Whitehead had been in the house and lit it up for her. Hot water flowed out of the long narrow pipe over the sink. What more did she need?

She found the meters for the gas and electricity and took shilling coins from her purse. She was used to saving them for the meters in her digs and put a couple in each meter, carefully placing one in reserve on top of each meter. It was no joke when the electricity went off and you had no coins. She must remember to get some more change on the way home. After all, she now had to keep two sets of meters running, for a week at least.

All the cupboards and drawers in the kitchen were opened in turn. She couldn't believe her luck. Almost everything she needed was there; knives and forks, cups and saucers, pots and pans. One drawer had tea towels, all neatly ironed and folded and in a bottom cupboard she even found old newspapers and wood for kindling. She put on the kettle to make herself a cup of tea and got the sandwiches.

"Here, Nina, come and sit in your trolley and have something to eat."

Her mind was racing. The whole place needed cleaning. All the drawers needed to be wiped out and the contents of all the cupboards needed sorting. Aunt Mary had always drummed into her,

"When you are cleaning, you start from the top and work down."

Old habits die hard and she knew she ought to start in the bathroom and bedrooms. Nevertheless, she wanted to make her little house look as smart as the others in the row.

To hell with it I'll start at the front and work backwards, or upwards, just as the fancy takes me. After all, this is my house and I can do things the way I want.

She found a bucket and another sweeping brush, this one was obviously intended for use outside the house, and a pair of stepladders in the cupboard under the stairs. On a shelf in the cupboard she found a scrubbing brush and window leather rolled up in a screw top jar.

"Right, that's it," she said to Nina, "front path and windows. Let's make Mrs Phelan proud of us but let's have some lunch first."

After they'd eaten, Judy pushed Nina in her trolley through the house and settled her in the tiny front garden where she could watch what was happening. Judy set to with a will. She washed the front windows, inside and out, first taking down the dusty net curtains for washing. The path was swept and the step scrubbed thoroughly.

By this time, Nina was fast asleep so Judy pushed the trolley through to the backyard and settled it in the shade. Although the sun was really warm now, Judy gently folded a thin blanket over her and plumped up the pillow behind her head. Now she could really get on.

While she worked, she made her plans. She would come again tomorrow and this time, she would bring some soap powder so that she could start washing the curtains. She would bring a change of clothes and a couple of towels so that she and Nina could have a bath before they went back to Mrs Beacon's and then she could put Nina straight to bed. They need never brave that awful bath again.

Judy and Nina went to the house every day and by Thursday, had fallen into a routine. The weather had remained fine and dry and Judy managed to wash and dry all the curtains in the house. There was a fine supply of old, embroidered bed linen in the cupboards upstairs and most of that still needed washing but she had enough clean sheets and towels so that she could move in.

They'd been eating fairly makeshift meals but Judy thought it wouldn't hurt for a week. She could start cooking properly again as soon as they moved in. It was too expensive to eat this way for long and one thing that Aunt Mary had taught her was to cook tasty, sustaining food at very low cost.

Her hard won savings were dwindling too fast. The extra cleaning tackle, shillings for the meter and the daily bus fares had taken their toll and she'd had to buy a gate to keep Nina off the stairs. Never mind, they would soon be settled and she could economise then.

Judy had seen Miss Hartley on Sunday morning, obviously on her way home from church and she had stopped to chat for a few minutes.

"You're working wonders with the place," said Miss Hartley. "Perhaps when you move in you'll have time to pop in and see me. It can be a bit quiet in the evening sometimes and it will be lovely to have someone young around. By the way, where's the little one now? I still haven't seen her awake."

Judy said that she was having a nap in the yard but promised to bring her round to see Miss Hartley as soon as they were settled.

"I'll look forward to that. Don't work too hard now. You can always make the finishing touches after you move in."

She hadn't seen Miss Hartley since Sunday. She'd fallen into the habit of taking Nina into the park in the late afternoon so that she could get some fresh air and run off some energy after her rest. Nina's nap had been a godsend, giving Judy a clear hour in which to wash and peg out the clothes she had left to soak the previous evening and do any ironing left from the previous day.

She hadn't seen much of Mikey either but had the feeling that Mr Whitehead had given him strict instructions not to bother them. There would be time enough after they moved in.

Mr Whitehead had also been conspicuous by his absence but she thought she should call to see him on her way home tonight. She was grateful now for his offer of assistance with the move, a taxi would have cost a fortune.

As yet, she'd seen nothing of the couple living the other side of Miss Hartley although she sometimes felt as though someone was watching when they passed.

She still walked Nina everywhere she could even though she sometimes had to be prepared for a trip to take twice the normal time if Nina insisted on pushing the trolley instead of riding in it. They had wandered up and down the narrow streets between the two busy roads, looking for shortcuts and working out the quickest route to the small shops that were still open and, of course, to the park.

As she was locking up late Thursday afternoon, she caught sight of Mr Whitehead coming out of his front door.

"Hello, Mr Whitehead," she called across the garden walls. "Do you have a minute?"

"Of course, I was going to call anyway. How are things going?"

"Marvellous, the place looks lovely now. There are one or two things I still have to do but most of them can wait until we move in. By the way, thank you for lighting up the geysers for me. It's a real treat to have water for baths on tap, not to mention the washing. I'll have fingers like prunes if I carry on like this."

Mr Whitehead, though he said nothing, thought how much more cheerful and how much younger she looked than only a week before.

"I can come for you at about ten o'clock on Saturday morning, if that's convenient. Mikey's anxious to come up and help but I'm a bit concerned that there might not be room in the car for him after all. Have you a lot to bring?"

"Oh, no, I've been bringing bits and pieces with me every day. I'll leave the trolley here on Friday night so the biggest thing is Nina's high chair. Apart from that, there's just some clothes and a box of odds and ends. Do let Mikey come, I wouldn't want to disappoint him. I know he's longing to see Nina again and I suspect you've been keeping him away."

"Not exactly, he has a job at one of the factories down the Green. He sweeps up, makes tea and runs errands for the workmen and although they don't pay him much, it gives him his independence and makes him feel worthwhile. He gets himself up, good as gold, every morning and is there before eight o'clock and as he finishes at five, you've been gone by the time he gets home from work. However, he finishes at lunchtime on Friday, which is why he was at home last Friday afternoon, moving the carpet. I know he's looking forward to seeing you both again and he would like to help on Saturday, if you're sure you don't mind."

"Not a bit of it," said Judy warmly. "We'll be glad to see him. Nina seems to have taken to him and she can be difficult with strangers."

At the sound of her name, Nina, who'd been clutching tight at Judy's hand, started to tug at her.

"Park, Mummy, park," she said plaintively, bored with standing around.

"Well, I mustn't keep you. I can see you have an appointment with the swings. I'll see you on Saturday morning."

Mr Whitehead tipped his hat to Judy and then bent down to Nina, who was now pulling quite hard on Judy's hand.

"Bye bye, Nina. We'll see you on Saturday."

"Sat'day" muttered Nina, pushing against Judy, anxious to be off.

***

Saturday dawned at last. Judy had crept out of bed very early, moving quietly around so as not to wake Nina. She'd managed to clean their rooms the night before, after Nina had fallen asleep and had finished most of the packing. Two suitcases, a portable sewing machine, a couple of carrier bags and a large cardboard box stood ready by the door. By the time Nina woke, Judy was already washed and dressed and had breakfast on the table. Nina was, as usual, starving.

Judy washed and put away the breakfast things. Mrs Beacon had been in the evening before, sniffing her disapproval, but had been able to find no fault with the state of their rooms. No breakages, not that there was much to break, and the place was as clean as a whistle.

As Judy washed and dressed Nina, she couldn't help thinking, *Well, I could always get a job as a cleaning lady or a washerwoman. I've certainly had plenty of experience this week, Auntie Mary would be proud of me.*

She kept looking at her watch; the last half hour seemed to drag. She shook it to see if it was still going. Could it really only be five minutes since she last looked? Finally, she heard footsteps on the stairs. One foot put firmly in front of the other, that could only be Mr Whitehead. She opened the door just as he was about to knock.

"Good morning, my dear. Are we all ready to go? Look, here's Mikey. I think we'll let him carry that heavy suitcase."

Mikey came forward bashfully.

"Hello," he muttered shyly, "I'll carry the suitcase down first and then come back for the rest."

He went down on one knee so that his face was level with Nina's.

"Hello, Nina," he whispered. "Have you forgotten me already?"

Nina was clutching hard at Judy's trouser clad leg, a little overwhelmed, but she looked at Mikey out of the corner of her eye and smiled tremulously.

"That's grand, Nina. That's grand. You wait and see, we'll soon be pals."

Mikey picked up the heavy suitcase and Mr Whitehead the highchair and at Mr Whitehead's suggestion, Judy followed with Nina to wait in the car until everything was loaded. Just before she closed the door for the last time, she took one last look around the rooms where she and Nina had lived for more than two years. Not much, but it had been home to them. She turned resolutely and closed the door behind her. This was the end of one period in her life and she knew that another was just starting.

The new place had no memories of John, her husband, or of Auntie Mary, who'd been dead now for nearly four years. They were starting afresh and this was no time to look back. The future was what mattered now, the future for her and Nina.

She followed Mr Whitehead down the stairs. Sure enough, Mrs Beacon was hovering at the door of her sitting room on the ground floor.

'Here are the keys, Mrs. Beacon. I've written my forwarding address down for you. I'd be grateful if you'd send on any post that comes for me.'

Mrs Beacon almost snatched the keys out of her hand and narrowed her eyes to look at the address Judy had printed neatly on a postcard.

"Are you sure you know what you're doing? If this is where I think it is, all them houses'll be coming down before six months are out. You could find yourself on the street after that. And another thing, how well do you know those two fellas what are moving your stuff? One looks like a toff and t'other looks as though he's not all there. Are you sure you're doing the right thing?"

Despite Mrs Beacon's nosey manner, Judy could detect a touch of real concern. After all, she'd lived there quite some time. She touched Mrs Beacon on the arm reassuringly.

"Yes, I'm quite sure. I just know no harm will come to us. Don't you worry, Mrs Beacon, we'll be all right."

Surprising herself, she leaned forward and kissed Mrs Beacon quickly on the cheek.

"'Bye now," she said and, swooping Nina up into her arms, she went quickly down the hall.

"Well, if it don't turn out right for you, you can always come back. I haven't let them rooms yet. Come and see me if you're ever up this way," Mrs Beacon called up the hall to Judy's retreating back.

Mikey, who had already loaded the suitcase into the car, held Nina while Judy settled herself in the front seat and then passed her over.

"I'll just go and get the rest of the stuff," he said and charged off for the last bag which had been left on the landing at the top of the stairs.

"Well, you have to admire his energy,' said Mr Whitehead, who stood waiting for Mikey to reappear. 'Here we go now. Can you put that box on the back seat next to you Mikey? The boot's full."

They were off. Nina, delighted at her second car ride in a week, was leaning over Judy's shoulder and pointing.

"Look, Nina, bus. There's a big bus."

"Bus," responded Nina, chuckling.

Judy was grateful to Mikey for distracting Nina and keeping her happy. She was surprised to find that she was a little nervous and had a peculiar fluttering sensation in the pit of her stomach.

Was she doing the right thing? Mrs Beacon's words echoed in her head. What did she know about these two after all? Had she been too hasty?

Mr Whitehead sensed her unease.

"Don't you worry," he whispered to her between the bursts of laughter coming from Nina and Mikey, "you'll be quite safe with us."

Judy looked at him gratefully and blinked hard.

"I know that, Mr Whitehead. I think I've really known that all along."

41

They turned the corner into Tiverton Place. Now all the houses in the street looked immaculate, number five included. Miss Hartley was standing on the doorstep of number seven. It was Saturday, so the smart suit had gone and been replaced by a well cut pair of navy trousers and a pale blue lightweight sweater. She'd obviously been waiting for them and waved as the car pulled up.

"Hello, Judy," she said, smiling. "This must be Nina, awake at last. I'm just on my way to the shops but I wanted to welcome you both. I'm sure you'll be happy here. Can you wait just a moment?" she said, disappearing into the house.

Seconds later, she reappeared with a flowering plant in a pot wrapped in shiny paper.

"Just a little welcome present for you. I hope you won't be offended."

"What a lovely thought. I know just the place for it. Have you a minute to come in?"

Holding Nina firmly by the hand, she pulled out her keys and opened the front door.

"This is it, sweetheart," she murmured to Nina. "Here we are at last."

She stepped over the threshold and into the sitting room, leaving Miss Hartley to follow while the car was being unloaded.

"I'll put it here, out of Nina's reach," and she placed the plant in pride of place in the centre of the sideboard. It looked lovely, a bright splash of colour against the dark wood.

" I must say, you've worked wonders. The place looks marvellous. I know you must be wanting to settle in so I won't keep you. I'll leave you to get on with it and hope to see you later. Please don't hesitate to knock if you need anything. I'll only be out an hour or so."

Mr Whitehead was coming in as Miss Hartley was going out and Judy had to bite her lip to stop herself grinning as she watched them engaged in that strange ritual dance which sometimes occurs when people try to pass in a narrow space. They both stepped the same way so that they still couldn't pass each other and then both stepped the other way, finding themselves in the same fix.

Finally, Mr Whitehead stepped right back out on to the path and stepped aside to let Miss Hartley pass. Judy could tell he was a little hot under the collar but as Miss Hartley turned to wave goodbye, Judy could see the amusement in her eyes and her struggle for an impassive expression.

William turned and watched Miss Hartley's trim back disappear round the corner at the end of the street. She hadn't changed much physically in the years he'd known her. But even though she was smart and businesslike and often had a twinkle in her eye, she was far from the fun loving girl he had first met during the war.

***

He well remembered the first time he'd seen her, her head thrown back in laughter, her face glowing and her red curls bouncing round her shoulders. She had been absolutely stunning. He'd thought that she looked like Rita Hayworth but fresher somehow. What a lucky lad young David was to have captured such a girl.

David, a smart, good looking lad in his own right, had been a corporal in his regiment and looked likely to make sergeant before too long. He was the son of one of William's cousins and had been in the regiment for several months before approaching William to mention the connection. When William took him to task, he'd just said that he didn't want to look as though he was asking for preferential treatment. Even then, he'd asked William not to mention it to anyone else. William had, of course, respected his wishes but nevertheless had kept a fatherly eye on him.

There had been no need to make allowances. He was a fine young man who did his duty without a murmur and who got on well with the other lads in his unit. Having no close family of his own, William grew fond of the boy, almost regarding him as the son he'd never had.

In March of 1942, when they'd been on leave at the same time, William had been flattered when David asked him if he could come to town on Saturday to meet his girl. They had some shopping to do but would be glad if they could join him for afternoon tea.

William strolled through Piccadilly, touching his cap to Queen Victoria as he passed; he'd always thought she was a game old girl.

The trams rattled by and Market Street was bustling, with plenty of uniforms in evidence. The shops seemed to be quite busy although there was never much on the shelves. He glanced down the arcade as he passed Lewis's. No sign yet of the 'ladies of the night' who did a roaring trade after dark. Their business was flourishing despite, or perhaps because of, the blackout.

43

He pushed open the door to the Kardomah and the warm smell of freshly ground coffee made his nostrils twitch.

The waitresses, in their white caps and aprons were rushing around serving coffee and clearing tables. This was a popular place to meet, especially on Saturdays, and there were several couples waiting for tables. He peered through the crush, looking for David.

He saw them before they saw him. They'd been laughing, hands clasped, and he could see that their feet were touching under the table. He watched them for a minute. They were clearly in love, totally engrossed in each other, looking into each other's eyes, oblivious to the rest of the world.

David looked up and caught William's eye. He rose to his feet as William approached and introduced him to Margaret with pride. She had smiled and politely taken his proffered hand, murmuring how pleased she was to meet him. She was holding tight to David's hand and an engagement ring was prominently displayed.

"Are congratulations in order?"

David laughed

"Yes, you're not the first to know, we told our parents last night, but you're the first to see the ring. We bought it half an hour ago. I tell you, William, I think we've been in every jeweller's down Market Street."

"Well I don't care,' said Margaret stoutly. 'I'll be wearing this ring for a great many years so you can't blame me for wanting to find the right one."

"Of course not, sweetheart, but I'm certainly glad we don't have to go out for another one next week. All that traipsing around, in and out of shops, worse than route marches, not to mention the wear and tear on my pocket."

Margaret looked at David, the smile lighting up her eyes, and squeezed his fingers again. William looked at the two of them.

"What are your plans now? When's the wedding to be?"

"We haven't quite decided. In a way I'd rather wait. I'd hate for anything to happen to me and for Margaret to be left alone."

He'd struggled with his conscience, trying to be responsible, but she could be very persuasive.

"Well I wouldn't." interrupted Margaret. "I don't want to wait a minute more than necessary but it is difficult. There's no room for the two of us with my mum and dad and it's no better at David's digs and it's almost impossible to get rooms at the moment."

She looked at William, her face serious for a moment.

"Well, maybe I can help you there. It just so happens that I have a little house coming vacant at the weekend. The family is moving down South. They're moving in with her mother who has a big house and has just been widowed and wants her daughter near her.

If it suits, it's yours. I'm particular who my tenants are but I reckon you two will just about pass muster."

He watched Margaret's eyes light up with hope.

"When can we look at it?" she said eagerly.

"Now Margaret, don't get ahead of yourself. Even if this works out, you'll still have to square it with your mum and dad. You know they're not keen on us rushing things."

"I'll deal with mum and dad. Once my mind is made up, I usually get what I want and I know they won't stand in my way when they see how much I want this."

William decided to beat a hasty retreat and leave them to their discussions. It looked as though things could become stormy. He looked at the clock above the door.

"My goodness, we've been sitting here for over an hour. I must get along and leave you to your deliberations. I'll be in from about five o'clock onwards until about eight," he said, writing down the address for them.

"I don't want to rush you but if you could let me know either way by tomorrow evening. If you don't want it then I can make other arrangements but I would like to get it sorted out before I go back to my unit next Wednesday."

"Don't worry, we obviously have a lot to talk about now but we'll come round to see you later on and let you know definitely by tomorrow."

William stood up to leave, reluctant to be thanked, but David stood too and put out his hand.

"I can't tell you what this means to us William. It's a chance in a million and whatever we decide, we want to thank you for giving us first refusal. Thanks."

William looked at Margaret, whose eyes had filled. She swallowed hard.

"Thank you,' she whispered, 'thank you so much."

Later that afternoon, accompanied by Margaret's disapproving parents, they came along to look at the house. As William passed over the key to number seven, he looked at Margaret's determined little chin and the light of battle in her eye and had a feeling she would get her way, despite all opposition.

***

They'd been able to manage three days together in Yorkshire. Margaret had taken a day of her holidays and travelled by train. She was excited and a little apprehensive, she knew exactly what she had committed herself to but had made up her mind. Her dad had run her to the station, despite the petrol shortages, given her a kiss on the cheek and told her to have a good time, seemingly unaware that his little girl was travelling with the sole purpose of getting into bed with her chap. On the other hand, her mum had looked at her knowingly, causing her to flush, and whispered as she kissed her goodbye,

"You take care of yourself and be careful." Mum knew the score all right.

David had been on the station waiting for her, a broad beam on his face. They went along to the small hotel he'd booked and went straight up to the room. It wasn't very big and the eiderdown covered bed seemed to be staring them in the face. She put down her bag carefully on a straight backed chair and turned to face him.

David looked at her searchingly,

"Are you absolutely sure about this?"

She smiled and held out her arms.

"I've never been so sure of anything."

He kissed her deeply and could feel her responding. This was the first time they had been truly alone, without constraints. Their embraces so far had been restricted to the back row of the cinema, along with other courting couples, in the park or even more restricting, the stolen kisses in the porch at Margaret's house.

Margaret instinctively unfastened his jacket and slipped it off his shoulders, then she unbuttoned his shirt and slipped her hands inside, sliding her arms around him and holding him tight. The look of love on his face gave her confidence and in no time at all, they were lying naked, face to face on the bed and gazing into each other's eyes.

"You know I'd never do anything to hurt you, don't you?"

She nodded.

"It's not too late to stop."

"I don't want to stop, I want to go on. I want you to love me and let me show you how much I love you. I've been waiting for this, thinking about you like this for weeks. Show me what to do."

46

He put his arms around her and pulled her to him. She sighed and pressed against him. It all felt so right.

An hour later, they lay together relaxed and sated, and Margaret was filled with joy. It had been everything she'd expected and more and she felt so close to David, their love seemed so much richer. He was close to tears now.

"It means so much to me, to be together like this. I love you, I love you with all my heart."

She pulled his face into her neck and stroked his hair.

"I know, darling, and you know I love you too."

The weekend raced by. They surfaced for food and for quick walks but spent the rest of the time locked away in their room, exploring each other's bodies and learning to give each other pleasure. Margaret's initial shyness had evaporated and she was frank and open and unashamed. He loved her all the more for it.

As he put her on the train on Sunday evening, they were both bereft. She didn't want to go and he didn't want to let her. They clung to each other in the clamour of the station.

"Who knows when we'll be together again. It's so awkward in Manchester."

"Don't worry, we'll work something out, you'll see."

She leaned out of the carriage window and kissed him again and then waved as the train began to move. He stood on the platform and she waved until he was out of sight.

All over the country, decisions were being made in every strata of society. Much of the population was on the move, out of the cities and into the surrounding countryside. The parents of young couples were cautioning against hasty marriages but were unable to withstand their pleas and their chance for at least a fleeting happiness.

***

He was so engrossed in the past, he didn't notice Mr Goldman coming down the street until he heard a voice, the heavily accented English unmistakable.

"Hello there, Mr Whitehead. What's happening? New neighbours? That'll be nice. I'm sure Mrs Goldman will be pleased."

William turned and smiled. He was a funny little chap, no doubt about that. His shoulders sloped under the tightly belted raincoat and a trilby hat tilted cockily over one eye but his eyes were bright and his teeth gleamed below a trim moustache.

47

"Just a minute, I'll call her and you can meet her," and turning, he called up the path.

"Judy, can you spare a minute? I'd like you to meet someone."

Judy came to the front door, holding Nina by the hand.

"This is Mr Goldman who lives at number nine at the end of the row. We don't see too much of him as he works very hard but we sometimes see him on a Saturday, out doing with shopping with Mrs. Goldman."

Judy smiled shyly whilst Nina clutched her hand, half hidden behind her mother's legs.

"I'm very pleased to meet you," she said.

"Same here, I hope you can settle down here OK. Things is turning into a bit of a tip but we manage to muddle it through, isn't it, Mr Whitehead?"

"That's right," said William. "Please give my best to Mrs Goldman."

"Will do. See you some more. 'Bye now," he said as he struggled along the row with his brown paper parcel, heftily tied up with string, and clearly cutting deeply into his fingers.

"You won't see much of Mrs Goldman, Judy. She's a bit of a recluse and only leaves the house once a week when they go shopping. I doubt I've spoken more than a couple of dozen words to her all the time they've been living here. I think she's shy and finds it difficult to meet people but they're a devoted couple."

"He certainly seems very nice, even if his English is a bit tricky."

Whilst all this was going on, Mikey had continued to empty the car and trundle the cases and boxes up the path. He had taken Nina's chair and the boxes with the bits and pieces for the kitchen through to the back and put the suitcases at the bottom of the stairs.

"I've finished now, Judy. Would you like me to carry the cases up the stairs for you?"

Judy looked at William, who nodded his approval.

"That would be great. The smaller of the two is to go in the front bedroom and the other one is full of Nina's stuff. She has twice as much as I do, can you put that one in the back? Leave the sewing machine in the kitchen, would you? I'll have to find a home for it down here."

He rushed off again, anxious to please. She could hear him thundering up the stairs with the heavy cases, dashing first into one bedroom and then into the other and then thundering down again.

"That was quick. I can't thank you enough, Mikey. You've been a wonderful help. I don't know how I would have managed without you."

"That's right,' added William. 'It would have taken twice as long and you did a good job putting everything in the right place. Well done."

Mikey positively glowed.

"Come on then lad. It's time we cleared off and let these two lasses settle in. Judy will let you come and see Nina another time perhaps," looking at Judy enquiringly.

"Of course. If you're not doing anything tomorrow, you're welcome to come to the park with us, if it's not raining. We'll be going up about three o'clock, after Nina has had a sleep."

"Wow, I'd love that. I'll call for you about three then," he said disappearing down the path and along the row to his own house.

"I know you're kind hearted lass and you seem to have hit just the right balance with Mikey. I don't like to interfere but I don't want to see his feelings hurt. He can be a bit touchy.

It would be better if you make it quite clear from the start when he can call. Lay down some guidelines for him and stick to them. He's a willing lad and will be a good friend to you both, especially to Nina, but he needs to know where he stands. I don't want him to wear out his welcome."

"Don't worry," said Judy softly. "I can see what you mean and I'll be very careful with him. He's a nice lad and I wouldn't want to upset him."

William smiled at Judy. *She'll do.*

"Enough said then. I'll leave you to get yourself sorted out. Please let me know if you need any help at all. After all, you know where I live."

Judy watched him walk briskly down the path, shoulders back and almost marching. He raised his arm in half a wave as he turned into the pathway of number one.

She turned, and holding Nina's hand, went back into number five, closing the door behind her. Here she was. She suddenly swooped down, picked up Nina under the armpits and started to swing her from left to right, hopping from foot to foot herself.

"Here we are, sweetheart, and let's hope that here we stay."

49

She started to repeat it, singing it out loud to an old hymn tune. "Here we are, sweetheart, and let's hope that here we stay."

Nina laughed out loud, loving the game and unused to seeing her young mum so carefree. With a final swing, Judy put Nina down and said.

"Come along then. Let's get our stuff sorted out."

She went into the kitchen and put one of the boxes in front of Nina.

"There you are, you take all the things very carefully out of that box and pass them up to Mummy and we'll soon get things put away."

They soon had the kitchen straight and then went upstairs. By this time, Nina was showing signs of needing a sleep and Judy put her down for an hour in her own little bed, which she'd made up with clean sheets the day before. She sat with her until she fell asleep and then carefully fixed the gate across the bedroom doorway.

It didn't take her long to get everything else put away and then she went downstairs and made herself a cup of tea, sitting in the old rocking chair, pushing herself very gently backwards and forwards and holding the cup to her chest with both hands. She looked around the kitchen with satisfaction. She had a feeling that things were going to work out for them. Everyone was so nice, so friendly, that she didn't feel quite so isolated any more.

Chapter 4

She supposed now that maybe things hadn't been quite as idyllic as she remembered but surely, what mattered is that her memories of her parents were all glowing. If there had been any sticky patches, she must have pushed them away. She remembered only the warmth and the laughter.

Dad had been funny, clowning around and telling jokes. She remembered walking along the sands at Blackpool, Dad in the middle with an arm round each of 'his girls'. Mum had been so pretty; never cross, she'd always had time to talk to Judy. She was happy to have her friends for tea, make costumes for the school play or a dress for a special occasion, whip up something special for a treat.

Her face lost its cheerful expression and her features drooped as she thought of that awful day when Miss Hargreaves, the headmistress of her school, had come to fetch her half way through a maths lesson. She'd been twelve years old and in her first year at grammar school. She'd known straight away that something was wrong. Miss Hargreaves was a martinet, strict and severe, and the younger girls in the school appeared to be beneath her notice. They all kept out of her way as much as possible and were justifiably wary of her.

Miss Hargreaves was unusually gentle with her, walking along the narrow corridor towards her room with her hand on Judy's shoulder. Judy was terrified. She was terrified of Miss Hargreaves anyway and couldn't imagine what was going on. She didn't think she was in trouble but maybe she was. She couldn't think and so she concentrated on just putting one foot in front of the other.

Miss Hargreaves opened the door to her office and, placing her palm in the middle of Judy's back, gently propelled her inside. Judy came to a sudden halt, oblivious of Miss Hargreaves gently pushing her forward. Aunt Mary sat in a chair placed in front of Miss Hargreaves' desk. Judy's chin dropped. Aunt Mary looked ruffled and upset. Her hair was untidy and her hat was on a little crooked. Her gloves poked untidily from one of her coat pockets and she was clutching a handkerchief tightly in her right hand, dabbing at her eyes.

Judy didn't want to know. She didn't want to ask and she didn't want to hear. She knew it was going to be too awful to bear. Aunt Mary's voice seemed to be coming from a long way away. She was saying something about a road accident, something about 'instantaneous and couldn't have felt a thing'. What on earth was she talking about? Judy just looked stupidly at her aunt, who had raised her voice and was saying,

"Don't you understand? They're dead. I tried to tell you nicely but you don't seem to take it in. They're dead and now you'll have to come and live with me. What I'm going to do with you I've no idea but I'll do my duty by you, you can be sure of that. No-one can say I didn't do my duty by dear Harry's child."

Aunt Mary gave her nose a good blow, put her hanky in her bag and visibly pulled herself together.

"Well girl, you'd better go and get your coat and your bag. You'll be coming home with me tonight and tomorrow we'll have to go and get your things. Go along now."

Judy looked at Miss Hargreaves, who nodded her approval. As she was closing the door she could hear Miss Hargreaves murmuring about a "terrible tragedy" and "an awful shock for the child" and gently suggesting that Aunt Mary be a little patient with her.

She retrieved her bag quickly from the classroom after a whispered consultation with the maths teacher. She could hear the girls whispering; wondering what was going on but couldn't look at any of them. She just had to be alone for a minute.

She went into the cloakroom to get her coat. The rows of hooks and hanging coats looked endless and the place was eerily quiet without its hoards of chattering girls. She felt numb and couldn't grasp what was going on. She felt hot and sticky and rather sick and went into the toilets to get a drink of water. As she leaned over the sink she caught sight of herself in the mirror, irrelevant thoughts tumbled through her head. Is that what people meant when they said "white as a sheet?" Is that what they meant when they said "eyes like saucers?"

She fastened up her coat, picked up her bag and went back to Miss Hargreaves' office. There wasn't a soul in the corridors either, just murmuring voices from an odd classroom as she passed.

Aunt Mary was now quite composed and was never again to show any regret or grief. She now had a mission, to bring up young Judith, and by God, she was going to do it properly.

Judy lay that night in Aunt Mary's box room, bewildered and weeping gently. She still couldn't believe that her mum and dad were gone, that she'd never see them again. She wanted to talk to them; she had things to tell them and things to ask.

How could they leave her? How could they leave her with Aunt Mary?

She began to bang her head rhythmically against the wall. The pain in her head helped to distract her from the other pain but she still felt as though her chest would burst open and her heart would burst out. At last, she began to sob, great racking sobs, on and on, until she couldn't breathe and then great shuddering breaths, just enough to give her the air to start sobbing again. She was totally unaware of the noise she was making, that her nose was running and her eyes were streaming. She sat in bed, arms round her knees, rocking backwards and forwards, almost howling with pain.

The light went on. Aunt Mary strode in.

"That's enough of that. Pull yourself together. Look at the state of you. You're disgusting. Wipe your face, you look an absolute fright. You have to pull yourself together. It's not decent, carrying on like this. What will the neighbours think if they hear you?"

She pulled Judy's arms down and thrust a hanky into her hand. Judy swiped ineffectively round her face. She tried, but she could stop the sobs.

She knew she was making Aunt Mary angry but she couldn't stop and her hands rose again to her face. She put the hanky into her mouth and bit down hard but still she couldn't stop sobbing, her breath coming in great gulps.

She felt a stinging blow to her cheek. Aunt Mary had struck her. The shock shook her rigid and she even stopped breathing for a few moments. She'd never had a hand raised to her before and she stared up at Aunt Mary out of red, tear filled eyes.

Aunt Mary looked a little shamefaced.

"Hysteria, that's what it is. You were hysterical. I had to do something. Come on now, lie down again and try to sleep. We've a busy day tomorrow. We've got your things to get and we've to go to see the undertaker and the solicitor. There's a lot to sort out. We'll have to get organised."

She stepped back from the bed, turned towards the door and stood for a moment with her hand on the light switch.

"I hope we've seen the last of that kind of behaviour. It isn't ladylike and I won't stand for it. What your mother and father would have thought to see you behaving in this, this... abandoned fashion, I can't think. Just pull yourself together, my girl, and I'll see you in the morning."

It sounded like a threat and hung in the air as she turned off the light, firmly closing the door behind her.

**

She never did see that kind of behaviour from Judy again and congratulated herself that all the girl had needed was a firm hand. She didn't notice that a light had gone out behind Judy's eyes. She didn't notice that she rarely smiled, never laughed but did as she was bid in a quiet, obedient way.

Judy's teachers, on the other hand, became really concerned about her. Her schoolwork hadn't fallen off, in fact quite the opposite. Her marks, which had always been good, had become excellent but they found it difficult to reconcile this docile, almost listless child with the lively, cheerful girl they'd been teaching only weeks before.

The general feeling in the staff room was that she would come round in the course of time. Miss Hargreaves had her doubts about the treatment she was receiving at the hands of her aunt and although she'd had Judy in the office a couple of times to ask how things were going, Judy couldn't confide in her. She could only satisfy herself that no actual physical mistreatment was taking place.

After a few months, most people seemed to have forgotten what Judy used to be like and just accepted the serious, studious girl they now had in their midst. Some of the teachers even wished for a few more pupils like her.

Judy's life had become drudgery. She wasn't allowed out in the evening and every late appearance from school led to tight lips and clipped tones even when she'd told her aunt in advance that she would be home late. Gradually, she dropped all her outside interests. She didn't try out for the netball team the following September although she'd previously been on the team. She dropped out of the school choir and despite encouragement from the staff, showed no interest in the school play. She didn't want to be involved in any capacity, either in front of or behind the scenes. Eventually, people stopped asking her to participate in anything outside school hours.

Her life now consisted only of work; housework and school work, in that order. She had a very strict rota of jobs to be done. She didn't know which worse, accompanying Aunt Mary to the shops at the weekend or working in the kitchen being taught how to make good, nourishing meals on a shoestring. Once out of school uniform, she invariably dressed in old fashioned clothes which Aunt Mary chose for her. They were good quality and all bought at least two sizes too big so she could 'grow into them.'

Her only escape, and then only when Aunt Mary was grudgingly satisfied that all the chores had been completed to her satisfaction, was to go up to her bedroom to do her homework and study. Her only recreation was a visit to the library and even then, Aunt Mary vetted everything she read.

*** *** ***

The years slid uneventfully by until Judy's last year at school when Aunt Mary was summoned once again to the headmistress's office. As she'd shown little or no interest in Judy's academic achievements, she was a little surprised to hear that there was an excellent chance that Judy would be offered a university scholarship.

Judy sat outside Miss Hargreaves' room. She could hear the murmur of voices and hoped against hope that should she be offered a place, Aunt Mary would agree to let her go.

In the office, Miss Hargreaves was handling Aunt Mary with kid gloves. She knew a bully when she saw one but she was careful initially to point out only what an honour this would be for the school and what a credit to her upbringing of the child and how, after university, Judy would be in a position to earn a great deal more money than if she left school immediately and found a job.

She was playing Aunt Mary like a violin. She knew her strengths and her weaknesses and although she disliked doing it, for the sake of the child, she flattered Aunt Mary unmercifully.

Only when Aunt Mary started to flutter about the cost, did she show her true steel. She fixed her with a gimlet eye and suggested that there would, perhaps, be money available from her parents' estate. She'd known them well and surely there would have been insurance policies and money from the house in trust for Judy. Yes, yes, she knew that it was expensive these days bringing up a child but Judy had never been demanding, why she didn't even have a bike and Miss Hargreaves knew she walked to school in all weathers, even though the school bus passed the end of her road.

Aunt Mary had the grace to flush slightly and, without meeting Miss Hargreaves' eyes, stuttered out about how she was only thinking of Judy's future and she had to make provisions, she wasn't getting any younger herself, after all. Miss Hargreaves pounced.

"Exactly, Miss Minshull. I knew you'd see it my way and would have Judy's best interests at heart. What better investment for the future than in the girl's education. Why, God forbid that anything should happen to you, but what a relief it would be for you to know that she was able to take care of herself and earn her own living."

She could see that Aunt Mary was weakening, torn between retaining her control of Judy and the money that was invested for her and the wish to retain the appearance of the saintly aunt and good fairy she felt she presented to the world. She was unaware that the world saw her quite differently.

"Well, Miss Minshull, I am as certain as I can be that Judith will get a place so I feel it would be advisable for us to discuss, at this stage, exactly what it would cost. As Judith is fast becoming a young woman, I feel that an allowance of the same figure each month for her to control herself would be the ideal solution. That way, she will learn how to budget and how to manage for herself."

Difficult as Aunt Mary was, Miss Hargreaves knew that she prided herself on keeping her word and would abide by any decision made. It was imperative that all the details be nailed down now before Aunt Mary had a chance to go home and think it over. Mentally grinding her teeth, she ploughed on, pushing Aunt Mary for one concession after another until she felt she could push no further without jeopardising everything she had already gained. Even though she hadn't achieved everything she wanted, she wasn't entirely dissatisfied with the outcome and had gained some huge concessions on Judy's behalf.   Unfortunately, although Miss Hargreaves had made great steps in gaining some freedom of movement and some financial independence for Judy, she'd been unable to achieve the concession she had wanted most.

Aunt Mary's heels were firmly dug in. She had agreed to everything except that Judy should go away to college. That really was unnecessary expense when there was a perfectly good university within easy reach. Why pay out good money for rented accommodation when she had a home already provided with everything she could wish for.

Miss Hargreaves smiled grimly but decided there was nothing more to be gained.

"Let's have Judith in then, shall we? We can tell her the good news. I'll send for Judy's form mistress as well, she has a free period just now and she'll be happy to hear of your plans."

She knew well enough that she must strike while the iron was hot, go over the ground again to reinforce in Aunt Mary's mind the agreements already made. Perhaps it was a little underhand but vitally necessary for Judy's future. She knew that she wouldn't go back on promises made now, in front of two people, apart from Judy, both of them 'official' figures.

It was more than Judy had hoped for and for the first time in a very long time, Miss Hargreaves was happy to see a smile on that serious little face and some animation in her expression. Judy thanked Aunt Mary dutifully and then Miss Hargreaves for the interest she had shown in her. As Aunt Mary turned to leave the office, Miss Hargreaves had, without any other change in her expression, dropped one eyelid in a compliant wink. It was the funniest thing Judy had seen in years and later that evening, she lay in bed smiling to herself.

Over the next few days, every time she thought of it, she smiled again. She knew she owed her soon to be found freedom to Miss Hargreaves' shrewd negotiations but now suspected that Miss Hargreaves did, in fact, have a side to her character of which the pupils were totally unaware.

Never, in all her wildest dreams, did she imagine that one day, in the not too distant future, she would have good cause to thank Aunt Mary for teaching her thrift, good household management and above all, self sufficiency.

***

University life suited her. She worked hard and largely kept herself to herself. She had, however, taken charge of her own wardrobe and to her amazement, some of the gear Aunt Mary had earlier insisted upon was quite acceptable, even desirable, within the bounds of the student population.

She was gradually able to shuffle off the stuff she hated most and although she had to shop very carefully and account for every penny, she had more room to manoeuvre than she could ever remember. Her mother had been a talented dressmaker and Judy seemed to have inherited the knack. She could run up a skirt or blouse in short order and Aunt Mary, rather impatiently, had taught her to knit. A new jumper or skirt was no problem when she could afford to buy fabric or wool.

Even better, she now had friends. Not close friends in whom she could really confide but people on her course with whom she could sit during the coffee breaks. Some of them were young men and a couple of them actually asked her out, though she hadn't had the confidence to accept an offer.

Gradually, she noticed that one young man in particular, John Freeman, made a point to sit next to her whenever he could. He seemed to be as shy as she was but he had a wry sense of humour and she occasionally found herself giggling at one of his quiet remarks, delivered with a deadpan expression. Over a period of weeks they became good friends and when he did finally pluck up the courage to ask her to the cinema, she hadn't the heart to turn him down and was surprised to find she didn't want to.

Aunt Mary had actually mellowed a little over the last year or so. She seemed to be slowing down and occasionally huffed and puffed about not getting any younger but she was still as exacting as ever as far as Judy's household duties were concerned. Although her mouth still went into a stiff, straight line when Judy went out in the evening, she made no verbal objection and seemed happy, if she could ever be said to be happy, with a token gesture of disapproval.

Judy had avoided nights out with the rest of the crowd, the rowdy pub life just wasn't for her. She found it unbearably loud and very threatening but a night at the cinema with John or occasionally in the cheapest seats in the theatre with other friends seemed harmless. For the first time in years she began to enjoy herself.

She and John began to spend more time together and although they were equally inexperienced, managed to progress to holding hands in the cinema and then a kiss in the shadows at the end of her road.

Although she'd read countless romantic novels surreptitiously over the years, wrapping them in plain covers and keeping them hidden from Aunt Mary, she couldn't somehow equate this gentle pressure of lips with the tumultuous emotions experienced by the heroines in the novels. It was quite pleasant and John seemed to enjoy it too, although he sometimes did push himself closer against her than she liked. She waited and waited but her heart never started thumping and she never felt the giddy loss of control she felt she ought to feel. Was there something wrong with her?

It's difficult to say how their relationship might have developed had things been allowed to run their natural course. Perhaps they would have tired of each other and each gone on to someone else, gaining experience and maturity as they went along. Perhaps they would have had a chance to grow closer together, learning about each other and maturing together but, unfortunately, events overtook them and they rushed into a decision they would later learn to regret.

Chapter 5

One morning, Judy opened her eyes and saw that the sun was shining outside. She squinted at the clock on the bedside cabinet, eight o'clock. It couldn't be. She listened carefully, not a sound from downstairs. Normally, Aunt Mary would have called her half an hour ago but everything was silent.

She jumped out of bed and pulled on her tatty old dressing gown over the flannel nightie Aunt Mary insisted she wore. Pushing her feet into her slippers, she opened the door, still no sound. What on earth was going on?

She ran quickly downstairs, calling Aunt Mary as she went into the kitchen. The table was set for breakfast as it was when she came down every morning. She'd set it herself the night before. There was still no sign of Aunt Mary, no kettle on to boil, no newspaper on the table, no milk bottle brought in, nothing.

Suddenly she whirled and tore up the stairs at full speed, slowing only at the top in front of Aunt Mary's door. Heaven forbid there was really nothing wrong and Aunt Mary caught her panicking. She pulled herself together and tapped gently on the door.

'Aunt Mary, Aunt Mary, are you in there? Are you all right?'

Nothing. She tapped again, a little harder and this time put her ear right against the door, trying to hear some response. Still nothing. Finally she gritted her teeth and opened the door into the darkened room. Even in these circumstances, the years of discipline held sway. She couldn't switch a light on when it was broad daylight outside. She looked towards the bed where Aunt Mary was lying quite still and then stepped over to the window and pulled back one of the curtains.

Aunt Mary hadn't moved. Judy shook her gently by the shoulder. She couldn't ever remember having touched her before except accidentally.

"Aunt Mary, what's the matter? It's after eight o'clock, are you ill?"

With a dreadful grimace, Aunt Mary opened one eye and stared at Judy. She grunted and tried to move but one side of her face seemed to be pulled down as if dragged by an invisible hand.

Judy touched her hand; she was icy cold and obviously very ill indeed. Now Judy did panic. She ran into her own bedroom and tugged off the eiderdown, running back to throw it over Aunt Mary and babbling all the time.

"Now just wait there, Aunt Mary. I'll fetch the doctor. You'll be all right, just wait and see. It will take me five minutes to get dressed and run over to the 'phone box. I'll come straight back, don't worry."

She barged back into her own room, throwing off her nightie and throwing on the first clothes that came to hand. She grabbed her purse and galloped down the stairs and out the front door. Sin of sins, she'd left the front door open behind her but she couldn't worry about that now and charged across the road to the 'phone box.

Aunt Mary was in the hospital within the hour but Judy waited two hours before one of the nurses remembered she was still waiting for news. She came down the ward holding a cup of tea, which she pushed into Judy's hand. She could see the child was suffering from shock and felt guilty for having forgotten her.

"The doctor will come and have a word with you in a few minutes. You've had an awful shock, is there anyone else we could contact, another relative or a friend perhaps?"

Judy shook her head, murmuring that there was really just the two of them. Although the nurse felt sorry for her, she could hear matron calling; they were rushed off their feet this morning.

"The doctor will be down in a few minutes, dear, and then perhaps you'll be able to see her."

Half an hour later, the doctor appeared. A serious stroke, he told her, but with a good chance of at least a partial recovery. She was in the best hands now and perhaps she would just like to have a peep before she left. Judy tiptoed down the hushed ward where the nurse was pointing to a drawn curtain. She pulled the curtains gently apart and looked in. It looked like Aunt Mary but she was lying very still and looked quite peaceful. The nurse came over and put a hand on Judy's shoulder.

"Look here, love. There's nothing you can do now. We've given her something to make her rest and she won't wake up for hours. Go home and come back again this evening. Visiting is from seven to eight and you can bring her a few things; a clean nightie, her toothbrush and wash bag, you know the kind of thing. There's nothing to be gained by waiting around here. Go home and have something to eat, try to get a little rest and try not to worry, we'll look after her."

She opened the front door. All was silent, no signs of life and no sound at all. She went straight upstairs to the bathroom, passing Aunt Mary's open door on the way. She could never remember seeing it left open before and as she glanced in, she could see the rumpled bedclothes, the half drawn curtains and the slippers placed neatly side by side under the bed. It was like the 'Marie Celeste' and she half expected to hear Aunt Mary's voice demanding to know what she was doing, dawdling around on the landing.

She suddenly realised, guiltily, that she was famished and as she passed on her way back down the stairs, she closed the offending door firmly and thought,

I'll deal with that later but I must eat something first.

It felt very strange to be alone in the house. She couldn't remember ever having been there without Aunt Mary's presence hovering somewhere nearby. She had been surprised to find she was so hungry and although it felt odd to be rummaging around and pleasing herself what she ate, she had nevertheless knocked up some scrambled eggs on toast and devoured two pieces of the fruit cake she had found in the tin in the pantry.

She sat in the kitchen nursing a cup of tea between cupped hands, watching the hands of the clock on the wall moving around. She only had a few hours and it would be time to go back to the hospital. She decided to have a bath and wash her hair and make some effort to dress up a little for her visit. She knew Aunt Mary would have plenty to say if she arrived at the hospital looking unkempt and untidy.

She still had the bag to pack and dreaded going back into that room. Nevertheless, thanks to Aunt Mary, she knew her duty and, gritting her teeth, went back upstairs to the closed door.

The room smelled a little musty now the sun had come round so she drew back the curtains and opened the window as wide as it would go. She pulled back the eiderdown and blankets over the chair at the end of the bed and stripped off the sheets and pillowcases, throwing them on to the landing. She would wash them later.

She felt like an intruder, poking around Aunt Mary's clothes and she felt slightly queasy handling underwear and nightwear. She pulled out a canvas bag from the bottom of the wardrobe and carefully packed the night clothes and slippers. Then she went into the bathroom for her wash things and that was even worse. She had to wash her hands before she did anything else. She carried the bag downstairs, picked out a couple of nice apples and carefully wrapped a large slice of cake in grease proof paper and put them into the bag.

Anything else? She knew it was extremely unlikely that she'd get it right. If she took food in, Aunt Mary would say it was a waste. If she didn't, she would be a thoughtless child who didn't consider her elders. Heaven help her if she forgot anything that Aunt Mary actually did need. She'd never hear the last of it. She went over the list again in her mind. She thought she had everything.

Two hours later, she was walking up the road towards Withington Hospital. It had been a workhouse in a previous life and its gloomy facade echoed its grim past. The seemingly endless and poorly lit hospital corridor was busy with dozens of other people visiting friends and relatives. Most of them looked quite cheerful and were chatting and smiling, all carrying parcels or flowers and turning off as they reached the wards they wanted.

Judy looked up. Ward 7B, this was it. She turned into the ward and found there were people waiting outside the double doors, which were firmly closed. Not quite seven o'clock but there was to be no entry until the hands of the clock reached seven precisely. The matrons ran the wards like regimental sergeant majors and not a single visitor was allowed through the doors until every patient was in bed, every counterpane neatly stretched and tucked and every patient was washed, combed and tidied up.

The other visitors were beginning to mutter, it was just turned seven, what was happening? One of the nurses came and pulled back the heavy door, fixing it securely before she stood aside to let the visitors pass.

Judy was just walking through, looking anxiously towards the end of the ward where she had last seen Aunt Mary, when the nurse caught her gently by the elbow.

"Oh, there you are. I was looking out for you. Come along, love, Matron would like a word with you. This way, she's waiting in her office."

Judy followed obediently, looking neither to left or right. This all seemed so familiar somehow. She'd felt this way once before, gone through the same motions, only this time it wasn't Miss Hargreaves' office but the matron's. It was like a slow motion re-run of some dreadful recurring nightmare.

The nurse caught her by the arm and led her gently inside, guiding her towards the straight backed chair in front of the matron's desk. The matron sat unsmiling in her navy dress and white cap and apron.

"Sit down, won't you? I can tell by your face that you already suspect the worst and I'm so sorry to have to tell you that you're right. Nurse, go and fetch us a cup of tea, plenty of sugar, and close the door behind you."

"Now then, Miss Minshull, I'm sorry to have to tell you that your Aunt died a short time ago. Unfortunately, she had another massive stroke and there was nothing we could do."

"Did she ask for me or did she say anything at all?"

"No, not a word we could understand. She was pretty incoherent, the first stroke had left her paralysed as you saw this morning and although she was mumbling a little, no-one could tell what she was saying."

"I can't believe it. I thought she was indestructible. She never said that she was feeling ill, I had no idea."

"That's the way it is with strokes and it may be of some comfort for you to know that it's unlikely she would have recovered all her faculties after the first stroke. She would probably have needed a lot of nursing and would never have been truly independent again. I somehow feel that that wouldn't have suited her at all."

She leaned forward and gently placed her palm on Judy's tightly clasped hands resting on the desk in front of her.

"Here's the tea. Drink it up now. You've had a dreadful shock. Would you like me to leave you alone for a few minutes?"

Judy nodded soundlessly and put the cup and saucer down on the desk. She sat there, rigid, unable to move and unable to think until the matron came back.

"Would you like to see her or would that upset you too much?"

"I think I'd better get it over with. I won't believe she's really gone until I do and then I won't have to do it again."

Matron took Judy along to a small room next to hers where the curtains were drawn so that nobody passing along the corridor could look in. She opened the door and ushered Judy inside. There was a figure on the bed, totally covered with a white sheet. Matron gently folded the sheet back from the face. Judy steeled herself and looked down. All the harsh lines were gone and she looked younger. There was nothing frightening about her and Judy suddenly wished she had had the chance to see her Mum and Dad after they'd died. Perhaps it would have made it easier. Matron nodded and pulled the sheet back up.

"There, that wasn't so bad was it? You can see how peaceful she looks and she has no more worries anymore. Will you be all right? Shall I call a taxi to take you home?

There are various formalities to complete but it might be better if you could come back tomorrow morning when you're rested. We can start to sort out the paper work and I'll arrange for the almoner to be here to help you."

Judy shook her head.

"No, I can get home all right on the bus. I suppose I'd better take back that bag I brought with me. Aunt Mary won't need any of that stuff now, will she?"

Matron retrieved the holdall from her office and handed it to Judy.

"I'll see you tomorrow then. Any time after eleven o'clock and before one. Try and make it between those times as the almoner is on duty and you'll need some guidance on what to do next."

She patted Judy on the shoulder and turned back to the ward. Judy was dismissed. She hardly knew what to do next but trudged back the way she'd come only a short time earlier, lugging the bag along with her. It felt much heavier now. In a flash of temper, with energy she didn't know she had, she hurled the bag into the next rubbish bin she found. There was no point in carting that all the way home, was there? It was no use to anybody now.

***

Although she'd been too numb to take in much when her parents died, she had vague memories of the funeral. There had been dozens and dozens of people at the service, huge swathes of flowers and wreaths and many kind, sympathetic faces. Some of them had tried to keep in touch with Judy but had been firmly discouraged by Aunt Mary, who had said it would be better for her to put the past behind her. Gradually, in the face of such discouragement, they had all lost touch.

This funeral was quite different, even more awful, if that were possible. Instead of crowds of people, there were just four mourners; Judy, the family solicitor, Mr Hughes, Miss Hargreaves from the school and John Freeman.

65

Judy had chosen the simplest, and cheapest, wreath she could find, even now the thrift imposed on her by Aunt Mary at the forefront of her mind. There were bouquets each from Miss Hargreaves and Mr Hughes and John had brought along a cellophane wrapped arrangement with a card signed by some of the other students. Nevertheless, the floral tributes looked extremely sparse lying on top of the coffin. The chapel was cold and echoing in the face of so few mourners and although the local vicar kept the service as brief as possible, it was a relief to have it over with.

Judy stood and watched as the curtains in front of the coffin gently swished closed, silently saying goodbye. For the first time ever, she felt rather sorry for Aunt Mary, so few people to mourn her and only Judy herself to whom her passing would make any difference at all.

They stood at the door of the chapel, not knowing quite how to take their leave of each other. It had seemed pointless to arrange anything for after the funeral as so few people were coming and Judy didn't know quite how to bring the proceedings to an end.

Finally, Mr Hughes put out his hand.

"Please ring me tomorrow and we'll make an appointment so that we can tie up all the loose ends. We need to get this done as soon as possible so that you will know where you stand financially and so that I can release some cash to you."

"I will, I'll do that. Perhaps now I can begin to sort myself out and make some decisions. Things have been at sixes and sevens all week but I realise that I need to get myself organised."

Mr Hughes offered Miss Hargreaves a lift and they went off together towards the cemetery gates, leaving John and Judy standing in the porch. The undertakers had already left, the vicar was still in the chapel and they could see the next funeral cortege coming down the drive towards them.

Judy gripped John's arm.

"Come on, let's get out of here. It's driving me crazy."

The sky had been a heavy, threatening grey all morning and now the rain was lashing down across the long stretches of headstones. They scrunched along the gravel, huddled under Judy's umbrella, and passed the oncoming cortege. There were at least half a dozen cars packed with mourners, all solemn and sombre. At least the deceased had a decent turnout, unlike poor Aunt Mary.

John insisted on riding home on the bus with Judy and walking with her right to the gate. He asked her if she wanted him to come in for a while but Judy couldn't face it. It seemed sacrilegious to have a man in Aunt Mary's house. She squeezed his hand gently.

"No, I don't think so. I think I'd rather be on my own. I'll be back to classes in a couple of days. I'll see you then. Thanks for coming, it meant a lot to me to have you there but I've got some hard thinking to do. I'll see you later in the week. You get off now."

Judy stood at the gate. John looked quite different in a suit and a black tie, more mature, sort of. She smiled as he turned at the corner and waved and then disappeared out of sight. She squared her shoulders, went up the path towards the front door and went inside. Now she really was on her own and the thought was rather frightening.

Chapter 6

Three months later they were married. What remained of her parents'
money and the little left by Aunt Mary had been invested to give her a
small, regular income. Aunt Mary's house was in a good area and
although a little old fashioned, had been well maintained. Mr Hughes
had recommended keeping this as a rental property to increase her
income while she was at university. After that, they could think again.

Mr Hughes had taken care of all the details; the tenancy
agreement and the investments and together, they had calculated that
she would have just enough to live on. She rented a decent sized
room, with access to a kitchen and bathroom shared with another girl,
and threw herself back into her studies.

She hadn't expected to feel lonely, she had been lonely for
such a long time, but this was different. She felt more isolated than
ever and began to spend more and more time with John, who said he
wanted to look after her.

He was kind and gentle and now she no longer had the
constraints laid on her by having to go home to Aunt Mary, their
relationship had changed. For the first few weeks, she hadn't wanted
any physical contact at all and he had said he understood, just kissing
her gently as they parted.

Now things were changing again. They often sat close
together on the lumpy old settee in Judy's room and John gradually
began to show his feelings. Sometimes he held her quite passionately
and when she stopped him trying to unfasten her blouse or firmly
removing his hand from her thigh, he would jump up and start either
pacing the room, running his fingers wildly through his hair, or grab
his jacket and leave.

Judy liked the feeling of closeness. It was wonderful to be
held and cuddled and she liked the kissing but she was frightened to
let things go any further. She just didn't know what to
do, how to go about things. Her background had hardly prepared her
for physical intimacy and she had no-one to ask for advice. She
would have been too embarrassed anyway.

There were girls at university who were pretty free and easy,
who had a bad name but were in constant demand from the boys and
looked down on by the other girls. She didn't want to finish up like
one of them, did she? Anyway, she'd heard enough of her girl

friends' moaning about the lads trying it on and being 'only after one thing and when they've had it, they throw you over.' She had thought John was a bit different but it seemed to be true that the boys had stronger urges than the girls and had more difficulty controlling them.

John, in the meantime, was becoming more and more frustrated. One evening, after they had tussled on the settee for an hour or more as she constantly pushed away his hands, he'd jumped up and gone into the bathroom. He was missing for ages and when he came back, had obviously washed his face and combed his hair.

He was rather pale but composed now and stood, warming his back at the electric fire, hands in pockets.

"I can't stand this any longer. Let's get married."

Judy was stunned. It had never crossed her mind and she just sat, hands braced on the settee either side of her and gaped at him, opening her mouth to speak and then realising she didn't know what to say.

"Look,' he said. 'I've thought it all out. I know we're young but we're not that young. Plenty of people our age get married. You've got nobody and my parents don't care much what I do as long as I don't bother them. We could share things, study together and keep each other warm at night. I'm sick of bailing out of here and having to run for the bus, uptight and upset because I've had to leave you again. We could look after one another, what do you think?"

Then he made the ultimate, irresistible plea.

"I love you, you know I do and I thought you loved me. I thought you wanted us to be together."

"But how would we manage. Could we afford it?"

Judy was just beginning to realise that he meant what he said, that this truly was a proposal of marriage.

"I've thought it all out. If we pool what we're paying for a room each, we could get something big enough to share. We'd be together then, all the time. I can't go on like this any longer. Either we get together permanently and properly or it might be better if we stopped seeing each other. We're going nowhere the way we're carrying on now. Well, say something."

She sat very still on the settee, looking up at him warily.

"I don't know what to say. I've never even thought about it and it's come as a bit of a shock. Let me get used to the idea. There's a lot for us to think about."

"Well, perhaps it's a bit sudden. I'm going home now unless you change your mind and let me stay the night. After all, we're practically engaged," he said in a phony French accent, leering at her playfully, and hand on hip and twirling an imaginary moustache.

"Not tonight, mon cher!" she responded in a high, squeaky voice. "Zees is all too, 'ow you say, sudden."

He picked up his jacket, gave Judy one last kiss and a tight hug and left, arranging to meet her the following day.

Judy fell into a heap on the lumpy settee. She must think this all out very carefully.

For the first time in a long time, she actively missed her mum. What often receded to a dull ache was transformed again into full blown grief and she sat sobbing and muttering.

"Oh Mum, what shall I do? I don't want to be alone any longer but I'm too young to get married. I don't want to lose him, he's all I've got in the world. He's the only one who cares tuppence what happens to me but he does love me and I think I love him too."

The sobs turned to gentle sniffs and when she awoke, stiff and cold, a couple of hours later, she had made up her mind.

***

The wedding was almost a repeat of the funeral, a very sombre affair. There were a few more people but not many.

Miss Hargreaves and Mr Hughes appeared. They were Judy's only guests. Mr and Mrs Freeman also arrived at the Registry Office bearing a totally inappropriate wedding gift of half a dozen beautiful crystal glasses.

She went through the wedding in a daze. She'd seen the wedding party before them leaving the All Saints Registry Office, lots of people, all laughing and throwing confetti, shouting out messages of good luck and slightly ribald remarks.

The room seemed enormous with just the six of them although the registrar was kind and did his best to put them at their ease. She'd always imagined, like most girls of her generation, floating down the aisle in a haze of white tulle, veil over her face, looking towards the handsome figure waiting at the altar.

By comparison, this seemed a little tawdry and her serviceable suit and small bunch of yellow roses were certainly a far cry from her earlier expectations. Although the room was imposing, with wood panelled walls and a lovely flower arrangement on the highly polished desk, it was very impersonal. She felt more as though she were applying for some official documentation than getting married.

Where was the excitement, the romance? It was all over before she knew it.

"That was nothing special," she thought. "It should have felt like a momentous occasion, uplifting or something."

She looked down at the ring on her finger, just a plain gold band but it tied her firmly to John and she had made a commitment for the rest of her life.

Fortunately, the sun was shining and Mr Freeman insisted they go into the park in front of the Registry Office to take some photos to 'mark the happy occasion.'

He'd had to slip a tramp five bob to move to the next bench so they could get a clear shot. He probably hung about in the park on a regular basis looking for the odd back-hander; a good way to put a couple of extra pints under his belt.

They'd booked a meal in a restaurant just a few minutes away down Wilmslow Road.. John got into his father's car so he could give directions and Judy got into the back with John's mother.

"I'm glad to have a little word with you on your own, my dear," she said in a low voice, leaning towards Judy and patting her hand on the seat between them.

"John can be very pig-headed when he wants to be and nothing would do but that the wedding was as soon as possible. You know that we've agreed to carry on paying his allowance until he finishes at university but there won't be any extra cash. We're pushed to the limit at the moment, with one thing and another."

Without looking at Judy, she patted her hand again and murmured,

"I hope there wasn't any specific reason why you had to rush into this, was there? John says not but I'd like to hear it from you. Women can be much more straightforward with each other, don't you think?"

Judy flushed to the roots of her hair. She could feel her face getting hotter and hotter and couldn't look Mrs Freeman in the face either. How dare she? What gave her the right to ask such a question? Surely she could see she was a decent girl.

She began to get angry, unusual for her, but this was John's mother and she didn't want to start a row on her wedding day. She pulled her hand from Mrs Freeman's and put it back in her lap. She turned her head and spoke quietly but firmly, looking Mrs Freeman straight in the eye.

71

"I know what you're insinuating but it isn't true. I was brought up to be a decent girl and that sort of thing is out of the question. Why, my mother and father would have been horrified to hear you even suggest it, let alone Aunt Mary, who must be turning in her grave."

"I only asked out of concern for you both. Heaven knows, marriage is hard enough. It's no piece of cake, believe you me. You're both very young and I shudder to think how you'd manage with a baby on the way."

"Well there isn't,' said Judy firmly, 'and there won't be for quite some time, at least until we've both graduated anyway. Now let's talk about something else, shall we?"

Little did she realise that she would have cause to eat her words. She hadn't even thought what people would say about such a rushed affair and realised that Miss Hargreaves and Mr Hughes probably thought the same as John's mother. She now also realised the reason for some of the knowing smiles and winks she had received from other students. She felt an absolute fool.

I really am as green as grass. But still, time will prove them all wrong, won't it and then they can smile on the other side of their faces.

The lunch went off well, if rather sedately, although Mr Hughes made a nice little speech wishing them both well and Mr Freeman stood up and wished them all the luck in the world. The party caught the eye of the other diners and they were treated to a round of applause as they stood up to leave.

John's father and mother were to run them down to the station where they were taking the afternoon train for Blackpool. They put their suitcases onto the train and stood on the platform until the station announcer called the departure of their train.

Judy could feel her cheeks glowing from the two unaccustomed glasses of wine and she felt a little giddy. Mr and Mrs Freeman both kissed her on the cheek, Mrs Freeman whispering, "no hard feelings?" into her ear as she did so.

Judy shook her head.

"Of course not," she murmured.

"Do come over and see us soon but don't forget to give us plenty of notice. We're out and about such a lot these days, you must ring and we'll fix something up."

Judy doubted they would ever fix anything up. She'd no desire to go and stay in their home and she really couldn't ever imagine calling them Mother and Dad as they'd suggested. Still, she put on a big smile and waved to them as the train pulled out.

She looked at John. He was her husband, how very strange. He was going to be with her now night and day. She shivered a little with apprehension or anticipation, she didn't know which.

***

It was years since Judy had been in a boarding house, not since before mum and dad died and then it had been slightly more upmarket than this but nevertheless, it was clean and welcoming and from the window, they could just see the sea between the roof tops.

John put the suitcases on the bed and Judy started to unpack. She knew she ought not to be but she was embarrassed. She wished she could have two minutes on her own to gather her thoughts and the room wasn't so big that the bed didn't seem to intrude wherever she looked.

They decided to go out for a walk before tea and changing out of their wedding clothes and into slacks and sweaters was torture for both of them. She changed with her back to John without realising he was doing the same and turned to catch him with his trousers half up. Even the backs of his ears were red.

This is awful. How are we going to manage? Perhaps he won't bother tonight but will give us both a chance to get used to the idea.

They went for a walk along the beach; the sun was shining and they had to thread their way between deckchairs and sandcastles to get down to the firmer sand where it was easier to walk. John took her hand but he didn't say much.

After tea they went for another walk, in the other direction. It seemed that anything was better than that bedroom with just the two of them in it. This time, they walked along the promenade. John bought Judy a silly hat and then won a small, rather tatty looking dog at one of the rifle ranges. This seemed to buck him up a bit. After all, surely it was a sign of masculinity to be able to shoot a rifle.

She looked at her watch, it was only nine o'clock. How on earth were they going to spend the time until bedtime? The next two hours loomed like two weeks but she hardly dared wish for it to pass quickly because she didn't know what to expect later.

John suggested going for a drink so they wandered along until they found a pub that looked as though it might suit them, not too

73

flashy but not too crowded either. They found a small table in a corner and sat there holding hands, sipping at their drinks.

Judy wasn't much of a drinker at the best of times and a couple of glasses of cider on top of the wine she'd consumed at lunch had given her a bit of a headache.

Goodness I haven't been married a full day yet and already I'm complaining of a headache.

She started to giggle but she couldn't tell John what was so funny but he was happy to see her laughing and began to laugh with her. He bought another round and Judy managed to swallow yet another glass of cider while John struggled manfully with another pint. It was approaching closing time and they would have to return to the boarding house.

Never mind, perhaps it will give us both a bit of Dutch courage.

She didn't realise that she was viewing her impending nuptials with feelings of fear and resignation. Romance had completely flown out the window and she was just gritting her teeth and praying for it to be over.

Perhaps when we've done it once it will be all right. At least I'll know what to expect and won't ever have to worry like this again.

When they got back to the bedroom, John picked up his towel and soap and said,

"You use the sink in here. I'll go along to the bathroom and give you time to get in bed."

Judy was thankful for the short respite and it would have been comical, had it not been so tragic, to see her running around at double speed. She threw off her clothes and dragged on her nightie. That was the worst over. She swiped a wet flannel round her face and scrubbed wildly at her teeth, trying to get into bed before John came back.

She suddenly realised she'd left her underwear on a chair. She jumped out of bed again to move it. She couldn't leave her knickers there for John to see. She began to panic, what should she do with them. She hurriedly pulled out her case from under the bed, thrust the offending article in and jumped back into bed, pulling the covers up to her chin. She waited, still no sign of John so she jumped out of bed and turned off the light. Back into bed as quick as a flash, covers up to the chin again. Her breathing had just steadied after all the dashing about when John opened the door. By this time, she was so frightened and so panicked that she even thought of pretending to be asleep.

"Oh good, I'm glad you're already in bed. There's enough light from the streetlights, so I won't switch the light on again."

She lay absolutely rigid; eyes shut tight and listened to him fumbling around in the half light. He bumped his toe on the end of the bed and cursed under his breath. She was so tense, if she'd giggled, it would have been near hysteria. It might have broken the ice but she didn't dare. She swallowed hard, she knew she couldn't allow John to lose his dignity, he might go off in a huff and then things would be even worse.

Finally, she felt his weight on the edge of the mattress, felt him lift the bedclothes and slide in next to her. She was lying on her back, legs stretched straight out and hands clasped tightly together. Nervous people often don't know what to do with their hands but she'd never thought that it might apply in bed. She turned her head slightly; John was almost leaning over her, his weight supported on one elbow. She could see him smiling in the dim light.

"Don't look so worried. I'm as nervous as you are. I've never done this before either but people have been managing ever since the world began and we can learn as we go along."

Reassured, Judy put her arm up around his neck and pulled his face down to hers. He kissed her very tentatively and she opened her lips slightly and welcomed him with a slightly open mouth. She felt his tongue gently pushing between her teeth. She liked this; although why they called it 'French kissing' she had no idea. She could feel his tongue moving gently in her mouth and moved her own to meet it.

He carefully unbuttoned her nightie to the waist, pushing it almost off one shoulder and slid his hand over her breast. This was all new ground, they'd never gone this far before. She could feel the roughness of his pyjama jacket against her skin, it wasn't unpleasant but the feel of his fingers against her nipples was starting up all sorts of tingling feelings. She sucked his tongue deeper into her mouth, her breathing deepening. She was becoming aroused. She'd read plenty of romantic novels, some of them fairly explicit, but she was unprepared for her own body's reaction to this kind of stimulation.

He lowered himself gently until his face was against her ear, still keeping up the gentle pressure on her breast. She heard him swallow.

"Take off the nightie," he said hoarsely, "I want to see you."

Judy was reluctant to break the spell but she sat up and whipped the nightie over her head, chucking it carelessly on the floor. She didn't have time to be embarrassed now. She lay back and watched as John unfastened the cord of his pyjama pants and slid them off under the bedclothes. She watched him take something from the pocket of his pyjama jacket and put it under the pillow. The jacket followed the pyjama pants on to the floor.

She felt much more relaxed now as they turned towards each other. She gasped as his body touched hers; the feeling of skin on skin was electric so she put her arms around him, feeling the smoothness of his back, running her hand up and down from neck to buttocks.

She'd no idea that men could be so smooth, she thought only women were supposed to have skin like silk.

He put his head into the hollow between neck and shoulders and kissed her there, taking up again the gentle motion of his hand on her breast. She could feel that both nipples were sticking up now; it felt strange but exciting. So far so good, but she didn't know what to do next and continued gently stroking his back, waiting for him to make the next move.

He kissed her mouth again, thrusting his tongue backwards and forwards and moving his hand from her breast down to her thighs. This was more new territory and she had to overcome her instinct to push him away.

"I'm married now, it's all right," she told herself, wondering fleetingly how something could be sinful one day and her duty the next.

She could feel him now, pushing against her leg. He felt enormous and he took her hand and put it against him. She grasped him loosely and he shook slightly. The pressure of his lips became firmer, the thrusting of his tongue more pronounced as he gently pushed her legs apart. She kissed him back, aroused by his mouth and dazed by the sensation of what was happening in various parts of her body. The throbbing sensation continued from her mouth to her breasts and downwards and she could feel that she was wet and getting wetter.

John's fingers probed her gently and she suddenly gasped in turn, his finger was pushing inside her and she could feel he was shaking too.

With a groan, he sat up and groped under the pillow. He tore at the packet with his teeth and she shut her eyes when he started to

76

fumble around his own body, holding something small and white between his fingers.

He pushed her on to her back, pushed her legs wide apart and, supporting himself with his arms either side of her head, thrust himself inside her. She felt the pain like a knife and bit her lip so as not to cry out. All feeling of arousal had disappeared as soon as the pain started and she was aware only of John pumping up and down on top of her, rubbing her sore. It lasted only seconds and with a great shudder and a strangled moan, John's whole body went rigid above her. She opened her eyes for a moment. John's face looked as though he was in pain, all scrunched up, eyes closed tight, and mouth in the grimace of a grin.

Suddenly, he stopped moving and pulled away from her, rolling on to his back. She now felt very sticky and wondered whether she was bleeding, trying to pluck up courage to have a crafty look without alerting John to her fears. Her embarrassment had returned in full force and she felt slightly bruised and battered. All pleasure had fled.

John lay on his back breathing heavily as she swung her leg over the edge of the bed.

"What's up?" he asked, raising himself slightly. "How do you feel? They say it always hurts the woman a bit the first time but the worst is over now. It'll be better for you next time, I'm sure."

Judy kept her back towards him and reached to get her housecoat from the end of the bed. She pushed her arms into it before she stood up and whispered that she was just going along to the bathroom.

She quickly picked up her soap and towel and opening the bedroom door slightly, checked that there was no-one in the corridor. All clear, thanks heavens the bathroom was only next door but one. She made a dash for it and closed and bolted the door behind her.

As she suspected, she had bled, but only slightly, so she cleaned herself up, sniffling a bit as she did so. She unbolted the bathroom door, checked the corridor again and sped back to the bedroom.

John was lying on his side with his back towards her. He didn't speak and neither did she and as she slipped into bed beside him, she realised he was sound asleep.

***

By lunchtime on Monday they were back home. They'd set up house in a large, rambling place near the Longsight market and on the bus route for the university.

They had two rooms, double the space they'd had originally, living apart, but Judy soon found that her living space seemed smaller than ever. John was dreadfully untidy and left his stuff lying all over the place, soiled underwear on the floor or kicked under the bed, clothes over chairs and books constantly spread out all over the table. If he even made himself so much as a coffee, the cup was left standing and he always seemed to spill a little and drip the water so there was a sticky, unsightly mess in the small kitchen area.

Heaven knows, she tried not to nag him but it did get on her nerves, constantly picking up after him. Living on his own, his idea of a balanced meal had been either beans on toast or fish and chips. He soon became accustomed to Judy's cooking and even put a little weight on his skinny frame but he remained obstinately oblivious of the work involved.

Being married had given him some confidence, a little standing with the 'boys' and he now insisted that they went out to the pub more often, where Judy was left sitting with the other girls while he stood at the bar, with an air of bravado, telling smutty jokes and having serious discussions about United's line up for the coming season.

After a couple of months, Judy was falling behind with her studies, the workload was just too great, with all the extra washing and shopping, not to mention the cooking and constantly picking up after John. He even muttered under his breath when she asked him to stop on the way home to pick up a loaf or a pint of milk. She might have kept up had she been left in peace to get on with it in the evening but John wanted to go out so often. They were saving on the rent; the cost of their two rooms was less than those they had rented individually but the difference was swallowed by John's ever increasing insistence on being in the pub. Judy wondered what on earth she had got herself into. John had wanted to look after her but she soon realised that she was looking after him and there seemed no respite.

The best part of being married was lying in bed first thing in the morning while John was still asleep. She could lie up close against his back, her arm thrown over his chest and for a while at least, she felt some comfort from his presence.

She'd become more or less resigned to the rest of her conjugal duties. John had said that they would learn together but he seemed to have learned all he wanted. He'd learned just enough to arouse her sufficiently to make penetration relatively easy and that was it. The early promise was never fulfilled although Judy occasionally remembered their first tentative love making. She wondered whether she was odd or whether there could perhaps be a way of creating or prolonging pleasure for her not just for John who more often than not these days, just rolled over and fell asleep, sometimes without even saying goodnight.

After a few weeks, desperate for a little solitude and anxious to catch up with her studies, she started to suggest that he went out alone. What bliss, as she heard him clatter down the uncarpeted stairs and bang the front door behind him. She would make a fresh coffee and, piling John's books all together, would spread her own over the table and, pencil and notebook at the ready, would crack on, and work steadily to try to catch up.

She did try to keep an eye on the clock so that she could be in bed and 'asleep' before John came home. It didn't always work and sometimes he woke her up, his breath smelling of beer so that she turned her face away from his kisses but it was generally easier to just let him get on with it than to try to reason with him.

Any pleasure she might have felt during their earlier courtship had now flown out the window. Love-making, like all the other paraphernalia which came with living with John, had become just another chore, something to be got through so that she could get on to something else.

She was unaware that she'd missed a period until she felt queasy several mornings on the trot. One morning, she had been out of bed only a few minutes when she had to rush to the bathroom to throw up. As she leaned over the toilet bowl, she also noticed that her breasts were a little tender. She sat back on her heels, wiping her mouth with the back of her hand when her eyes flew wide open and she groaned. No, it couldn't be, surely not, please God not. She pushed herself up and rose slowly to her feet, leaning against the wall with one hand over her eyes. Oh God, no. Don't let it be true.

She walked unsteadily back into the bedroom and lay down, thoughts whirling. She wouldn't tell John about her suspicions. It was no use putting the cat amongst the pigeons unnecessarily. She'd skip her first class and go down to the doctor's surgery. It might be nothing at all. It might be just some kind of tummy bug going around. She would wait and see, not cross bridges before she got to them. It might be nothing at all.

John had finally gone off in a thoroughly foul temper because he was up late and had to rush around to find his stuff for the day, moaning and muttering under his breath and chucking books and clothes around. She tidied the rooms, glad at least that she would be able to come home and find the place presentable.

There were only two people in front of her in the doctor's waiting room when she went up to give her name at the window. Maybe she wouldn't have to wait too long. She sat staring at an old poster on the green painted wall, hands in her coat pockets and fingers crossed.

The doctor was detached and impersonal and the examination uncomfortable and embarrassing. His eyes flickered over her stricken face as he confirmed her worst fears.

"Come in in four weeks and we'll have another look at you." He said coolly. He had already checked for a wedding ring but these days you never knew.

Then she was back on the street, walking back towards the flat. She couldn't face a class; she had to have an hour's peace to gather her thoughts. She half stumbled up the stairs, fumbled with the keys and then stood with her back to the door, pressed tight against it. She felt as though she wanted to keep everyone out, just for a little while.

Finally, she roused herself. The sickly feeling had now passed and she managed to get down a plain biscuit and a cup of weak tea. 'Well so much for John's safe method,' she thought bitterly. More than once during the last few weeks he had come in slightly the worse for drink and even though she knew their supply of contraceptives had run out, had insisted that he knew what he was doing. It was quite safe and he'd pull out in good time. Now she realised how irresponsible he'd been and had the fleeting thought that she would soon have two children to look after. How on earth would they manage?

***

The next few months were difficult for Judy. At first, John had been delighted, preening himself and reporting almost boastingly to his friends that he was going to be a father. He seemed proud of the fact although Judy couldn't see what he had to be proud of, he'd just been inconsiderate and careless and it was she and the baby who would bear the brunt of his childishness. They'd be terribly short of money.

She would just about finish her first year as the baby was due during the summer holidays, but it looked as though her education was at an end.

She tried to console herself with promises of returning to college when the child was old enough for nursery school or even infant school but she wasn't convinced.

John had moved from the first euphoria into a phase of being dreadfully impatient with her. She hadn't felt too well during the first part of her pregnancy and was struggling to keep up with her academic work. John studied spasmodically but his practice of going for a pint with the lads hadn't diminished. He was still out several nights a week and Judy was at her wits' end trying to save a little cash for all the things she would need for the baby.

She hid pound notes away where he wouldn't find them and then told him there was no cash left. He'd always been happy for Judy to manage the finances and had had cash doled out to him like a child with his pocket money. The food became plainer and plainer and all the little luxuries had disappeared from their larder while Judy scrimped and saved and then carefully hid away the stuff she bought for the baby under sweaters and underwear.

One night, she had finally succumbed and given him the last coins in her purse. He'd been grizzling for an hour and she gave him the last of her cash just to see the back of him. She wanted him out of the flat and, if she were honest, out of her sight altogether for an hour or two. She had little to occupy her now that the holidays had started. It was just as well really, she was large and very unwieldy and tired quickly. Just the shopping and keeping their home in order was enough for her now. It was very warm and all the windows were open to take advantage of what little breeze there was.

She sat on the sofa with her feet up and a book on her knee. It was really too hot to concentrate on anything and she leaned back and closed her eyes, one hand resting on her bulging stomach. She really ought to get into bed before John got back but she was too tired, she couldn't be bothered and it was even hotter in the bedroom than out here.

The first twinge caught her by surprise, that's all it was really, you couldn't call it a pain although her stomach felt as hard as a board. Could this be it? She was rather frightened and at the same time exhilarated that something was happening. She sat very still for maybe half an hour or so. Had she been mistaken? Was it was the nurses called 'false labour'? Finally, when nothing more seemed to be happening, she pushed herself to her feet and went into the kitchen to put the kettle on. She was reaching up onto the shelf for the tea caddy when she felt the strangest sensation. Water was rushing down her legs and all over her bare feet and she was standing in a puddle.

This was no false alarm. Something was definitely happening. Trust John to be missing when she needed him and she tried to think calmly. She couldn't afford to panic now.

After all, I'm only having a baby, I'm not seriously ill.

She mopped up the puddle, checked to see that her case, which had been packed for a week, was still on the chair in the bedroom and slowly and steadily made her way to the door and down the stairs. Mrs Beacon, the landlady, was the only person in the house with a telephone, she'd try there first.

As she reached the ground floor and made her way down the hallway she could, thankfully, hear the sound of a radio as she tapped gently on the closed door.

Mrs Beacon took one look at her face and drew her inside.

"It's your time, isn't it, love? What do you want me to do, ring for a taxi?"

Judy nodded weakly, both hands on her stomach, in the throes of the next contraction, a bit stronger this time. Mrs Beacon went upstairs to Judy's flat and brought down the case while they were waiting for the taxi, which came within ten minutes.

"Would you like me to come with you, love?"

"No, no thanks, I'll be OK. Perhaps you could let John know what's happened when he comes in. He'll be wondering where I am."

Mrs Beacon sniffed sharply.

"Oh aye, I'll let him know. Don't you worry about that? Now off you go. Let me carry that case for you and get you into the taxi. The driver won't mess about getting you to the hospital; he'll be terrified you'll have the baby in the cab. Best of luck, love, best of luck."

The next few hours passed in a blur, one contraction after another, coming closer and closer together. She gave a fleeting thought to John and wondered where he was. Fathers weren't encouraged on labour wards, the nurses regarded them as a nuisance and they were always banished to the waiting room long before there was any sign of the actual birth.

She remembered thinking,

no wonder they call it labour, it's bloody hard work.

She was tired now, falling asleep after a contraction and waking with the onslaught of the next. She could see the clock at the end of the ward and was amazed to see that she was falling sound asleep for only a couple of minutes at a time.

The nurse wiped her face with a soft cloth and took her hand.

"Don't worry Mrs Freeman, it won't be long now. Here's the doctor to have another look at you."

Half an hour later, Judy was the mother of a seven pound baby girl. She was exhausted and sore but exultant. She looked down at the baby in her arms and gently pulled away the blanket to check the fingers and toes. The little face was very red and very screwed up but the wave of emotion that engulfed Judy was overpowering, bringing tears to her eyes. Her own child, someone of her very own to love and take care of. John no longer existed for her, just the baby. As she looked at the little face she made a silent promise that this child would never suffer from lack of love or lack of attention but would grow up secure in the knowledge of her mother's love.

"We may not have much money, my darling," she whispered, kissing the baby's brow, "but you'll never go short of love. We'll manage somehow, I'll look after you."

Chapter 7

The other houses within the boundaries of the two major roads continued to empty, with more people leaving every week. Most of them were being moved to the newly built council estate way out in the country, a full hour's bus journey from the city centre. Some of the families, particularly those with young children, moved joyfully, looking forward to bathrooms and gardens and fresh air for the kids.

Others though, mainly the older people, were filled with gloom. They muttered about being uprooted and cutting ties with places where they, and their parents, had grown up. All the mod cons in the world wouldn't compensate them for the loss of their homes and the upheaval they were going through against their wishes.

The streets became more deserted by the day as the number of houses being boarded up increased. It looked and felt like a ghost town and the decrease in population and the empty streets began to affect William. There was still no news from the Town Hall and despite constantly assuring himself that no news is good news, he was becoming depressed and increasingly doubtful he was doing the right thing.

Things were pretty awful now but what would it be like when they actually started pulling down the houses? Was he putting his tenants through an ordeal which would have no favourable outcome? Was he just being pig-headed and should he bow gracefully to the inevitable? He waited for the postman every day, fearful that when the letter came it would be bad news and he knew he was becoming more and more irritable.

Much of his time had been spent maintaining his own and the other houses in the row but now it hardly seemed worthwhile to do anything when they might pull down the whole shebang in a couple of months. He saw himself as a man of action and the uncertainty and inactivity were wearing him down. If only there was something he could do, if only he had a decision one way or the other.

He could make no plans to go forward in either direction and the guilt he was suffering about his tenants was difficult to cope with.

He'd regarded himself almost as a father figure, certainly to Mikey since his parents died and, to a certain extent, to Miss Hartley even though she was so self sufficient and independent. He had no fears that Margaret wouldn't adjust to the change and he would have to bring pressure to bear that Mikey was offered accommodation near to him so he could keep an eye on him.

Heaven only knows what would happen to the Goldmans. The poor woman was scarcely able to leave the house unless her husband was with her. Though he wasn't a sentimental man, he had to admit being touched by the sight of the two of them going down the street towards the shops to do the weekend shopping. Her hand always rested in the crook of his elbow as he leaned towards her, speaking gently and patting her hand at regular intervals to encourage and reassure.

He knew a little of their history but no real details. He'd originally been approached about renting his house to them by a fellow officer, Bruce Marks. Bruce was a pleasant enough fellow with whom he'd enjoyed a few pleasant drinks in the officers' mess when they were waiting for their postings.

Although there was some anti-semitism amongst the officers, William himself had heard rumours about what was happening to the Jews in Germany. As the rumours increased in frequency, he had begun to believe that, horrible though they seemed, they may have some foundation in fact. It was all too terrible to be the figment of someone's tortured imagination.

He'd been in a crowd at the bar one evening when one of the company referred to Bruce as a 'kike' and seemed totally taken aback when William took exception. William looked him straight in the eye, faced him down and then turned on his heel and walked to the other end of the bar where Bruce was drinking in self-imposed isolation.

"Have another drink, old man," he said. "We'll have little enough opportunity when our orders come through, we could be up to our knees in mud or rubbing sand out of our eyes in the desert."

Bruce just smiled and nodded. He was, of course, aware of the little scene that had just taken place at the other end of the bar and could still hear old Gerald blustering a bit.

"This may not do you any good amongst the chaps, you know,' he said wryly. 'Gerald Moody can be a pretty awkward customer when he puts his mind to it. He could make things fairly unpleasant for you."

"I'm not too worried about Moody although he certainly needs watching. I've heard one or two whispers about his treatment of some of the lads but nothing specific, as yet. He can't do me any harm, he's just a bag of wind at the best of times. Now let's order up and get stuck into some serious drinking."

They found, surprisingly, that they had a lot in common and that they had actually joined the army within a week of each other. Bruce's father was also in the property business although in a much bigger way than William's row of terraces. He owned a great many properties in Cheetham Hill on the north side of the city where most of the Jewish population had settled.

Bruce had worked for his father in the family business and had some experience, not only dealing with tenants, problem and otherwise, but had done a lot of the actual maintenance of the properties, giving him a further link with William who fancied himself an expert in building repairs and joinery.

They finished the evening in a rather inebriated state and left the mess almost holding each other up and then walking very slowly and very carefully back to their rooms. William was not too drunk to hear Moody mutter, 'Jew lover' as they left the mess together but realised that he was altogether too drunk to challenge him. Drunk or sober, he didn't care much what Gerald thought.

A week later, their postings came through and their units moved out. Although correspondence was difficult because of the censors, they kept in spasmodic touch over the next few months and William wasn't too surprised to receive a letter of greater than usual length from Bruce. He was asking him whether any of the houses in the row were available for rent for his aunt and uncle who had escaped from Austria a few months ago. They'd apparently had an extremely narrow escape and there was some personal tragedy involved although he didn't feel free to go into detail.

His father had, of course, put them into one of his own houses but Aunt Luisa seemed unable to settle. The Jewish faces, accents and culture in which she found herself failed to reassure her. On the contrary, she felt threatened by them and wanted now to live where there were no Jews, where nobody knew them and where they would be left alone. Uncle Jakob would do anything to make Aunt Luisa happy and so, if there were an empty house in William's row, would he consider letting it to them?

People were moving around the country anyway because of the war. Number nine would be vacant within the month so he had no hesitation in writing to Bruce's father to give him the go-ahead and instructions to contact Jim Bradshaw at number three. Jim had a dicky heart and wouldn't be conscripted so he'd agreed to look after the properties for the duration. Just as well, as they'd discovered that their young child, Mikey, would have learning difficulties and his wife was struggling to cope.

. There was little for Jim to do except hold the keys and collect the rents but William knew he was reliable. Little maintenance would be done as there was a severe shortage of building materials anyway.

The Goldmans had moved into number nine and had lived there quietly ever since. He didn't even meet them until he came home on leave in the summer of 1943. Jim Bradshaw had written to him that they kept themselves very much to themselves but the rent was always paid on time and they kept the place in good order.

***

Nearly twenty years later, little had changed. Despite having left his own thriving showroom in Vienna, where he'd made clothes for the rich and famous, he'd adapted well to his life in Manchester. He now worked as a humble tailor in Cheetham Hill and carried garments home in parcels for Luisa to hand finish.

Mr Goldman had become more friendly as his English improved and stopped to pass the time of day with the neighbours if he met them on the street. Mrs Goldman still rarely left the house. Most of the tenants knew she watched their comings and goings but didn't seem to mind. Her privacy was respected and the working class ethic of minding your own business and letting other folks get on with theirs was ever present amongst the neighbours.

During the last few weeks, however, Mrs Goldman had found something new to watch. She'd become engrossed in the activities of Judy and Nina, especially Nina. She could just see into the yard of number five from the back bedroom window. From the lines of washing hung out almost daily, she could tell that Judy had washed every piece of linen and every curtain in the house. Nina's little jumpers and dungarees were pegged out on the line and the garden had been tidied up. Sometimes, if the kitchen door was open, she could hear Nina chattering and playing in the yard or Judy talking to her and sometimes even singing.

When they walked past number five on Saturdays, she noticed that the tiny front garden had been tidied up, the paintwork and front steps were clean and the net curtains were freshly washed.

She often watched Judy and Nina coming and going from the park in the afternoon, Judy holding Nina's hand and chatting to her.

87

She always looked so patient and so loving with the child that, despite her better judgement, she felt herself warming towards them.

The weather had been fine for most of the time. On the few days it was too wet to venture out and Judy and Nina stayed at home, Luisa found she had an empty feeling, as though she had missed a promised treat.

She'd gradually got into the habit of making sure she was at the window around the time they went out and rarely missed them. Even though the streets around were emptying, the sound of a child laughing cheered her. Although she was still desperately worried about the outcome of Mr Whitehead's application, she felt more cheerful than she had for years. Jakob had noticed the difference and had several times remarked on her smile when he came home at night.

"You should smile more often, Liebling. You are so lovely when you smile and you know that when you are happy, you make me happy too."

They never spoke of the past, it hurt too much. The only day they let their sadness show was on Yom Kippur, when Luisa steeled herself to cross the city by bus to say Kaddish, the Jewish prayer for the dead, with Bruce's family in their local synagogue. For a few days before, they were both subdued, Jakob because of his own very real feelings of grief and because of his concern for Luisa. Luisa, in turn, couldn't resist the rush of memories which she pushed away for the rest of the year and the impending ordeal of the journey and the meeting with so many of her relatives weighed on her mind.

Now Luisa had something to look forward to every day. She'd started to tell Jakob about the little things she heard Nina and Judy saying and how bright the child was, how lively, how pretty. Jakob wisely just smiled and listened but made no comment. Although it had taken many years, Luisa was becoming involved in the outside world again despite herself. The next step would be to get Luisa into the street on a Saturday at the same time as Judy so that they couldn't avoid meeting face to face. It could do no harm and might just do some good.

***

It was Monday morning, quarter to nine. Margaret always preferred to be in the office early so she could gather her thoughts before the rest of the staff started hurtling down the narrow corridors.

She took off her jacket, hung it carefully on a hanger and checked her hair and make-up in her compact mirror. She checked the diary for reminders and Mr Robinson's appointments for the week. A few minutes respite before the post arrived and then the day's work would start in earnest. Leaning back in her chair, she let her thoughts wander. She was becoming increasingly concerned about William. She rarely saw him these days, the busy man seemed to have disappeared. She never saw him doing repair jobs and he'd even missed cleaning and polishing his car for the last couple of Sundays. When she did see him, he seemed short tempered and disinclined to even pass the time of day.

Although a little worried about the future herself, she had taken William's assurances that the houses would be safe at face value. She now began to wonder whether things were so clear cut. Her thoughts were interrupted by the buzzer on her telephone. The unexpected loud noise startled her, it wasn't even nine o'clock but Mr Robinson was buzzing. She hurriedly picked up the 'phone.

"Yes, Mr Robinson?"

"Margaret, I'm glad you're in early, I wanted to have a quiet word with you, can you come in?"

"Of course, I'll be right there."

Mr Robinson was sitting behind his desk with his back to the window. Despite the bandage on his hand and the plaster on his forehead he looked smart; beautifully ironed white poplin shirt and striped tie, navy jacket unbuttoned. He did, however, look paler than usual and the hand playing with the paper knife shook slightly.

"Whatever happened, Mr Robinson? Are you sure you should be in the office?"

"Yes, Margaret, I'm quite sure. In fact, I've never been surer of anything. I wanted to have a private word with you before the telephone starts ringing and people start popping in and out. I'm well aware that I've created problems for you over the last few months. I know I've been difficult, to say the least, and I want you to know how much I appreciate what you've been doing."

Margaret flushed, slightly embarrassed. Although she had worked for Robinson for several years now, personal exchanges had always been kept to a minimum. She spoke occasionally to his wife and knew he had a young daughter and that he lived in the suburbs in Hale, quite a 'posh' area. He knew approximately where she lived and that she lived alone but very little else.

"I've only been doing my job, Mr Robinson. That's what the company pays me for."

"That isn't entirely true, Margaret, and you know it. We'll speak about this frankly now and then we never have to mention it again. Do you agree?"

Margaret nodded, wondering what on earth was coming.

"As I'm sure you've noticed, my drinking has recently got out of hand. What for years had been a quick drink at lunchtime and then a couple on the way home has escalated beyond control. I realise now that I've been throwing an intolerable burden on you, that you've been covering for me and shielding me from the effects of my own foolishness."

"It's not quite that bad."

"Yes it is and I want you to know that I appreciate your loyalty under what must have been extremely difficult circumstances."

Margaret opened her mouth to speak but he held up his hand, palm outwards.

"Let me finish, Margaret. This isn't easy for me, you know. Very briefly, I had far too much to drink on Friday night on my way home and pranged my car. I was too drunk to realise how bad it was and managed to stagger home on foot. I didn't even realise I was injured until my daughter screamed at the blood running down my face and dripping on to the hall carpet.

My wife patched me up as best she could and got me into bed to sleep it off. On Saturday morning, I couldn't face breakfast, not even coffee. My head was splitting and my throat was raw. I didn't want to wake my wife. She'd been dreadfully upset the night before so I walked down to the end of the road to see what damage I'd done. I wasn't sure what I'd hit or exactly where I'd left the car."

She could see this was difficult for him but he struggled on.

"It only amazes me that I didn't kill myself. The car's a write off. I'd skidded off the road and hit a beech tree head on. The front of the car is completely mangled and it took the men with the breakdown lorry hours to unwrap it from the tree. I've heard it said that the Lord looks after children and drunks and in my case, this is certainly true.

The most horrifying aspect of all, is that the tree I hit is no more than twenty yards from a pedestrian crossing. The children use it coming and going from school and the people from the old folks' home at the end of the lane use it spasmodically all day. True, there isn't much foot traffic around at night but I could just as easily have killed someone else as well as killing myself."

He set his jaw and continued grimly.

"I started back to the house. All I could see was the front of that car wrapped around the tree and I couldn't help imagining first a child and then an old lady trapped behind the car. I just made the bathroom before being violently ill. I realised that this might be my last chance to recover what has been steadily slipping away me; my wife and child, my home, my job and the respect of people I care about.

I vowed there and then that things would change. I feel I've been given another chance. My wife is prepared to try and make a fresh start and, thanks to you, things haven't slipped too badly here. They haven't, have they?"

He looked directly into Margaret's eyes so she gave it to him straight from the shoulder.

"I'll be honest, Mr Robinson, since you've been so honest with me. One or two whispers have been going the rounds. I've squashed them whenever and wherever possible and I'm fairly sure they haven't reached the top floor yet although, as you know, in this place, it's only a matter of time, Nevertheless, you've always been well respected by most of the staff and I've heard nothing much beyond the level of idle gossip. If you go carefully and are able to grasp the reins firmly, I think you'll get away with it. Of course, I'll do everything I can to help"

If anything, his face was even whiter and he swallowed hard.

"I know that and you know how much I appreciate what you've been doing. It's a crazy state of affairs but had you not been a woman in a man's world, I think you'd be running the whole company by now. You've a better head on your shoulders than half the management."

Margaret flushed again. She'd always known that Mr Robinson appreciated her work but this was high praise indeed.

"As you can see, I'm still a little shaky but I've been in to see my doctor and he suggested one or two ways I can help myself. I don't think another few days with you still standing watch will do any harm and I need some time to pick up the pieces. Perhaps you could go through the backlog and bring me in anything that needs urgent attention. Once I've looked through it, we'll go over it together to see what needs to be done."

Margaret stood up, smoothed her skirt and said briskly,

"I'll start on that now. There are one or two urgent matters where a quick decision from you will show that you're still very much in charge. I'll bring them in straight away."

The next few days were fairly hectic. She was, it was true, still fielding many of the telephone calls and dealing with more routine matters herself but gradually, Mr Robinson was proving that he was back at the helm. Instead of disappearing at twelve thirty for lunch and coming back a couple of hours later a little the worse for wear, he was now lunching on a sandwich at his desk.

She'd never been a clock watcher, preferring to stay an extra few minutes in the evening to finish a job or organise her work for the morning. Now, increasingly, Mr Robinson was still hard at it when she put her coat on to leave for the day.

Each morning, as soon as the post was sorted, she was called in for dictation and by Friday afternoon, things were nearly back on track. She'd taken in the post to be signed and half an hour later, he buzzed to let her know it was ready for mailing. She went into his office and picked up the mail folder. Mr Robinson looked up from the file on his desk.

"Sit down for a minute, Margaret."

She perched on the edge of the chair, knowing that if the letters weren't in the post room by four thirty there'd be hell to pay from the post boy, who was always anxious to be away on time on Friday.

"I won't keep you a minute. I just wanted to thank you again for all you've done. Things are almost completely under control and I know I have you to thank. I want you to know how much I appreciate your help and if there's ever any way I can help you, either at work or personally, you only need to ask."

"Thank you, Mr Robinson. I'll bear that in mind and I'd also like to say what a pleasure it is to see you looking like your old self again. By the end of next week, if we carry on like we have this week, things will be back to normal."

She smiled reassuringly..

"I hope you're right. Anyway, why don't you go home now. I'm sure you can find something to do with an extra hour on such a fine evening."

"Thank you, I will. I'll drop off the post on my way out. Have a nice weekend and I'll see you on Monday."

She quickly pushed letters into envelopes, put a rubber band round them and grabbed her jacket. She would walk through Piccadilly Gardens on her way home and look at the flowers. She might even sit on a bench with an ice cream and watch the world go by for half an hour. It had been a hard week and she deserved a break.

***

Judy and Nina had settled into the little community. Their life was now so different, so much less restricted. She and Margaret Hartley had become firm friends and Margaret often popped in for an hour after Nina was in bed. Although Judy wasn't exactly lonely, evenings could seem long.

There was always of basket of mending as Nina was hard on her clothes and was growing fast. Judy knitted her jumpers and ran up dungarees but shoes cost a fortune. She had her radio and still read avidly but was grateful for a little adult company. Though Nina was a darling, stimulating conversation wasn't her strongest point.

It was early Friday evening and Judy was in the kitchen washing through the clothes that Nina had worn that day. It was still hot and the back door was open to let in the sunshine and the fresh air. She heard a tap at the front door and went to open it.

"Hello, Margaret, I wondered if you'd call in tonight. Isn't it a lovely evening."

"Gorgeous. If you've nothing else planned, I thought we might have a little treat. Are you busy just now?"

"Nothing I can't leave 'til morning,' said Judy. 'I'm amazed there's any soil left in the garden at all, considering the amount on the knees and backside of Nina's pants. They'll be better for soaking anyway and I'll rinse them through tomorrow."

She gestured Margaret inside, glad to see her, but Margaret said,

"That's good. I've had such a funny week at work, I feel like doing nothing very much and I wouldn't mind a bit of company while I'm doing it. You put out the chairs and I'll be back in a tick," she said, disappearing back the way she'd come but leaving the door open behind her.

93

Judy pulled the rickety tables and chairs into the early evening sunlight. It was still warm and the air was laden with the smell of honeysuckle and roses.

"Shall I put the kettle on?" she called as she heard Margaret coming through the front door.

"Not tonight, love. I've bought us a little treat by way of a minor celebration."

She plonked her shopping bag on the table and pulled out a couple of bottles of beer and large lemonade.

"Shandy for us tonight, this weather is just right for it. Come, get the glasses and let's get started."

She poured two tumblers half full of beer and topped them off with lemonade and then put the contents of a couple of packets of crisps into a bowl.

"There, you take the glasses and I'll bring the crisps,' she said, following Judy into the garden."

"Wonderful, like nectar,' said Judy, putting down the glass from which she'd just taken a hefty drink. 'What are we celebrating anyway?"

"I can't say too much but things at work have suddenly taken a turn for the better. It's been a bit of a struggle keeping up this week. I've been home late a couple of times but I really think we've got the problem licked."

"I'm so glad, Margaret. I could tell you've been worried and I'm glad things are working out. You deserve it, you seem to work so hard. I hope your boss appreciates you."

Margaret smiled. "Oh, yes. I think he does, at least he's not one of those bosses that treat you like a piece of furniture."

"You know, it's really funny. I was so scared that I was doing the wrong thing when I moved down here. I didn't know Mr Whitehead from Adam but just took him on face value. Not like me at all but I was so desperate to get out of those top floor rooms and give Nina the chance of a little freedom."

She paused, trying to formulate her thoughts.

"Our lives have changed so dramatically. For the first time ever, I have some space of my own. True, I did have my own little bedsit after Aunt Mary died but John was there every five minutes and then after we married, the confined space with someone constantly underfoot drove me mad."

"You've never spoken about Nina's father. Does he ever come to see her?" asked Margaret, not wishing to intrude but fascinated nevertheless.

"Not since he left. He sends cash, to salve his conscience I suppose, but on the whole, I'd rather he stayed away. For Nina's sake, I'd rather she had no father than one she can't rely on and he is rather selfish. I suppose he's just immature really and perhaps he'll grow up one day. Still, in all fairness, I'm grateful for the money.

I feel so safe here. There are people around all the time and I've made friends for the first time since Nina was born. You've no idea what it means to me to have you living so close, always willing to stop for a chat. Then there's Mr Whitehead, who's been so helpful with the bits and bobs of repairs I've needed. As for Mikey, Nina has him wrapped firmly round her little finger. But he's such a lovely boy, so willing to fetch and carry and ...."

She couldn't go on. Her eyes had filled with tears and a great lump had risen in her throat. Margaret stood up and briefly bent to put her arm round Judy's shoulders, giving her a quick hug.

"Come on now. No tears, this is supposed to be a celebration. Pass me the glasses and I'll top them up."

She went back into the kitchen and re-filled the glasses, giving Judy time to compose herself a little. She went back into the garden and put the glass in Judy's hand.

"Now then, you must tell me what Nina's been up to this week. I haven't seen her since Sunday. She's so quick, she's learning something new every day so tell me the latest."

Judy was only too happy to launch into an account of their week and Margaret was only too happy to listen. She didn't mind living alone, she had no wish for someone to replace David but as she got older, she regretted more and more that she had never had a chance to have children of her own. Little Nina, living next door, was an absolute Godsend and it was fascinating to watch her develop and grow, week by week.

Margaret sat back and looked down the garden.

"You've done wonders out here,' she said, subtly changing the subject. 'It's an absolute picture now and the scent's almost overpowering."

The little garden was back to its former glory. What had been a tangle of rampant growth had turned out to be honeysuckle, which laid its perfume across the small space to the house.

Although Judy had no experience of gardening as such, that having been Aunt Mary's domain, she had taken to it like a duck to water. She'd borrowed a couple of books from the library and faithfully followed the instructions. The flower beds were filled with colourful annuals planted from seeds bought on the market and they were all thriving.

"I must admit I'm delighted with it. When I first started, Mr Whitehead was really helpful. He re-fixed the trellis against the back wall and showed me how to cut back the plants. I didn't even know it was honeysuckle until he told me and I've managed to identify the rest and sort out what I should be doing with them.

I particularly love that rose and it flowers and flowers. I can't tell you what a pleasure it is to come downstairs in the morning and walk into a kitchen scented with roses. I'll cut you a couple to take home with you."

Margaret sniffed appreciatively.

"You must have green fingers. It's a pity Mrs Goldman isn't a bit more sociable, poor thing. Her garden's lovely too and I think she manages to grow a few vegetables. Talking of Mr Whitehead, have you seen much of him recently?"

"Now that you mention it, I've hardly seen him at all for a couple of weeks. He always stops and makes a great fuss of Nina when we do see him but he doesn't seem to be around much at the moment."

"Quite honestly, I'm a little worried about him. He's far from his usual self and I wonder whether things are getting on top of him a bit. You know, this business with the Town Hall. He seemed so sure that everything would work out but the longer it drags on, the more it seems to be getting him down. If I know William, he's more worried about letting us down that he is about losing his own home."

Judy frowned a little as she cast her mind back.

"It's funny you should say that. The last time I saw him to speak to, a couple of weeks ago, he told me we'd be taken care of. He's been down specially and found that if the worst should happen, I'll be offered council accommodation of some description, either a flat or a small house, even though I've been living here such a short time."

She just hoped that if the worse did come to the worst, they'd offer her something she could afford but hesitated to voice her concern.

"That's a relief at least. I don't know how much choice we'll be offered as to area and I can tell you that there are some places I wouldn't even look at. Surely, they can't ship everybody off to Wythenshawe, there *are* other council estates after all. Let's hope it doesn't come to that. Communities are being torn up by their roots, they're pulling down old houses and scattering people who've been neighbours for years to the four winds."

As Margaret lay in bed that night, tossing and turning and trying to sleep, she couldn't shake off Judy's words, they kept going round and round in her head. She'd become very fond of Judy and, she must admit, little Nina but she'd had it brought home to her just how isolated Judy's life had been since the birth of her child.

For the past two years, she'd had only casual contact with other adults; shop keepers, her landlady, perhaps occasionally another young mother in the park. She knew only too well about loneliness, she'd suffered her share of that but she couldn't imagine living a life where she was almost virtually isolated from the rest of adult society. Poor Judy, poor brave Judy.

Well at least she had friends now and Margaret's brain jumped into full organisational mode. There was no reason that Judy couldn't go out occasionally although if she has no friends, where could she or would she want to go? She probably hadn't been out in the evening since the child was born.

She and I could go to the pictures occasionally. I can't suggest it too often because I know she's on a tight budget and I know she wouldn't stand for me paying for both of us. There again, if she and I go out together, who'd look after Nina? Well, at a pinch, William would do it, I suppose, and then there's always Mikey. He's sensible enough to be left in charge. If Nina should wake up, which is seldom enough, at least she knows him. I'm not sure how Judy would take to that idea. I'll have to be careful how I put it to her. I'll think about that tomorrow, perhaps a chance will just come up in conversation. I'll play it by ear.

Satisfied with her plans, Margaret turned on her side, pulled the pillow down into the hollow between neck and shoulder and slowly but surely drifted off to sleep.

***

Mikey had become a firm favourite with Nina and often dropped in on his way home from work to play with her for half an hour. He had the patience of a saint and was happy to be a horse and carry Nina on his back or be a visitor at a doll's tea party and drink 'pretend' tea and eat 'pretend' cake and enjoy it.

Judy often heard them chortling and giggling together. Nina had learned half a dozen nursery rhymes from Mikey and she often sat on his knee and they said them out loud together. Mikey had obviously learned them from repetition as a child and was teaching them to Nina the same way. Their comical sing song choruses kept both them, and Judy, amused for half an hour at a time.

She noticed too that Mikey spoke to her quite freely, if still haltingly. He told her cheerfully about what had happened at work and what the foreman had said about his plans for a week's holiday in September. When he chattered with Nina, however, his stammer completely disappeared.

Judy had overcome her first irrational jealousy of Mikey's attraction for Nina. She realised how important it was for Nina to have a wider acquaintanceship, particularly other adults. Anyway, nobody could take exception to Mikey. He so obviously enjoyed every minute he spent with them. He had never, contrary to Mr Whitehead's misgivings, outstayed his welcome. He seemed to have an inbuilt sense of tact, of when to go home, and Judy had come to rely on this.

Nina, on the other hand, adored Mikey and often lifted her arms for him to pick her up as soon as he came through the front door. She'd had gone through a phase of being rather imperious and treating Mikey like a willing slave and Judy had become rather concerned. She wasn't too happy to notice Nina becoming bossier and bossier around Mikey.

Still a baby and already such a little madam. She certainly seems to have the female instinct to subjugate the male that I never had in my whole life, as far as I know.

She held off for a few days, perhaps it would pass without her interference. She had no intention of allowing Nina to take advantage of Mikey and would nip it in the bud, if she had to. One afternoon, she was in the kitchen making Mikey a cup of tea and Nina and Mikey were in the garden on an old blanket. Waiting for the tea to brew, she listened idly to their chatter.

They'd built a tower of building blocks, one of Nina's favourite games, second only to knocking it down when all the bricks were stacked. She heard Mikey laughing,

"There we go, Nina. All the bricks are used up, we can't get it any higher. Ready... steady ... go!"

Nina gave a shout and a wallop and down went the bricks. She'd hit them harder than usual and they'd scattered virtually all over the garden. She and Mikey were laughing at the mess and Judy heard Nina's usual plea, "again, Mikey, again."

"All right, let's get all the bricks."

Judy looked through the window. Mikey was gathering together all the bricks nearest him, ready to build another tower.

"Mikey, bwicks there. Mikey get bwicks."

"No, Nina, you get the bricks. You're nearer than I am."

Nina's voice started to rise, she was almost shouting now.

"Bwicks, Mikey bring bwicks. I want bwicks. I want tower."

Her face was getting redder and redder, her eyes screwed up. She looked ready to burst into tears.

Mikey sat back on his heels and looked at her, rather surprised.

"Now then, Nina. It's no use pulling those faces at me. I'll help you build another tower, if that's what you want but if you don't fetch the bricks, no tower for you, my lady. And, if you haven't got a smile for me, I'll go inside and talk to your Mummy instead."

She looked at Mikey from under her eyelashes. Did he mean it? Yes he did. She put her hands flat on the blanket, pushed her bottom into the air and then stood up. Without another word, off she went across the small patch of garden to retrieve the missing bricks.

Judy stood in the kitchen, hand over her mouth so she shouldn't laugh aloud and tip them off that she'd been listening. She picked up the teapot to pour Mikey's tea, still smiling.

Chapter 8

William cocked his head when he heard the snap of the letter box and the slap of the post on the mat. Would it be today?

He wearily put down his morning paper and with both palms on the kitchen table, pushed himself up and went down the hall. There were three letters, with a gas bill on top. He shuffled it to the back; the latest list from the book club, again shuffled to the back and there it was, the dreaded buff envelope with the Town Hall crest on the back.

He walked back down the hall and dropped into his chair, studying the envelope as though his eyes could bore through the paper and see the contents without opening it. This was it, at least now he would know the worst. Quickly and purposefully he ripped the envelope open and pulled out the letter.

Dear Sir,
We regret to inform you...........

He closed his eyes as if in pain. He really need read no further although he ploughed on to the end, noting his right to appeal. etc., etc.

The cat is truly amongst the pigeons now. I can't keep this news from them any longer. They have a right to know what's happening and a say in what happens next.

He frowned, consideration, his options.

It's a bit revolutionary for Ardwick but I think my only course of action is to call a meeting. I'll try to get it organised for later in the week.

He'd carried the worry alone for so long, in a way it would be a relief to pass some of the responsibility for a decision on to the rest of the tenants. He could see no alternative and felt a twinge of guilt about burdening them.

On the other hand, their homes were at risk and they deserved a say in their own future. It rather surprised him to find he felt better than he'd done for weeks. At least now he could take some kind of action, there was something constructive he could do.

It was only eight thirty, too soon to start calling on people. He'd catch Judy sometime during the day and call on the others after tea. He gave a hollow laugh.

They may as well have a last meal in peace. Heaven only knows what they'll say when they hear the news.

He washed up his few dishes, tidied the kitchen and then went upstairs to make his bed. He liked everything in its place and when he'd finished his chores, he went into the bathroom to wash and shave.

He looked at the kitchen clock again, it was still only a quarter to ten but he decided to go and see Judy anyway. She'd probably been up and about for hours and it might be as well to catch her before she went to the shops.

Judy heard the knock on the front door and dashed to open it.

The rain was hammering down as he stood on Judy's path under a huge black umbrella.

"Oh, Mr Whitehead," she half wailed. "I'm so glad to see you. I've been trying to get out of the house for an hour or so but I can't leave Nina for a minute. She's really not well and I don't know what to do."

"Where is she?" he asked quietly. "Let's have a little look at her."

"She's on the settee in here. I've been up and down with her all night and I've just carried her downstairs so I can keep a better eye on her. Earlier on, she was just a bit restless and a bit warm but now I'm really worried. She seems to have got so much worse in the last hour. What do you think?"

William went into the tiny sitting room. Nina was lying listlessly on the settee, her eyes half closed and her face flushed. William put his hand gently on her forehead.

"She's burning up. I'll go and telephone for the doctor. In the meantime, try sponging her forehead with a cold cloth, that might cool her down."

He let himself out and Judy ran into the kitchen for a bowl of cold water and a cloth. She wrung out the cloth and placed it gently on Nina's head.

She whispered to her all the time.

"You'll soon feel better, darling, you'll soon feel better, darling," keeping her voice as steady as she could. She was terrified.

Nina had never known a day's illness and now she was obviously very sick indeed. Judy forced herself to keep her panic under control. Her heart had risen halfway up her chest and was now

101

in a solid mass just behind her breastbone. She took the cloth from Nina's head, it was already warm so she quickly wet it in the cold water and replaced it.

She carried on stroking Nina's hair. She didn't know what else to do, she felt so helpless. Where was Mr Whitehead? Where was the doctor?

She muttered under her breath,

"Oh, please let her be all right. Please let her get better. Please help me, she's all I've got. Please, please, please"

Her litany was interrupted by Mr Whitehead coming back through the front door. She looked up.

"Is he coming? What time will he be here, did they say?"

"Unfortunately, he's already out on his calls and they aren't expecting him back until lunchtime. They promised to pass on the message the minute he came in and I know him well, he'll come straight away but that doesn't help us for the moment. Let me think for a minute. There must be something we can do."

Judy jumped to her feet and was wringing her hands. She was as pale as Nina was flushed. She looked at Mr Whitehead, her eyes haunted.

"I've got it. Leave it with me for a minute. I won't be long."

He went out again and Judy sat down. Nina looked almost lifeless and Judy could feel the tears trickling down her cheeks. My God, what could she do?

William went along the street and up the short path to the door of number nine. He could just barely see Mrs Goldman's outline through the net curtains and knew she could see him but he tapped on the door anyway. It seemed an age until she reluctantly opened the door.

"Mr Hartley, what can I do for you? Is it about the houses? It might be better if you come back later when Jakob's home and tell him all about it."

William spoke to her very calmly and very gently.

"Mrs Goldman, I badly need your help. The little lass at number five is really poorly and her mother is making herself ill with worry. I've 'phoned the doctor but it could be a couple of hours before he gets here. Now you know I'm not one to panic but I'm worried myself, she doesn't look too good at all. I really hate to disturb you but I'm at my wits' end."

Mrs Goldman took a deep breath and turned back into the sitting room. William thought she was turning him down until she said over her shoulder,

"I just get my keys and lock the front door. I be right with you."

They hurried up the street, close together under the umbrella, and pushed open the door to number five. Judy looked distraught and Mrs Goldman took in the scene at one glance. The overwrought young mother was sitting on the edge of the settee, leaning over her daughter and stroking her lank hair and the child was now restless and muttering a little.

Mrs Goldman removed the damp cloth and put her hand to the child's head; too hot, far too hot.

She wasted no time on preliminaries or niceties.

"Does she seem worse?" she asked Judy.

"It's hard to tell, she's become very restless and keeps talking to herself. I think she's delirious. I just don't know what to do, it could be hours before the doctor gets here."

"She's very hot, too hot. Have you a thermometer?"

Judy shook her head despairingly.

"It doesn't matter. I've seen enough children with fevers to know that this one has to come down, quick as we can do something.

You've been doing the right thing so far. The cold cloth on the head is good, very good but she's so hot, we have to do something more and we have to do it fast. You won't like it, she'll probably scream and cry but it's got to be done. Have you hot water?"

Judy nodded, just grateful that someone seemed to know what needed to be done.

"Go upstairs and run four inches of cold water into the bath. Then put in just enough hot to make the water tepid. Not cold, tepid and call out when it's ready."

Judy rushed upstairs and started to run the bath.

"Listen here, Mr Whitehead. I want you to keep the mother down here for a few minutes. The child will be distressed but it's the only way I know to get her fever down fast. I'll get her upstairs and you ask her mother to get her a drink and some clean pyjamas."

Judy called from the top of the stairs.

Mr Whitehead lifted Nina.

"I'll carry her, she's grown a lot in the last few weeks and she's too heavy for you."

He picked Nina up, cradling her against his chest. He looked desperately worried too as he carried the child tenderly upstairs and into the bathroom. Mrs Goldman followed.

She tested the water with her fingertips.

"That's just right," she said approvingly to Judy.

She sat on the little chair in the bathroom and held out her arms.

"I take her now. I want you both to go downstairs. She's going to cry but I'll be down with her in about fifteen minutes and you can comfort her then."

She looked meaningfully at Mr Whitehead. He took Judy's arm.

"Yes, come on Judy. She'll need a drink and some clean clothes. I can promise you she's in safe hands now. Come along, my dear. Let Mrs Goldman get on with it."

Judy reluctantly left the bathroom, turning at the door for one last look at her baby and William followed. Mrs Goldman could hear him speaking soothingly to her all the way down the stairs.

She checked there was a clean bath towel on the rail and then quickly stripped off Nina's little pink pyjamas. The child started to shiver almost immediately, mewing at the discomfort like a distressed kitten.

In her anxiety, Mrs Goldman lapsed back into German but she kept up a low, reassuring murmur whilst she picked Nina up and lowered her gently into the water. As the water closed around her lower limbs, Nina went rigid. She held her breath until she couldn't hold it any longer and then let out a hair raising howl.

"Shush, Liebling, shush, shush."

She picked up a sponge and squeeze water slowly but surely all over Nina. She washed her all over, rotating the cold sponge from back to front, under the arms, round the back of the neck. Nina was heavy and beginning to struggle, whimpering, but she carried on with the bathing, finishing up with rubbing her head with the wet sponge.

"That should be enough now, Liebling, I think is enough."

She called down the stairs and Judy came rushing up two at a time.

"Is she all right?" Nina was still whimpering.

"She will be better in a few minutes. I think you should hold her now. Put the towel on your knee and I will lift her out."

Judy sat on the chair and as Mrs Goldman placed Nina on her lap, she wrapped her tightly in the large bath towel and hugged her.

Mrs Goldman took a hand towel and lightly rubbed it over Nina's damp hair.

"Let us go back down the stairs. She should be drinking as much as you can give her now. She needs to have liquids, as much as possible."

Judy nodded as she stroked back Nina's hair. She wasn't nearly so hot. She bundled her in the towel and took her down the stairs, carrying her as though she were made of china.

Mr Whitehead was still waiting in the sitting room, hands in pockets, but with a hopeful expression.

"What do you think? Does she seem better?"

"Well she's certainly not so hot. Come on darling, try and have a little drink for mummy."

Judy held the beaker to Nina's lips. Nina was still hiccupping a little but her sobs had subsided and she took a couple of gulps of water.'

"That's a good girl, that's a big brave girl. Come on sweetheart, have a little more."

Judy settled Nina back on to the settee and covered her with a cotton sheet, stroking her gently.

The three of them sat almost in silence until they realised that Nina was sound asleep and breathing deeply and easily.

Mrs Goodman rose.

"I think you don't have to worry so much now. She's sleeping properly and the doctor will be here soon. Mr Whitehead, you should go to the chemist and buy a thermometer and something to bring down a child's temperature. He will know what to give you. I will go home now but if you need me, you call for me. I will leave open the back door so you can go into the yard and shout. I will hear you."

She picked up her keys, nodded at Mr Whitehead, and left.

"I'll be off to the chemist. I've got my orders but I'll only be ten minutes and then I'll wait with you until the doctor comes."

"She seems so much better, I can't believe it. I'd have thought the shock of that water would kill her when she was burning up but it's like a miracle. She's so much cooler now. How did Mrs Goldman know what to do?"

"I believe she has some nursing experience. I'm off now but I'll be as quick as I can and then when the doctor's been, I'll go and get the prescription for you."

The doctor arrived a couple of hours later. After having a good look at Nina, taking her temperature and listening to her chest, he got out his prescription pad and started scribbling.

William held out his hand for the prescription and left straight away to collect the medicine.

"Her throat is very inflamed and her glands are swollen but she should start to improve quite quickly. Children are very resilient you know, try not to worry. Give her one spoonful of the medicine as soon as possible, another at teatime and then again about ten o'clock. In the meantime, if you're at all worried, don't hesitate to ring the surgery. I'll be there between five and seven thirty and if it's later than that, they know where to get hold of me."

He put his instruments back in his bag.

"Incidentally, whoever was responsible for the cold bath knew exactly what they were doing. It's upsetting and uncomfortable for the patient but very, very effective and extremely high temperatures can be dangerous, as you probably know. Don't worry too much about food but make sure she takes plenty of fluid over the next day or so. It wouldn't hurt for you to try to get some rest yourself, you look very washed out. I don't expect you got much sleep last night and it won't help the child if you make yourself ill."

The medicine was collected and Judy managed to get a spoonful into Nina without too much fuss, along with another drink and then settled her down on the settee again, where she dropped off to sleep.

Judy made herself a cup of tea and sat in an armchair where she could watch Nina. She awakened with a start half an hour later and realised there was a gentle tapping at the door. She looked at Nina, she was still sleeping soundly and her tea was stone cold, still balanced on the arm of her chair. She went quickly to the door and found Mrs Goldman on the step.

"Do come in. Nina is asleep for the moment but she seems better already. Please come through to the kitchen, if you don't mind. I don't want to wake her."

She led the way and Mrs Goldman looked around the kitchen approvingly. She had noticed that the sitting room was clean and tidy and that the furniture was polished to a high gloss. The kitchen was a little more untidy but obviously only with things that had been used that morning.

"Will you have a cup of tea, Mrs. Goldman? I didn't get chance to thank you properly this morning but the doctor had nothing but praise for you."

"No, no thanks, no tea. I came back because you looked so worried and tired this morning. I want you now to go upstairs and lie on your bed for a little while. You need to rest. I promise you, you will need your energy to keep Nina happy for the next few days. I will sit with her while you rest and I promise to come and wake you if she wants you. I can stay for a while, until it is time to cook Jakob's evening meal. You go upstairs now, go now."

Judy had never felt so tired, she had never been so heart-wrenchingly worried before and reaction was setting in. She wanted to protest that Mrs Goldman had done enough already but she felt so weary. Mrs Goldman shooed her upstairs with one hand.

"Go, rest. I will watch, she is safe."

Two hours later, Judy was woken by someone gently shaking her by the shoulder. She looked up, disorientated for a moment, who was it? Mrs Goldman had put a cup of tea on the bedside table.

"She woke for a little while, only a minute or two really, so I gave her a drink and she dropped off again. Here, drink your tea. I hope you don't mind I went into your kitchen. She still sleeps but I have to go in a few minutes."

She went quickly down the stairs. She obviously wasn't eager to enter into conversation and Judy, remembering what she had heard about her shyness, didn't try to keep her.

She sat up on the bed with her back against the headboard and sipped at the hot tea. She stayed there until she heard the front door close behind Mrs Goldman and then she put on her shoes and went downstairs. The kitchen was tidy now. Everything that had been in the bowl in the sink had been washed and neatly stacked on the kitchen table and the pyjamas, which Judy had left folded on a kitchen chair, were hanging on the washing line in the garden.

How kind, how unbelievably kind.

She went quickly through to the sitting room. Nina was beginning to stir. Judy sat on the edge of the settee and pushed back the hair from Nina's face. She opened her eyes and blinked a couple of times.

"Hello, mummy, Nina want drink." Judy put her arms around her little daughter and hugged her tight. She was going to be all right.

William lay in wait for Mikey to stop him from calling at Judy's on the way home from work. Mikey looked upset but William soothed him with assurances that she was on the mend.

"Look, Mikey, she won't want hoards of visitors at the moment. I promise to come and tell you the news when I've been and I'll let you know the minute she's fit to have visitors. The best thing you can do for her is let her rest until she's feeling better."

He waited until early evening before calling round to see Margaret Hartley and, looking rather surprised, she invited him in. The tenants in the row weren't in the habit of popping in and out of each other's house. In the culture which governed terraced streets, neighbours could be relied on in times of trouble. However, the formality was greater than would have been expected and free movement of people between houses, unless they were blood related, just wasn't part of the normal pattern.

This custom was only breached occasionally at Christmas or on New Year's Eve although the community could be relied on to come together on occasions of great moment. At the end of the war, each street had held its own party, and mothers filled long stretches of trestle tables with sandwiches and homemade cakes and jellies.

Bonfire night was another occasion when the streets acted as a unit, the older boys collecting wood for the 'bonny' for weeks in advance. The wood was stashed up and down the street in various backyards and the bonfire was built on the cobbles in the middle of the street only on the actual day. The unlit bonfire was under guard against mischief makers and raids on the wood from other streets until it was time to light it.

There were very few streets in which all the inhabitants didn't turn out to see the Guy placed on top of the bonfire and the almost ceremonial lighting which followed. Most of the families contributed something to the party atmosphere; parkin, treacle toffee and potatoes to go into the fire for baking. There were plenty of people to keep an eye on the younger children and the fireworks were usually given into the charge of a couple of the fathers who were able to keep the older boys in check.

***

Mr Whitehead rarely called on Miss Hartley and even more rarely went into her house, especially if she were alone. It just wasn't expected and even in these enlightened times, he was conscious of the need to protect her reputation as a respectable woman. Brief exchanges were generally carried out with him standing on the step and her inside the house.

"Come in, come in. I'm not too worried about what the neighbours might say. Good heavens, I've lived on this row for twenty years so if they don't know I'm respectable by now, they never will."

William went into the sitting room. Although all the houses apart from his were the same dimensions, they all looked so different when you walked through the front door. Margaret's house looked light and airy. The walls of the sitting room were painted pale cream. She'd ignored the current trend to put patterned wallpaper everywhere and had kept the walls plain, as they had been when she moved in.

The curtains were patterned with roses and cushions covered in the same fabric were piled on the settee and the armchairs. There was little other furniture in the room, just two small, bow fronted cabinets filled with china figures she'd brought from her parents' home and which William suspected were worth a pretty penny. A nicely framed mirror hung over the mantle and the whole effect was restful and very pleasant.

"Sit down William. I'll put the kettle on. It won't take a minute."

She came back to find William perched on the edge of a chair looking a little uncomfortable. She passed him his tea in a beautiful china cup and saucer.

"You'd better tell me what's the matter. I can see you're upset, so come on."

William explained what had happened that morning and how worried they'd all been when Nina was so poorly.

"The poor child," said Margaret sympathetically, "and I don't mean Nina. How are they both now, do you know? Do they need anything or is there anything I can do?"

"To answer all your questions, Nina already looks better and now that Judy isn't so worried, she looks better too. They don't need anything at the moment. Judy's a good little manager and seems to have her cupboards well stocked. If she can't get out in a couple of days, she'll need some fresh fruit and vegetables but we can sort that out between us so there's nothing you can do at the moment."

He spoke reassuringly.

"I'll just have a quick word later on and I think we should leave them to it tonight. I'll call again tomorrow to see how things are and I'll let you know when you get home from work. Mikey is champing at the bit wanting to see his little sweetheart but I've managed to put him off for a couple of days."

"Everything seems to be under control then. Thank goodness she was here and not in those dreadful rooms up the road."

"I can only second that. Apart from that Margaret, there was something else I wanted to talk to you about."

She looked at him enquiringly although she already suspected that he had some news about the compulsory purchase order.

"I had a letter from the Town Hall this morning and they've turned down my application to be excluded from the compulsory purchase order."

"Oh my goodness, what are you going to do, have you decided?"

"I had intended to get everyone together either tomorrow evening or the evening after but in view of the upset with Nina, I think we'll have to postpone it for a day or two. I don't want to worry Judy unnecessarily on top of what she's been through today."

"No, I'm sure you're right. Why don't you leave it until the weekend, a few more days can't matter either way but what did you have in mind?"

"I just think it would be the fairest thing all round if I put it to the tenants and for them to decide what they want to do."

"William, nobody could ever accuse you of being anything but fair. I'm sure we'd all be glad to know what's going on and to have some kind of decision made. Sometimes, it's the not knowing that drives you mad."

"Don't I know it. I've been in a bit of a funk for weeks because of the uncertainty but at least now I know where we're up to."

Margaret smiled.

"Really, William? Never mind, let's say for the moment we could all meet early next week, providing Nina is better. I'll fall in with whatever night is most convenient. I've nothing planned at the moment."

William finished his tea and handed the delicate china carefully back to Margaret. He rose to leave.

"I'll call on my way home from work to see how Nina is. Judy doesn't need for us all to be knocking on her door in turn but when you see her, please tell her I'll be thinking of her and be happy to call as soon as she's ready for some company."

"I'll do that. Goodnight, Margaret. See you tomorrow."

Margaret followed him to the door to let him out and wished him goodnight. She went back into the kitchen to tidy up..

Poor Nina, poor Judy and come to think of it, poor old William. Still he looked more positive tonight than I've seen him for ages and that's something.

***

Jakob noticed immediately he came through the door that Luisa was brimming with excitement.

"Come on, Liebling, tell it to me. What has happened?"

"Jakob, you never guess. That young girl, that Judy at number five was in such a state, poor girl. Her baby was so sick, really hot, with a high fever. The doctor he couldn't come for a long time and so Mr Whitehead, he came to fetch me to see if there is anything I can do."

"Did you go then?" said Jakob, trying to suppress his smile.

"What a question. Of course I went," replied Luisa indignantly. "Anyway, I help her and then I stay for a little while so the mother, poor girl, could get some sleep. You could see she had been awake half the night.

The child was already much better when I left but she is a lovely little thing. The house is lovely too, all Mrs Phelan's old things still there but all polished and the whole house is spotless clean."

She was stumbling over her words, trying to get out her news.

"Bright as a new needle," said Jakob. "I'm glad you went. You have a good heart and now maybe, you have a new friend. I'm sure that Judy is so happy you could help and you should maybe go again tomorrow or day after to see how it goes with the little one."

"I don't know if I could. This morning was different, I didn't have time to think. Mr Whitehead said 'come' and I did and then I could do something so it was all right. I don't know if I can go again when she don't need me."

"My love, of course you can. Think of Judy. Maybe she have to stay in the house all day for many days until the child is better. She be glad to see another grown up face. You know, you chose to be alone all day and not see anybody but your old man when he come home but this don't suit everybody."

"We'll see, we'll see. Come on now Jakob, all this talk, talk, talk and your meal is in the kitchen spoiling. Come now, come eat."

111

"Yes, yes. Let's eat and I tell you what happened today. I just wash my hands and then we sit down, yes?"

He decided to say no more. He knew his Luisa, she couldn't be pushed. She disliked speaking to strangers and her reserve could only be broken down by need, strangely enough, other peoples' needs, never her own. So far as he knew, the only other house in the row she had been in before today apart from their own, was Mrs Phelan's. Then too, William Whitehead had come to fetch her when the old lady broke her hip and she had looked after her and tried to make her comfortable until the ambulance arrived.

Although the neighbours had taken turns to go to the hospital to see the old lady, Luisa didn't go. She always sent her best wishes and insisted that Mrs Phelan's nighties came to her for washing and ironing. She just couldn't face the bus journey and all those new faces at the hospital.

He fervently wished that she would make contact with Judy and the little girl. After all, it was only next door but one, a few yards down the street but he knew that in Luisa's eyes, it might have been fifty miles.

Nina continued to improve and when the doctor came again the following morning, she was busy with her building blocks.

"No need to ask how our young patient is this morning, I can see for myself. Children are amazing, one day they have you terrified that they'll never recover and the next you'd hardly think they'd been ill."

He examined Nina and managed to get a look down her throat.

"Her throat is still inflamed but she's definitely on the mend. Keep on with the medicine and the fluids and just let her eat whatever she fancies. She'll be right as ninepence in no time. Keep her in a couple of days and then bring her to the surgery on Monday and I'll have another look at her."

Mrs Goldman was back at her post in the bay window. She watched the doctor arrive and leave. He didn't look concerned, surely the child was on the mend. She watched Mr Whitehead go up to the door of number five. He was only there a minute or two and he didn't look worried either, or not more than he'd done over the last few weeks. She thought he might just have called to let her know how the child was this morning but he marched back off to his own end of the row without even turning towards her window.

She continued to sit in her straight backed chair in the window for the rest of the morning. She finished all the work that Jakob had brought home the evening before and folded it all neatly and packed it into a parcel for him to take back the following morning. It didn't bring in much, outworkers were notoriously poorly paid, but then again, they didn't need much and it kept her busy. Jakob's wages paid the rent and other expenses more than adequately and covered the cost of their food. They didn't go out and spent little money on clothes. The few shillings that Mrs Goldman earned were carefully hoarded and sent at intervals to the synagogue in the north of the city. A special collection was taken there twice a year and the proceeds were sent on to Israel where the cash was used to support students who'd had lost their parents in the camps. Israel needed trained people in every sphere and this project helped some of them complete their education, particularly in the medical profession, a cause very dear to Luisa's heart.

She finished her housework, listening to the radio while she worked and noticed when she looked out of the back bedroom window that Judy had some small items of washing on the line. Surely the child must be better

She was torn with indecision. The only way she could find out for sure was to actually go and enquire but the thought of knocking on a door uninvited made her break out in a cold sweat. She just didn't think she could do it. She went back downstairs and sat down to listen to the radio. She couldn't settle, couldn't concentrate on anything. She stood up suddenly.

"That's it, I go ask, she don't bite."

She hurried around the kitchen, leaving herself no time to change her mind. She filled a small basin with soup she'd made the previous day and covered it with a cloth. Putting a cardigan round her shoulders, she picked up the basin, checked for her keys and closed the front door behind her.

Taking a deep breath, she walked the few steps to number five and knocked on the door. Judy opened it almost immediately, giving her no time to change her mind and run for it.

"Mrs Goodman, please come in. I'm so glad to see you. I didn't have a chance to thank you properly yesterday."

"Nothing to thank. Look, I hope you don't mind I brought you a little soup, my special recipe from my home. Maybe you not have time to cook and maybe the little one can take some soup for dinner. There's enough for two. How is she today? I see the doctor come and go, she must be better, no?"

Judy gently drew Mrs Goldman into the house, relieving her of the basin and pressing her gently down into one of the armchairs. Nina had played happily for an hour or so and had then become a little cranky so Judy had put her to bed for a nap, crooning to her until she fell asleep.

"She's so much better. It's hard to believe she was so ill yesterday. The doctor was very complimentary about you too, he said you really know what you're doing."

"I was a nurse in Vienna for several years and liked most to nurse the children."

"You know, Mrs Goldman, I can't tell you what it meant to me to have people around who were willing to help. I was so very frightened. To anybody else, it would seem like nothing now that she's so much better but yesterday, I was sick with worry. I know now it was just a throat infection but I had all sorts of things going round in my head. You know, I was scared to admit it but at one stage, I thought I was going to lose her. It might seem hard to understand but she's all I have."

Mrs Goldman reached out and comfortingly put her hand over Judy's, patting her gently.

"I know what it's like to have this kind of worry. I too had a sick child and didn't know which way to turn. I tell you something now that nobody knows except me and my Jakob. It was just before the Germans entered Austria, they called it the 'Anschluss' to connect the two countries. We heard so many stories about what was happening to the Jews in Germany. It all sounded like rumours and I don't want to believe it. All our friends say it blows over, we could survive, we was respectable people and hard workers."

She paused and looked at Judy.

"Jakob, he did believe it. He had cousins in Berlin who just disappeared and also friends in Munich who suddenly didn't write no more. We tried telephoning, impossible. No-one could give us news.

Jakob, he say to me "it's time we leave. We go to Switzerland first and then later to my father's family in England. You and the baby be safe there. We make our plans, we don't tell nobody and we just leave as if for holiday."

I didn't want to go. We have no close family in Vienna but still all our friends, place where we grew up, beautiful city, beautiful countryside. Jakob insist. "No argument. You want to take chance with baby's life? We start again in England. I can work and family there will help. I will arrange everything. You just start to pick out what we take, as if for holiday."

She paused, twisting her hankie in nervous hands. This was obviously very hard to tell.

"I don't know how, he got us travel papers. He took most but not all money from bank as if for holiday. We tell friends we go to mountains for a week for fresh air and walking. We close up our apartment and we leave and get train for Switzerland. It was very long journey. I was frightened and then my baby, my little Ernst, became sick on train, burning with fever. There was nothing I could do. I had some medicine but it didn't help and the train not stop for hours until we reach Switzerland. We were afraid to stop train for emergency because of false papers. We were helpless."

Judy could hardly believe what she was hearing She grasped Mrs Goldman's hands in hers.

"Go on,' she whispered, 'what happened?"

"We got safe to Switzerland and rushed straight to hospital with the baby. The doctor he look and shake his head. Meningitis, he say, not much hope. We stay in hospital three days and then little Ernst, only eight months old, he die in my arms. We have to bury him next day, is Jewish law, and we have to leave him in Switzerland."

She was struggling to continue.

"I don't remember much about coming to England. I was sick myself with despair but Jakob, who was suffering too, he look after me and bring me to this city but on the other side, where he have family.

I can't stand it there, every Jewish face I see remind me what I lost. I don't want to be with them anymore, I don't want pity, I want to be alone with my Jakob and so we find this house and come here. We go there only one time in year to synagogue when all family say prayers for the dead. Otherwise, I never see them."

Judy's eyes had filled with tears and she put her arm round Mrs Goldman's shoulders.

"It's hard for someone like me to imagine what it must have been like but I'm so sorry about your baby. I'm glad you told me but I promise I won't tell anyone else."

"Anyway, one good thing come from all. We hear after war so many people were killed. Many, many of our friends and all Jakob's family in Germany, even the children, little babies. Maybe

Ernst get sick even if we don't leave and at least he die in his mama's arms and not in a gas chamber. I try always to remember that."

***

Several days passed and Nina made a rapid recovery. By the end of the week, William felt able to go and have a word with Judy about the decision from the Town Hall.

"It's a blow but not entirely unexpected. We still have the chance to appeal but I want you to think very carefully about what you want to do. You know you'll be re-housed anyway and you should think whether you can face living round here with a young child with all the demolition work going on."

"I'll think about it, Mr Whitehead, but I'm sure I'll feel the same in a few days as I feel now. I don't want to move. Have you told the others, what do they say?"

"I'm going to talk to everyone else tonight, as and when they come home from work, but we should, perhaps, all get together and put it to the vote."

"That's a brilliant idea. Look, if it wouldn't be presumptuous, why not ask everybody to come here to number five about eight o'clock on Tuesday night. If you meet anywhere else, I won't be able to come because of Nina but she'll be in bed and fast asleep by eight and won't disturb us. I would like to speak to the others and see what they have in mind."

"Right, done," said William decisively, "Tuesday at eight. I'll tell the others."

William felt better than he had in weeks. The outcome wasn't what he'd wanted but at least he could take some kind of action instead of just waiting around.

Chapter 9

It was Monday morning and Margaret was on the bus on her way to work. It was packed solid, every seat was taken and there were standing passengers in the aisle. Buses into the city were fairly full by the time Margaret got on. Her house was only a few stops from the town centre. Although the ride was short, it was invariably fairly uncomfortable, too hot in the summer and freezing in the winter. The sun was streaming through the windows, raising the temperature inside the bus. All the windows were open but this did little to help circulate the air. It looked as though it was going to be another lovely, sunny day, much too nice to spend sitting in an office. Still, the weekends had been fine recently and that made a change and at least she could go for a walk in the park in the evening or sit out for a couple of hours after work. Her thoughts strayed.

Perhaps by next summer I'll be living somewhere completely different. I wonder what's going to happen. I suppose the meeting tomorrow night will decide whether William appeals or not but we'll still be hanging in limbo for months. At least he seems to have cheered up a bit now he knows where he stands and that's something.

She looked through the window, her stop next. She started to squeeze her way along the aisle to the platform. The bus stopped and spilled passengers on to the busy pavements. The streets weren't too crowded as yet. Margaret was always a little early but in twenty minutes or so they would be full of people, all in a hurry to get to work on time. They'd start getting off buses and coming down from London Road Station in droves and disappear singly and in groups into various office buildings, as though swallowed up. Half an hour later, the streets would be comparatively empty until the shoppers started to arrive. Then at lunchtime, the office buildings would disgorge their workers until the streets and shops were crowded.

Margaret walked up the steps of the building in which she worked.

"Good morning, Jim," she said briskly to the commissionaire, who held the door open for her.

"Good morning, Miss Hartley, looks like it's going to be another scorcher."

"I think you're right but it's been a lovely weekend."

"That it has, Miss Hartley."

She took the lift to the third floor. She often walked up but it had been so hot on the bus and she didn't want to get even hotter slogging up the stairs. Although it was a little cooler inside the building, she could feel her blouse beginning to stick to her back and it wasn't even nine o'clock yet.

In her office, she hung up the jacket she'd been carrying over her arm and put her handbag in the bottom drawer of her desk. She opened the diary. Mondays were always busy and although they were now up to date with almost everything, she would no doubt have plenty to do. She worked on steadily, sorting out the post and getting on with routine jobs until Mr Robinson buzzed her to come in for dictation about ten thirty. She picked up her pen and notepad and went in.

"Good morning, Margaret. Nice weekend?"

"Yes, thank you, and you?"

"Very pleasant indeed. Shall we get cracking? I'll give you the urgent stuff first. There are about half a dozen letters which need to go out tonight, so make them a priority. I'll be working on the six monthly report for Head Office for the rest of the morning and I'll want to dictate that straight after lunch."

"That's fine," said Margaret, opening the notepad on her knee. Mr Robinson dictated clearly, with a minimum of humming and hawing between sentences, and she wrote rapidly in her neat Pitman's shorthand.

Her previous boss had driven her mad, didn't know what he wanted to say and couldn't say it clearly anyway. She often thought that if he said 'What did I say?' one more time, she'd crown him with the nearest plant pot. Fortunately, it hadn't come to that and she had been promoted to Mr Robinson's office.

He dealt briskly and efficiently with the urgent post. What a difference from the shambling wreck who'd been sitting at the desk just a few weeks earlier. He really was his old self again and she had to admit, it was a huge relief to hand back the responsibility she'd been forced to take on so recently.

She picked up the folder containing the letters to which replies had just been dictated and glanced at the clock on her office wall, just after eleven o'clock. She sat down in front of her typewriter and wound in the first letterhead, complete with carbon and copy paper. Flicking back the pages in her notebook, she set to. Letter followed letter, her pace now rapid and steady, the pile of completed correspondence growing whilst the pile not yet dealt with diminished.

With a flourish, she pulled the last letter out of the typewriter, separated the carbon and put the letter on the pile. She'd just have time to do the envelopes before lunch.

More often than not, she had lunch in the canteen in the basement. The food wasn't bad, not haute cuisine, of course, but good plain food, reasonably well cooked. Besides, if she had a cooked meal at lunchtime, it saved cooking in the evening and she could manage with a snack.

Not today, though, she couldn't face the heat or the noise. If she was quick off the mark, she could get herself a quick sandwich and be into the Gardens before the crowds. She picked up her handbag and a magazine and made for the door. An hour in the park would make a welcome break, she had a hard afternoon in front of her.

She was lucky enough to get a seat on a bench and watched as the park began to fill with escapees from offices and shops. All the benches were soon filled and people were sitting or lying on the sloping lawns, unpacking their sandwiches, some of them with flasks of tea or cold drinks. The ice cream van at the entrance to the Gardens was doing a roaring trade. One couple, hand in hand, were looking for somewhere to sit. They found a space under a tree and sat close together. He put his arm around her shoulder and whispered into her ear. The girl turned her head to look intently into his eyes. How young they looked, yet they were obviously very much in love and were probably stealing an hour together in the middle of the day.

I must be getting old. It's not only the policemen who look young but even young lovers look younger every year.

She looked away, not wanting to pry.

Her thoughts strayed back to the house situation.

It must be on my mind more than I realised. The more I think about it, the less I want to move. I know they'll give me a more modern property but I could finish up with an hour's ride into town every day instead of ten minutes. That's adding two hours to my working day. I probably won't know a soul either and it's not easy for a single woman to make friends. Funny, I'd not thought about it before but I'd be losing my last tie to David too.

That house held so many memories for her. They'd taken the keys from William the same day. Her mum and dad weren't all that keen but she managed to talk them round and once they'd submitted to the inevitable, they set to with a will.

Her dad had managed to buy or scrounge enough paint to do the whole place and had set to at the weekend. She'd learned pretty quickly how best to get the distemper on the walls.

Because they'd made such progress, when David appeared on weekend leave, he'd decided to give up his digs to save the rent and move straight in. He was there when they arrived in the morning, already working, and the three of them made rapid progress through the house. Her mum was, in the meantime, cutting down curtains she'd had stored to put up at the windows. Stuff like paint and fabric were increasingly difficult to come by.

They guessed David's posting was close when Margaret received a letter announcing a week's leave and she immediately put in a holiday application. Although she was sorry that poor old Auntie Maud had died in Brighton, she was relieved to know that her mum and dad would be out of the way for the whole week. They'd decided to stay over after the funeral and have a few days by the sea.

On Friday morning, Margaret locked up her parents' house and took a small suitcase with her to work. She was at sixes and sevens all day, this was the first chance they'd really had to be together since the weekend in Yorkshire. She couldn't concentrate on what she was doing, having to re-type several documents, all fingers and thumbs but at last, the working day was over.

She practically danced her way to the bus stop, striding out and swinging her bag. She looked so happy, several people responded to her obvious joy and found themselves smiling.

Pushing open the front door, she saw David's kitbag. He was already here. She flew through the house, calling his name and they met in the kitchen, flinging their arms around each other. He held her so tight, she could scarcely breathe and she loved it.

She looked straight into his eyes; she felt safe and confident.

"Let's go upstairs. I want to be with you properly."

Laughing back at him, she ran full tilt at the stairs and he was right behind her.

"What hussy you are, who would have thought it?"

Then there was no time for words, the clothes were gone and they were together, just feeling the warmth of each other's bodies, responding to each other's caresses, urgent need demanding fulfilment, all thought banished.

They spent the week playing house, pretending it was permanent and would never end. David finished the last few jobs, fixing door handles and putting up curtain rails while Margaret cooked and cleaned. They couldn't bear to be parted, even for a minute and did everything together. They shopped for food, carefully counting coupons, and went for walks in the park.

They bathed together, a tight fit in a small bath, but they managed, unable to resist the feel of wet skin, slicked with soap bubbles and slow, tantalising stroking. Rubbing each other dry invariably led to more kisses and more embraces, which led to a step across the landing to the bedroom for more serious endeavours. They knew each other now and each knew how to arouse the other, they just learned as they went along.

Their last morning came and David had packed his bag and was ready to leave.

"Don't come to the station. I don't want to see you weeping on the platform, I want to think of you here, in this little house, where we've been so happy. I'll hang on to that thought while I'm away and remember the week we've spent together."

She nodded and went with him to the door. He kissed her quickly, a lump in his throat. He knew if he spoke he'd be in tears so he slung his bag over his shoulder and set off down the street. Margaret stood on the step watching him go, he turned at the corner and waved and she lifted her hand in acknowledgement, the tears streaming unchecked down her face.

She never saw him again.

***

She spent the next two years living behind glass, nothing seemed to touch her. She'd distanced herself from life and was going through the motions. She got up and went to work, she came home and switched on the radio only to find she hadn't heard a word in an hour.

Her mum and dad begged and pleaded with her to go back home. She wouldn't even consider it. More than anything, though they meant well, she couldn't bear their constant solicitude, the fussing, the advice to 'get on with her life.'

She just wanted to be left alone and it was a long and lonely journey before she really began to live again.

She pulled herself back to the present and looked at her watch, time she started back to work. She'd been sitting woolgathering for far too long. She rose and brushed the crumbs off her skirt and set off back to the office.

The afternoon passed quickly and just before five, she went in to Mr Robinson's office to ask him about his schedule for the following day.

"Come in, Margaret, and sit down for a minute. I know you've been busy but I couldn't help but notice that you look worried. Is there anything I can do? Would you like to tell me about it?"

"I don't think so. It's a personal problem really, nothing at all to do with work."

"Well, unless it's something really private, perhaps it would help to talk about it."

"No, it's nothing I can't talk about and perhaps it would help to tell someone. The problem started about a year ago when the house in which I live fell under a compulsory purchase order. The landlord's been trying to get the houses removed from the list but heard at the end of last week that he'd been turned down."

She rested her hands on the ever present notebook.

"He still has an opportunity to appeal but quite frankly, I have my doubts about his chances of success. I don't think any of us, there are five houses in all, really want to move but we're all meeting tomorrow evening to talk it over. The final decision will, of course, be Mr Whitehead's, the landlord, but I know he'll take our views into account.

It's really a question of how many, if any, of the people who live in the houses want to carry on to a court case, bearing in mind that many of the surrounding houses are already empty and boarded up. Even if we're successful, we'll have to stay where we are while the houses around us are being demolished and it might be too much for some of the tenants."

Mr Robinson leaned forward, elbows on the desk, waiting for her to finish.

"As you can imagine, the uncertainty is getting to all of us in one way or another and the landlord, who actually lives on the row, has been under a dreadful strain for the last few months. The authorities will, of course, rehouse all of us but I've lived in that house a long time and I don't want to lose my home."

Her normally calm manner was now seriously under threat and she was embarrassed to find that her voice wasn't steady.

Mr Robinson stood up and walked to the window, giving her a chance to regain her composure.

"All the time you've been coping here almost single handed, you've had this worry on top of everything. Why didn't you say something before?"

"There didn't seem to be much point. I don't think there's anything anybody can do, we seem to be completely at the mercy of the powers that be."

"I'm not so sure about that. It may be a question of how the case is handled. What's really needed here is a detailed plan of action and some strategy. There's usually more than one way to skin a cat. Once the tenants have decided whether to go ahead or not, and that should be clear by tomorrow evening, you can start to make plans. In the meantime, let me think about it for a couple of days, say until Wednesday, and see what I can come up with."

* * *

Tuesday evening and the neighbours began to arrive at Judy's door, Mr Whitehead first with Mikey, bringing with him a couple of packets of biscuits.

"I thought these might go down well with a cup of tea later on."

"You really shouldn't have bothered but it was a kind thought."

"No doubt young Nina will make short work of any that are left."

Judy was just taking the biscuits through to the kitchen when there was another knock at the door.

"Can you get that, Mr Whitehead."

William opened the door to find Margaret Hartley on the doorstep.

"I'm not the last, am I?"

"No, the Goldmans aren't here yet but I don't know whether they'll both come. I wouldn't be surprised if Mr Goldman came on his own."

Margaret went through to the kitchen.

"Here you are Judy. I've brought an extra pint of milk in case you run short with so many extra mouths in the house."

Judy accepted the contributions gracefully. They weren't to know that she had been out and bought extra milk and biscuits, just in

123

case. They weren't being patronising, she realised, just kind. How different from the neighbourhood where she had lived with Aunt Mary where her Aunt had carried on a policy of 'keeping herself to herself' and was just barely civil to the neighbours.

She went back into the sitting room to hear another knock at the front door. Both Mr and Mrs Goldman were on the step, Mrs Goldman holding tight to her husband's arm with one hand and balancing a cake on a plate in the other.

"How nice to see you both, do come in and sit down."

"Thank you. Mrs Goldman has brought for you a cake for later, one of her special ones. I hope you don't mind."

"Not at all, I'm very grateful. I'll just take it through to the kitchen. Do have a seat."

Mr Goldman sat on the settee with his wife next to him. Margaret was in one armchair and Mikey in the other while Mr Whitehead stood with his back to the empty grate, hands in pockets. Judy perched on the arm of Margaret's chair and they all looked expectantly at William. He cleared his throat, obviously a little nervous.

"You all know why we're here. I've finally had news from the Town Hall and I'm afraid it isn't good news. They've turned down my application. This means that unless I take some action, the compulsory purchase order will be enforced and we'll all be rehoused.

Before I go any further with this, I wanted to ask you how you feel. I can go ahead with an appeal, which means that we carry on living here even though everybody else is moving out. We might even still be here when they start to pull down the houses, with all the mess and upset that will cause. Even then, we could still lose and have gone through all that for nothing.

Alternatively, we can bow to the inevitable now and start by seeing what the Council will offer us in the way of alternative accommodation. I want you to know I will abide by your decision, whatever it is."

They looked at William, shocked but not really surprised by his news. Nobody seemed to want to start and they all looked at each other, waiting for someone to speak.

"It's important that you say what you think. Everybody here has a vote."

He looked at Margaret hopefully.

"What do you think, Margaret, what do you want to do?"

"I know what I don't want to do. I don't want to move into a soulless council estate where I don't know anybody."

"Here, here,' agreed Judy, surprising herself. 'I know I haven't lived here long and all of you have been here for many years but I would like to say a word, if nobody minds."

Mr Whitehead looked around. Nobody spoke.

"No, go ahead, say what you think."

"All right, we have nothing to lose and everything to gain. I'm prepared to put up with the upset and the mess until we're absolutely sure there's nothing else we can do."

"Well said," responded William. "Mr Goldman, how do you feel?"

Mr Goldman carried on patting his wife's hand gently.

"I speak for both, you understand. We don't want to go, not even to new house with big garden and I don't know what else. This is our home and we want to stay with our friends. Anyway, we give up now, how we know we wouldn't have won? Nobody going to care if we don't care. I say we fight."

Mrs Goldman nodded her head vigorously to indicate her approval.

"I agree," she finally managed to squeak.

"Mikey, you have the last vote. What do you think?"

Mikey blushed to the roots of his hair and started to wring his hands together.

"Come on, Mikey, just say what you think, son. You're among friends here and you are just as important as any of us."

"I don't want to move, Uncle William. I want to s.s.s. stay here like everyone else."

"Well done, Mikey, that's all we wanted to know."

He looked around the room at all their faces, one by one, and finally nodded.

"That's settled then. I'll go ahead. It means that we'll be in limbo for another few weeks at least but then we'll know one way or the other."

Margaret caught his eye.

"May I say a few words?"

William nodded.

"I want you to know, and I'm sure I speak for everybody, how much we appreciate what you're doing. Much the easiest way for you would have been to take the money and leave, instead of which you've been carrying the burden of worry for months now, all on your

125

own. I know this is our last chance to save our homes and I'd like to know if I, or any of us for that matter, can do anything at all to help."

"Yes, yes," chimed in Mr Goldman. "We want to help, can we something do?" His English tended to become a little erratic when he was excited.

Margaret didn't know what, if anything, Mr Robinson would come up with to help their situation but she did know it was crucial now to enable William to leave a door open for any help that may be forthcoming, from any direction. She didn't want to leave him to continue to carry all the worry alone but knew it could be sticky trying to get him to accept help, particularly outside help.

"How much time do we have?" she asked him gently.

"I need to check it first but I'm fairly sure we have to take action by October first, which gives us just over six weeks. There's just the paperwork to complete, I don't know what else we can do."

"There must be something. I don't get angry very often but I tell you now, I'm getting tired of being steam-rollered by the Council. I'm not going to lie down under this. I want to make some kind of a fight of it."

Margaret was delighted to see William's expression change. His back seemed straighter and a glint had appeared in his eye.

"You know, you might be right. What do you suggest?"

"I don't know yet, give me a day or two to come up with some ideas. In the meantime, let's all give it some thought. We might be able to think of something. Judy, can we use your sitting room again later in the week?"

"Of course, I'm only too happy to have you. What about Friday?"

She looked around the room, everybody agreed.

"That's fine then, same time Friday?"

They all nodded their agreement. 'Right then, I'll put the kettle on and by the way, there's no need to make contributions, you've all brought enough for half a dozen meetings.'

Although Margaret felt a bit of a traitor going for outside help without consulting William, she'd bought a couple of days' grace. Anyway, who could tell what they would come up with, they were almost certain to have a bright idea or two between them.

* * *

126

When Margaret arrived in her office the following morning, the door to the inner office was open and she could see Mr Robinson already at his desk.

"Can I have a quick word," he called as she walked in.

"Of course." She went into the office, still carrying her jacket and handbag.

"Is something wrong?"

"Nothing at all, I've been giving your problem some serious thought over the last couple of days and came to the conclusion that what's needed here is a marketing operation."

"I'm not sure what you mean, marketing?"

"You need to broaden your audience, make people want to help you and go after your opposition with all the force you can muster. In short, you need some publicity."

Margaret gasped, "Publicity?"

"Yes, publicity and some solid back up."

"What did you have in mind?"

"I hope you don't mind but I've been in touch with some people I know. They owe me a couple of favours and when I explained what was happening they both seemed keen to help. Could you be available at lunchtime to meet one of them? He'd like to talk to you to fill in some background information."

Things had taken a far different turn than Margaret had imagined, and far more quickly too.

"Yes, of course."

"That's settled then. I'll just ring to confirm and we'll meet him for lunch. The Queen's suit you?"

Margaret nodded, speechless.'

"Good, now I suppose we'd better get down to some work."

The sun was shining as they walked through Piccadilly Gardens and although Margaret was a little apprehensive, she was looking forward to the meeting. As they walked into the entrance, they were almost immediately hailed.

"Hello there, Norman. Come on through to the bar and have a drink while we're waiting to order."

Mr Robinson lightly guiding Margaret by the elbow, followed. They found a corner table and Mr Robinson held out a chair for Margaret.

"Cyril, this is the lady I was telling you about, my secretary, Margaret Hartley. Margaret, Cyril Black."

"Orange juice, please."

Margaret glanced anxiously at Mr Robinson, holding her breath. He intercepted her glance and smiled slightly.

"Same for me, please, with plenty of ice."

"Oh, ye of little faith," she thought and Mr Robinson watched her perceptibly relax.

Cyril Black was a charmer, no doubt about that, and that he was quite taken with Margaret was in no doubt either. Nevertheless, he listened attentively to her story.

"There are several points that strike me and I'd just like to run through them quickly.

First of all, I think it's essential that the actual appeal is handled very carefully. You've got this far without legal advice but I think at this point you need a solicitor. This may, of course, lead to a substantial cash outlay and you may need to consider how to raise the cash for this.'

He spoke quickly and clearly.

"Then I think you need to raise public consciousness, start making a fuss, creating disturbances, petitions, pickets, whatever you can think of."

Margaret was completely engrossed while Mr Robinson watched her, smiling.

"I know Norman has spoken to Charley McDonald at the 'News' and provided you let him know how and where you are campaigning, he'll probably be able to give you some "coverage. They're always looking for local interest stories and if you can make it good enough, they'll be happy to back you.

You have to cover every angle you can think of, try to keep the matter in the public eye to maintain pressure on the Council. They hate any kind of publicity. They want to get this pushed through with the minimum of fuss and it's up to you to resist whenever and wherever possible. In short, "raise hell", if you'll pardon the terminology."

His brown eyes twinkled.

By jingo, she's a corker, a real lady.

Margaret leaned forward, her hands clutched together on the table in front of her. She was aware of his appraising eye and was suddenly grateful she was wearing one of her better suits, the dark blue one with a pretty brooch in the collar and the cream blouse with the lace inset down the front. She felt a little flustered by his intentness which she knew was not altogether directed at the matter in hand.

128

"Quite honestly, Mr Black, I'd never thought of quite this kind of action. The tenants are all reserved people but I do see your point. I don't know how they'll take this but I'm prepared to give it a go. I'll put it to them at the weekend but I'll have to go very carefully. I wouldn't want Mr Whitehead to think I was going over his head. He's a bit of a stickler for doing the right thing."

She felt a little disloyal talking about William in those terms but it was true, William would need careful handling.

"Why not raise these ideas at the next meeting and see how they take it. You can't do anything on your own anyway. You'll need their full support and commitment. Just put the bones of the idea to the rest and see what combined ideas you come up with. Between us, we have a fair few contacts in this city and maybe there are strings which can be pulled."

"Yes, I'll do that and I'll let you know how they take it."

Their main course arrived, served by a very proficient waitress in a black dress and white lace cap and apron. Margaret took a moment to look around. All the waitresses were being monitored by the immaculately dressed head waiter stationed at the door to the restaurant. He was obviously keeping a close eye on both the staff, who lowered their eyes as they passed him, and on the food emerging from the kitchens.

It was years since Margaret had been in this place but nothing much had changed. The walls were covered with wood panelling which was so highly polished it reflected the light from the tall windows on two sides of the room. The table cloths and napkins were white, snowy white, and the silver and glasses shone in the sunlight. Margaret looked around appreciatively. She loved the quiet, understated elegance, the starkness broken subtly by the lush parlour palms at the base of the columns supporting the moulded ceiling and the tiny vase with a single rose in the centre of each table.

She and David had been here for a celebratory meal the night they got engaged. She pushed the memories away reluctantly.

She glanced up from her plate. Cyril Black was watching her again although his gaze was far from critical. She could feel her cheeks colouring. Really, this was getting quite embarrassing. She addressed him directly,

"I'm very grateful for your advice and I promise I'll do the best I can with it."

He smiled, "I'm sure you will, Miss Hartley. I'll give you a ring early next week to see how you're getting along."

129

He really was a bit of a rogue and she knew he was teasing her gently but to her surprise, she didn't mind a bit. In fact, she was quite enjoying it.

The following evening on her way home from work, she caught William on his doorstep just going into the house.

"Could I have a quick word," she called. "There's something I'd like to tell you."

"Of course, what can I do for you?"

Margaret knew that at this stage, she needed every ounce of tact and diplomacy she'd acquired over the years. William was a proud man, unused to being helpless and she knew that these last few months of waiting around at the mercy of factors beyond his control had taken their toll. The last thing she wanted was to undermine him further. Whatever action they took, they would need a strong man at their helm and William fitted the bill perfectly.

"I know you're giving constant thought to our next move and I know how easy it would have been for you just to take the money and move out and I want you to know how much I appreciate what you're doing."

William just cleared his throat and frowned. He didn't want thanks, it just embarrassed him.

"I'd hate you to think I've gone over your head but I've been discussing the situation with my boss and a colleague of his and they've come up with one or two ideas you might consider."

Margaret looked at him steadfastly. He made no verbal response but she could see he'd stiffened slightly.

"As I said, there are suggestions that never have occurred to me but it's a possible framework on which we could build our campaign. It needs your consideration and will need careful planning, timing and strategy if we go ahead."

"What sort of campaign and what sort of framework are we talking about?" he asked rather sharply.

Margaret took a deep breath and roughly outlined her conversation at lunchtime, watching carefully for William's reaction. He was concentrating on what she was saying. He didn't interrupt but heard her out to the end.

To her surprise, as she finished, a smile lit up his normally rather austere face.

"You know, it might just work. I'm all in favour of taking the fight into the enemy's camp but it will take some commitment from the others. We'll put it to them on Friday. In the meantime, I'll think on it and make a few notes. Let's see what we can dream up between us."

Margaret was so relieved at his reaction, she reached out and impulsively touched his hand, smiling warmly. Her already considerable respect for him had increased with his rapid grasp of the ideas and his acceptance of what he could have regarded as interference.

"Margaret, thank you. We both have plenty to think about now. I'll see you on Friday, bring a notebook, you've just been elected secretary."

On Friday evening, William arrived a little earlier than the others and Judy was surprised to see him on the doorstep with a blackboard under one arm and an easel under the other.

"I hope you don't mind, it won't take up much space and I think it will be a great help in making our plans."

Mystified, Judy made no objection as William erected the easel and put the blackboard on it, pulling a clean duster and a packet of chalks out of his pocket.

Within minutes, the rest of the neighbours had arrived and were all seated as at the previous meeting with William standing in front of the blackboard.

"Now then, we've all had time to think about what action we *can* take and Miss Hartley here has come up with one or two ideas. This means that we don't sit back and wait for the axe to fall, we take the fight to the Town Hall and start making a nuisance of ourselves.

I suggest we start to make a list of points to look at then we can take each point in turn to see what action can be taken. Who wants to start?"

They looked at each other, no-one was willing to take the initiative, nobody wishing to push themselves forward, everybody waiting for somebody else to start the ball rolling. Judy looked around, nobody else appeared to be going to speak.

"Mr Whitehead," she said tentatively, "I was wondering if it would be worthwhile to consult a solicitor."

Margaret was relieved that someone else had put that point forward without prompting.

"I know it would cost money but if we could find out roughly what it would cost, we could surely raise the cash between us, if it would give us a better chance."

The rest of the small group indicated their agreement.

"It's worth looking into. We can make enquiries so I'll put that down first for further discussion."

Margaret now spoke up.

"We might try to get some publicity. I have a possible contact at the 'Evening News' who might be prepared to take up a human interest story like this."

"What are they going to build here after they pull us all down?" chirped up Mr Goldman. "Maybe that make a difference. You know they already start with big blocks further up out of Town. They pull down many houses and now build flats for hundreds of people. If they have such plans for here, I think we for chop anyway and nothing we can do."

"Excellent point. I think you've hit on the one weak point in our plans and that should be dealt with first, even before the solicitor."

The list on the blackboard grew steadily as they gained confidence and they were becoming quite excited.

After half an hour, when suggestions had finally dried up, Mr Whitehead spoke again.

"Right now, let's look at the list item by item and see which jobs can be allocated to which people and how we can best tackle them."

Judy spoke reluctantly,

"I know a solicitor. He's been very kind to me in the past and even if he can't handle the case himself, I think there's probably somebody in his office that specialises in this kind of work. The trouble is, it's difficult for me to get out and about because of Nina, there's a limit to the number of places I can take her and a definite limit to the length of time she'll sit quietly. I do so want to help but I don't see how I can. I don't want someone else to fight my battles for me. I want to be involved, I want to do something. It's my home that's at stake too and I really want to go on living here."

They looked at Judy sympathetically, she was near tears.

The next contribution came from an unexpected quarter. Mrs Goldman spoke quietly but firmly, holding on to her husband's hand the whole time.

"I have idea. I'm not good at going places and seeing people and I don't even write English so good but Judy can do these things.

But I can look after child, if Judy trust me and that leave Judy free for other things. What you think, Judy?"

Judy looked at Mrs Goldman.

"Of course I trust you," she said warmly.

She wasn't as confident about her abilities as Mrs Goldman but she realised that this was the only contribution Mrs Goldman would be able to make. It was up to her to be generous enough to let her make it. It was true too, that the friendship and support she had received since she moved in had boosted her confidence no end and this was something she really believed in.

"That's fine then. That leaves me free to do whatever jobs are allocated to me. Thank you, Mrs Goldman, I really appreciate your offer."

"What about me, what can I do?" asked Mikey, all fired up with the excitement.

"Give us a chance, Mikey. We've only just started, there'll be plenty for you to do when we get more organised. Just hold your horses,' said William kindly. 'Some of the initial running around will be done by me and Judy. There are things to sort out that have to be done during working hours. Those that have jobs during the day will be kept informed about what's happening and what they can do as and when it arises. All right?"

Mikey nodded happily, glad he hadn't been singled out as the only one without a specific task. Miss Hartley and Mr Goldman were waiting for instructions too.

"Right then, are we all agreed? Judy and I will try to find out what the Planning Department have scheduled for this site and if that's favourable, we'll go along and see this solicitor chappie, see what he has to say. Maybe we should put off thinking about publicity until the ground is a little firmer. Let's see what we can find out at the Town Hall, we could go on Monday afternoon. Suit you Judy?"

Judy looked at Mrs Goldman, who nodded her agreement.

"That's fine then. I'll call for you at two. As for the rest of us, we'll meet again as soon as we have some news. Everyone agreed? Good. In the meantime, every plan can be adapted so if anyone has any bright ideas, let's have 'em."

The meeting broke up and everyone went along the row to their own homes. Although great uncertainty still hung over them, with the initiation of some positive action, their mood had lightened. Now that they were actually doing something constructive, every one of them felt better than they had for weeks.

133

Judy smiled wryly. She did want to help but had suddenly found herself elected to undertake jobs she'd never even considered. Her reticence had often been a problem in dealing with people she didn't know well but never before had she had anything, apart from Nina, about which she cared so passionately.

This is a chance for me to repay the kindness I've been shown since I moved here and now that Mrs Goldman's made it possible, I just can't let Mr Whitehead down, he needs all the help he can get.

Apart from anything else, it will do Nina no harm to be apart from me for a couple of hours now and then. I know I can trust Mrs Goldman and they could do each other the world of good. I may not be very forceful but I'm better in the outside world than poor Mrs Goldman. I'll just have to put in the time for both of us.

Mr and Mrs Goldman and Margaret Hartley left the house together and turned left and as they reached her path, Margaret impulsively reached out to Mrs Goldman.

"That was a wonderful offer. Judy will be a big help with all the running around there is to do and I think it's important for her to be able to help. You're making that possible by looking after Nina and I know you won't regret it, even though a toddler can be hard work."

"I'm glad to help, is least I can do – and I like little one, she very happy child, most times."

Margaret had never heard Mrs Goldman say so much at one time in all the years they'd lived next door to each other. Mr Goldman was looking at them benevolently, a big beam on his face.

"Goodnight to you both, I'll see you soon," she smiled.

"Goodnight," they murmured in unison, passing Margaret's bay window to reach their own front door.

Mr Whitehead and Mikey turned right as they came out of the front door and stopped briefly outside number three. Mikey looked a little unsettled, it was difficult to judge just how much Mikey understood about what was going on. William put his hand gently on Mikey's shoulder.

"What's the problem, Mikey?"

"Oh, I don't know, Uncle William. Everything s.s.seems to upside down. Will it be all right? Will we have to move?"

The time had come to be absolutely honest, there was no longer any benefit to trying to keep Mikey from worrying, he would only become more confused.

"Well, son, I don't really know but I can tell you this. If there's any way I can stop them pulling down these house, I will,' he said firmly, and then more kindly, 'Look, if the worse comes to the worst, I'll make sure that you're as near to me as possible so we can still keep an eye on each other. Us men have to stick together, you know."

"But Uncle William, what about Judy and Nina and Mr and Mrs Goldman and Miss Hartley, where will they all go?"

"I can't tell you at the moment. They'll all get somewhere to live, don't bother your head about that. I think what you're doing is crossing bridges before you come to them. You know what I mean, worrying about something that might never happen."

Mikey smiled tremulously.

"I think so, Uncle William. I'll try not to worry any more but you will tell me when there's a job for me to do won't you?"

"Of course I will. I'll be relying on you when the time comes. Now then, cut along, it's getting late and you have to be up for work in the morning."

Mikey said goodnight and then wandered slowly up the short path to his own front door. He turned and half raised his hand to William as he entered the house, closing the door behind him.

William heard the Goldmans saying goodnight to Margaret and as he turned to his own path, the street was now empty.

He went along the hall and sat down on the settee, shaking his head in wonderment. He was so heartened and encouraged by the response of the tenants and although he knew it was far from the truth, felt as though he'd taken control again. Who would have thought that they would all come through, practically falling over each other with ideas and offers of help.

He sat a little longer with one elbow supported by the arm of the settee. Margaret Hartley was absolutely marvellous. He knew he'd been 'handled with kid gloves' but only admired her for the way she'd done it. No doubt about it, he'd been eating out of her hand and it was absolutely painless. She had a good head on her shoulders and by golly, didn't she look good when she got her dander up. She'd looked ten years younger tonight, it really took him back.

Chapter 10

Monday morning brought Judy what she could only regard as a bombshell. She heard the postman coming along the street, she heard him every morning, his whistle was unmistakable. However, he rarely stopped at her door, who did she know who was likely to write to her?

She heard him coming up the path and then the letterbox rattled and the letter hit the door mat, just a plain white envelope, ordinary letter size, nothing official. She turned it over and recognised John's handwriting. She hadn't heard from him for a while, not since she'd left Mrs Beacon's. Perhaps he'd sent her some cash, heaven knows she might need extra now, she may need to contribute to the solicitor's bills for the appeal.

She tore open the envelope. Yes, there were four five pound notes inside. That would come in useful. She pushed the cash into her pocket while she sat down to read the letter.

'Dear Judy,

I am enclosing some cash, which I am sure you will be able to find a good use for. Sorry I haven't been in touch for so long but to be quite honest, I've been trying to screw up the courage to come and see you. When I finally did make it, Mrs Beacon told me you had moved and gave me your new address.

As I don't know your circumstances at the moment, I thought it might be better to write instead of calling.

There's no easy way to say this but I'd like a divorce. I have been offered a good job down South and will be starting in the next couple of months. I've met somebody else and we want to get married. I think it's best all round if we can make a new start and you will also then be completely free to get on with your life.

I have an appointment to see a solicitor next week and he will probably write to you direct. I'm really sorry about the way things worked out. I think I probably wasn't ready to get married and I know you did your best. None of it was your fault.

I think about Nina often but as she doesn't know me anyway, I think a clean break would be best. I'll send money as often as I can. I know it's little enough for me to do but I hope you can find it in your heart not to hate me.

Take care of yourself and of Nina.

John

PS My mother has been rather ill for the last few months but she often asks after Nina.'

Judy read the letter through again, clutching the envelope in her other hand.

What a nerve! He should have told the truth, he just hadn't had the courage to come and see her. No doubt Mrs Beacon had given him an earful for his desertion of his wife and child, she was good at that sort of thing.

Thinking of getting married? What, again? Twenty four years old and already married twice. For the sake of the 'someone else', I hope he's grown up a bit in the last two years or she's in for a hard time. Why should I worry? I wouldn't have him back if he came on his hands and knees.

At least the cash will come in handy. Thank heavens I don't have to rely on it though, it could be weeks before he sends any more. She was furious with John all over again, with his lack of courage, his self abasement and his downright immaturity. Look after Nina, would she be likely to do anything else? A clean break, what did he think it was when he walked out? No, not walked out, sneaked out. When had he last seen Nina anyway.

As for his mother, hardly the caring grandmother, asking after Nina, she could soon find out where they were if she really cared. She'd only seen her once anyway and that was when they came to the hospital two days after she was born.

Angrily, she snapped the letter back into its folds and stuffed it back in the envelope. She slung the envelope, now thoroughly crumpled, into a sideboard drawer and slammed it shut. There was nothing she could do now until she heard from his solicitor and then she'd have to go to see Mr Hughes for advice. Strange, she hadn't spoken to Mr Hughes for nearly two years and now there were two things she needed advice about.

She still felt rattled by lunchtime but she talked reassuringly to Nina, telling her that Mrs Goldman would be coming in the afternoon, that she would have a nice time, that Mummy wouldn't be long. To her surprise, when Mrs Goldman knocked on the door just before two, Nina held up her arms straight away to be lifted and put one arm round Mrs Goldman's neck. Mrs Goldman beamed.

"You go now, not to worry, she'll be fine, I look after her."

137

There didn't seem any point in hanging around. There was no point upsetting Nina with unnecessary fussing so she leaned over and kissed her cheek.

"See you later darling, 'Bye, Mrs Goodman, and thanks."

"See you later," lisped Nina and waved her hand. Judy turned and closed the front door behind her.

Mr Whitehead was already standing on his step. His car was in the road and garage door locked and padlocked.

"There you are. Is Nina all right?"

"Yes, she's fine, she seemed happy to see me go," said Judy, a little disgruntled.

Mr Whitehead smiled as he held open the car door for her to get in.

"That's good news, isn't it? Let's be off, shall we?"

They crossed the square and approached the Town Hall. Judy had never been inside before although she'd passed the huge Victorian Gothic Revival many, many times. Its blackened facade bore testimony to Manchester's domestic and industrial coal burning history.

She was impressed and a little overawed by the grandeur of the entrance hall, the mosaic covered floor with its pattern of bees to signify Manchester's industry and the double staircases sweeping to the upper floors.

They climbed the stairs to a narrow, rather gloomy corridor to the Planning Office. There was no natural light, just the borrowed light from the half glazed doors and partitions.

William knocked smartly on the door and went in. George Turner, a fair young man of about twenty six, was looking rather harassed behind a desk piled high with files and papers. Rolls of plans in cardboard tubes were precariously balanced against the wall to his right, one nudge and the whole lot would come tumbling down and probably roll all over the floor.

He looked up.

"Hello there, Mr Whitehead," he said in a friendly tone, glancing sideways at Judy and looking a little puzzled. "What can we do for you this morning?"

"I'll come straight to the point. We want to take action against the compulsory purchase order and would like some information so we can take it further. Don't we Judy?"

138

Mr Turner looked at Judy again.

"I thought it was you, don't you remember me? I haven't seen you since you were about twelve but you haven't changed at all."

Judy looked at him closely.

"George?" she said quizzically, "George Turner, Auntie May and Uncle Harold's son?"

"That's right. How are you? Mum and Dad will be so pleased to hear that I've seen you. They often talk about you and your Mum and Dad, especially at Christmas time."

He couldn't say how many times he had heard his mother wonder how that poor child was doing with that dreadful woman. The two families had spent Boxing Day together for several years but Aunt Mary had put a stop to that and George's mother had been reluctant to make a fuss in case she made things worse for Judy.

"I'm just fine, George. I live in one of Mr Whitehead's houses, so you can imagine that I'm keen to know what's going to happen."

Suddenly, the door to the inner office was flung wide, rattling the glass and wood panelling. A portly, red faced man in a beautifully cut dark serge suit came through the door, almost strutting. It was apparent that, in his own eyes at least, he was a very important chap.

"What's going on here? Ah, Mr Whitehead, it's you again. Still trying to resist council decisions, are we?" he said almost sneeringly.

His chest puffed out, filling his waistcoat and causing the gleaming watch chain strung between his waistcoat pockets to rise a little.

Mr Whitehead nodded stiffly.

"Yes, I am," he said shortly.

"Look man, don't you know when you're beaten? How you can expect to take on the authorities and win is beyond me. Why don't you just accept it gracefully and let us get on with our jobs, there's a good chap."

Judy could see William bristling. The man's overbearing and patronising manner was infuriating. She, surely one of the most non-violent people in the world, could have smacked him herself. She laid her hand restraining on William's arm. She surprised herself but knew that there was nothing to be gained by William losing his temper. She could see him struggling for control.

"I'll make up my own mind about that."

"Please yourself, please yourself. Turner, I'm sure you've got better things to do than sit around gossiping with all and sundry so why don't you see to Mr Whitehead and then you can get on with your work."

He left the office, banging the outer door behind him so that the polished brass latch rattled into place and they heard him clumping along the corridor.

It wasn't common knowledge but Gerald Moody, the erstwhile Captain Moody, had served under William during the war. A nasty incident, which William had regarded as outright bullying, had resulted in Moody being severely admonished and temporarily reduced in rank. William had thought he'd seen the last of him when the war ended and was galled to find him in a position of some power. Now, Moody felt he had the upper hand and gladly embraced the opportunity to flex his muscles and show William who was in charge.

Judy could hardly contain herself.

"What an objectionable man, how do you cope with it George?"

George smiled wryly.

"To be honest, it's not for much longer. Mr Moody isn't the easiest man to work for and I've applied for an internal transfer to another department and it looks as though I've got the job. It's a step up for me and the powers that be like their staff to have a wide experience within the Authority.

However, back to business, I'll have to check on the official procedure but I'll do that today and let you know as soon as I can, certainly before the end of the week."

"Thank you, that's fine,' said William, 'and by the way, there is one other thing I wanted to ask you while I'm here."

George Turner nodded, waiting for the question.

"Can you tell me what the plans are for this particular area? It isn't very big, so are they planning to build housing of some description?"

"It's a matter of public record and you could find out for yourself so I suppose it's not a breach of confidence. Up until about three weeks ago, the intention was to build more high rise flats on that site.

However, I happen to know that money is now running short and corners will have to be cut. Any money that's available will have to be spent on the new estate out at Wythenshawe. A lot of money has been lavished out there as it's supposed to be a 'show piece' for the rest of the country but of course the expenditure is enormous. You can't just build houses miles from anywhere, they need to build roads and schools and provide shops and even churches. As far as I know at the moment, your site has now been designated as 'open land' and will be landscaped and turfed and the plans show some tree planting."

"That's wonderful news. It couldn't suit us better and we're grateful for your help."

"May I give you another word of advice?" George asked diffidently.

"Of course, please do."

"If you haven't already done so, I'd strongly recommend that you retain a solicitor to act for you. They do cost money but they know the planning regulations and by-laws inside out and quite honestly, it could make the difference between win or lose. A solicitor would also be able to confirm officially the information I've just given you informally. As I said, it's a matter of public record but they know exactly how to go about these things."

Judy warmed to him, he was just a shade pompous for such a young man but he obviously meant well.

"In view of what you've just told us about the long term plans for the site, that's exactly what we intend to do. We'll make an appointment to see a solicitor as soon as possible. I don't mind telling you that ruffling that one's feathers will be a pleasure," said William gesturing with his head towards the recently slammed door.

"Hmm, you'll appreciate I can't comment on that."

"No, no, of course not. Well, thank you again for your help and you'll no doubt be hearing from us or our solicitors in the not too distant future. Goodbye."

Mr Whitehead was just opening the door to let Judy out when George called softly,

"Judy, could I have a quick word?"

Judy looked across at Mr Whitehead,

"Would you mind?"

"Not at all, you carry on. I'll wait out here," he said tactfully and went into the corridor, closing the door gently behind him.

George Turner looked a little ill at east and was reddening slightly around the ears.

"Look, Judy, I'd like to see you again to catch up a bit. Would it be possible for me to take you out, perhaps for a drive one night if the weather's good. After all, it's not as though we're total strangers and I know Mum and Dad will be delighted to hear that I've seen you."

Judy was reluctant to launch into explanations about broken marriages, babies and impending divorces in the middle of the council offices and took a moment or two to reply. Her first instinct was to turn him down flat, she really couldn't be bothered, she had too much on her mind. On the other hand, the thought of the cowardly letter she'd received that morning tipped the balance.

What had she to lose? She hadn't been out of the house on her own since Nina was born. Perhaps it was time for her to cut loose a little. She knew that someone, either Margaret or perhaps Mrs Goldman would babysit. She made a sudden decision.

"Why not? What did you have in mind?"

"What about Wednesday, I could either come and collect you, after all I know more or less where you live, or we can arrange to meet somewhere."

"Can I ring you and let you know? Is it all right for you to receive personal 'phone calls?"

"Of course it is, despite what you've seen this morning with you know who, we have moved out of the dark ages, even in the council offices."

He took a slip of paper and quickly wrote down his telephone number and extension.

"Here you are, you can reach me almost any time in working hours, apart from one 'til two. I'll look forward to hearing from you."

Judy took the slip of paper and smiled.

"I'd better not keep Mr Whitehead waiting any longer and I'm sure you've got plenty to do. I'll try to ring you sometime tomorrow and let you know. 'Bye now."

"I'll look forward to that, 'bye Judy."

William needed to clear his head so they called for a coffee in the basement Kardomah in the corner of Albert Square. The aroma of coffee rose to meet them but everything else had changed. It was all Formica and self service now and William couldn't see it as an improvement.

More signs of what they call progress, I suppose.

* * *

Not five minutes' walk away, Margaret was also about to be propositioned. She was ploughing through the letters and files piled on her desk when the telephone rang. She lifted the receiver quickly, holding the 'phone against her right shoulder and continuing to rifle through a file.

"Mr Robinson's office."

"Is that you, Miss Hartley? Cyril Black here."

"Good afternoon, Mr Black. How can I help you? I'm afraid Mr Robinson's not here right now, he's in a meeting that's likely to go at least another hour."

"No actually, it was you I wanted to speak to."

Margaret put down the file and took the receiver firmly in her right hand.

"I wondered what had happened at your meeting the other night and whether you'd decided to go ahead with the appeal."

"Yes, in theory, we all want to go ahead and Mr Whitehead, the landlord, is going to the Town Hall today to see what he can find out. We should have some definite news tonight."

"Good, good, once you have the go-ahead, we can perhaps arrange to make a start with the publicity. I'll have a word with Charley McDonald at the 'News' and see what he says."

"Actually, I think Mr Robinson has already spoken to him."

She was beginning to feel that if they weren't careful, Cyril Black would start to take over.

"That's fine then. I'll give you my number at the office and you could let me know what's happening or if there's anything else I can do to help."

He trotted out his number, which Margaret wrote down carefully in her telephone index.

"Thank you Mr Black. I'll certainly bear that in mind. You've been more than kind."

"Oh, before you go, Miss Hartley, I wonder if you'd care to come out for a drink one evening after work. You could give me an up-date then and perhaps I could make some suggestions."

Margaret hesitated. She wasn't in the habit of going out with men, either straight from work or otherwise. She did find him a trifle overpowering, it was true, but he certainly was charming. Subconsciously, she knew that Cyril Black found her attractive and she was flattered. It had been a long time since anyone had shown that kind of interest in her, most people just seemed to see capable and reliable old Margaret Hartley. What harm could it do? After all, it was only a quick drink on the way home.

"I don't see why not," she said cautiously.

Cyril Black believed in striking while the iron was hot.

"What about tonight?"

Margaret panicked slightly. This was all going a little too fast and anyway, although never less than smartly dressed for the office, she wished she were wearing her new navy suit instead of the grey, which was already a couple of years old.

"I'm sorry," she said firmly. "Tonight's not possible but any other evening this week."

At least she'd know in advance and could dress accordingly.

'Tomorrow then. I'll meet you outside your office at five thirty, OK?'

"Fine, I'll see you then. Goodbye."

Margaret replaced the receiver and noticed that her hand was shaking slightly. Good heavens, she was behaving like a teenager but she couldn't suppress the vague fluttering in her stomach or the blush that rose to her cheeks.

By the time she was on her way home, she'd managed to subdue her barely admitted excitement and was again being perfectly matter of fact. Absolutely nothing to get excited about, she'd wear her new suit, why not? She always prided herself on looking smart anyway. He was probably just being kind and wanted to know how things were developing with the appeal. As she was passing Judy's, the front door opened and Judy called out,

"Good evening, Margaret. I was watching for you, do you have a minute?"

Margaret walked up the short path and spotted Nina peeping out from behind the open front door. Margaret pretended she hadn't seen her.

"Hello there, where's Nina tonight, has she gone out for a walk?"

"I'm sure I don't know where she is but if you see her, will you please tell her her tea is ready and it's her favourite."

"Fine, I'll tell her."

Nina could resist no longer but almost fell out from behind the door giggling.'

"Here I am, here I am. I been a good girl today."

Judy bent down and picked her up, holding her on one hip in the way special to mothers the world over.

"Ah, there you are Nina. I'm glad to hear you've been such a good girl."

Margaret knew she'd been left with Mrs Goldman for the afternoon and she looked at Judy enquiringly.

"Yes, it was fine," Judy responded to the unasked question. "Look, if you're not busy tonight, why don't you pop back later. I'd dearly love a 'natter' and I can tell you what happened at the Town Hall."

"Fine, I'll see you later then.' She leaned forward and kissed Nina on the cheek. 'Bye poppet, see you later."

Nina and Judy watched her go down the path and along to her own house, waving to Mrs Goldman behind her net curtains on the way.

It was a couple of hours before she went back to Judy's. She had made a quick meal, washed the few dishes, tidied up the kitchen and pressed her clothes and polished her shoes and bag for the morning.

Judy opened the door before she had a chance to knock and gestured Margaret to come in.

"I've only just got Nina settled and she's really worn out. It's been an exciting day for her but she certainly seems to have had the time of her life with Mrs Goldman."

Margaret went into the small sitting room and took her usual seat in one of the armchairs.

"That's good. It's hard to believe that someone so shy could be so good with children. Still, I suppose kids have no pre-conceived ideas and just accept people as they are. They're easier than adults to get along with, especially if you're not too keen on talking your head off all the time. Well, I've been on pins all afternoon, what happened at the Town Hall?"

Judy gave her a brief summary of their visit to the Town Hall.

"The next major item is to organise a solicitor. Mr Whitehead seems happy enough to consult my parents' solicitor, Mr Hughes, and he said he'd ring him this afternoon to make an appointment for sometime next week. We'll just have to hope he can give us some idea of the cost. Honestly though, Margaret, I wish you could have seen Mr Whitehead's face when he spoke to that overbearing character. If I hadn't been so anxious, I think I would have laughed. I really thought Mr Whitehead was going to punch him on the nose."

She giggled a little at the memory, "I wouldn't have blamed him either, I could almost have thumped him myself."

Margaret noted the use of the 'we' when referring to the solicitor.   Obviously, Judy was going along too, provided Mrs Goldman would step into the breach again.   Judy's self assurance seemed to be expanding almost weekly, and about time too, thought Margaret.   She's been so wrapped up in just keeping herself and Nina going and now she has something broader to claim her interest.   It's the best thing that could have happened.   She was watching Judy carefully and saw her expression change, suddenly becoming serious and a little worried.

"What is it, Judy.   There's something else isn't there?"

Judy, who'd promised herself to keep the letter from John quiet until she knew something more concrete, suddenly spilled out the whole story, the letter, the money and the threatened divorce.

"The funny thing is, I scarcely know how I feel about it myself.   I was so mad this morning, I didn't know what to do with myself.   I don't think I would have been responsible for my actions if John had suddenly appeared.   But now, I just don't know.   He hasn't been near us for two years, just sent cash now and then.   I know I wouldn't want him back, Nina doesn't even know him but a divorce seems so final.   I feel sort of abandoned.   I've been on my own a long time now but once the divorce goes through, I'll really be on my own, apart from Nina, of course.   Silly, isn't it?"

Margaret leaned over and put her hand on Judy's arm.

"I expect it's for the best.   At least you'll be out of limbo and perhaps now is the time for you to start going out a little.   You're very young and you have your whole life in front of you.   It's not impossible that you should meet someone else."

"It's funny you should say that," laughed Judy.   "If you'd said that a week ago I'd have pooh-poohed the whole idea but now I'm not so sure."

She told Margaret about George Turner at the Town Hall and his invitation.

"I didn't say absolutely definitely.   I've got to ring him tomorrow and let him know.   What do you think, should I go?   He has no idea about John or Nina and I'd have all that to explain.   Is it worth it?   I haven't actually seen him or his parents since the Christmas before my parents died but they used to be good friends."

"Think about this, Judy.   Whoever you meet from now on, whether it's even vaguely romantic or not, will have to be told about

Nina at some stage. John too, for that matter, unless you want folk to think that you weren't married when you had her. Get some practice, go out with this young man, what did you say his name was, George? Get it off your chest as matter of factly and as soon as you can and then you'll both know where you're up to."

Judy had to acknowledge the soundness of Margaret's advice. She knew she couldn't devote the rest of her life exclusively to Nina, that wouldn't be fair to either of them. Still and all, perhaps this wasn't the right time, perhaps she should wait until the house situation was sorted out.

Margaret could see her wavering.

"Come on Judy, what have you got to lose? Before you raise your next objection, I'll sit with Nina for the evening, she never wakes up anyway once she's gone off. He sounds like a nice young man. Give him a chance. He's not asked you to marry him, he's only asked you out for a drink and if it doesn't work out, you don't have to see him again. Just take it as it comes and enjoy yourself."

Margaret could hear her own voice ringing prophetically in her ears. Practically everything she'd said to Judy applied to her too. She would take her own advice, take it as it comes, she wasn't committing herself to anything. Not only had she managed to reassure Judy, she had reassured herself as well.

"You're right, I'll do it. I'll ring him tomorrow and ask him to meet me in Town on Wednesday night about eight o'clock. Is that all right with you?"

Margaret agreed and they fell into a discussion about what Judy could wear. They were much more relaxed together now, had become friends. Despite the difference in their ages, each of them had recognised and acknowledged the qualities they admired in the other. A friendship based on mutual respect, it was almost certain to flourish.

"Let's have a look what you've got in that wardrobe of yours. I don't think I've ever seen you in anything but trousers. Do you actually have legs at all?"

They crept up the narrow stairs and peeped into Nina's room. She was lying flat on her back, arms flung up over her head, her hair curling in damp tendrils round her face. She'd kicked off the light blanket and Judy retrieved it from the foot of the bed and gently covered her with it. She beckoned to Margaret and they went across the landing into Judy's room.

"She looks so angelic when she's asleep, you wouldn't think she could be such a little monkey when she puts her mind to it."

"She's a little darling and you know it." Margaret looked knowingly at Judy. "Now then, let's have a look what you've got in that wardrobe."

They took out all the possibilities and spread them across the bed, trying one sweater with this skirt and then that one. Although the choice wasn't great, they agreed on a navy skirt and a pretty pink blouse and Margaret insisted Judy try the outfit on.

"After all, it's the only way to tell."

Judy struggled into the clothes they'd picked out and fished a pair of low heeled court shoes out of the bottom of the wardrobe.

'What do you think?' Judy flung herself into a film star pose, draped against the door frame, one hand clutching at the frame above her head and the other seductively on her hip.

Margaret fell back against the pillows at the head of the bed, laughing until her sides ached.

"I think you'll do very nicely,' she gulped when she was finally able to speak. 'He's a lucky young man."

"He did say he thought I was pretty," admitted Judy somewhat reluctantly.

"Not only a lucky young man but also a discerning young man as well," laughed Margaret.

"It's perhaps as well we've sorted through this stuff. If I'm going to be trolling around town with Mr Whitehead, I'll have to look my best. I did wear a skirt this afternoon but can you imagine his face if I turned up for the solicitors' appointment in trousers and a pullover and him all togged up in navy pinstripes."

"You must admit, he always looks smart," said Margaret, a trifle tartly. "He always looks tidy, even if he's only cleaning the car."

"My goodness, I didn't mean to ruffle your feathers. You're quite right, he always looks nice and he's a real gentleman too, one of the old school."

"He's not as old as all that,' said Margaret springing once more to his defence, 'not that much older than me, come to think of it."

"You seem determined to misunderstand me. I just meant that young men these days don't care so much about their appearance or their manners. I was paying Mr Whitehead a compliment, not criticising him."

Margaret regained her equilibrium. She was surprised at the speed of her rejection of even an implied criticism of William and the

148

swiftness of her defence but decided to let the matter drop. She went downstairs and into the kitchen.

She thought how long it had been since she'd had that kind of fun, not since she was a teenager, when she and her pal from school were constantly in and out of each other's bedrooms, borrowing clothes and make-up and only her shoes were safe because she had such tiny feet. She stood reflectively, waiting for the water to come to the boil as Judy came downstairs.

"Thank you for sorting me out. I really do appreciate it and I never intended to offend you."

"I know that, you goose."

She echoed Margaret's thoughts almost exactly.

"It's great to have someone to talk to about stuff like that. I never had a close friend when I was in my teens and I've missed out on all that girls' talk. I just muddled along as best I could. I really enjoyed that messing about, I haven't thought about my appearance since Nina was born. You've done me a power of good."

Margaret went home smiling. Judy had looked pretty with a little colour in her cheeks and her figure was surprisingly good in something other than the comfortable clothes she usually wore. She wondered whether there was anything in her wardrobe that would suit Judy and how she could offer it without offending. She could sort that out later, the main thing was for Judy to have a good time. She could hardly wait for the next instalment.

***

William put the 'phone down with satisfaction. A meeting had been arranged with Mr Hughes, Judy's solicitor, for Friday morning. Now the decision had been made, the sooner they could get into action the better. Now for a final check, William opened a drawer and took out the file of papers. Every communication and form was, of course, neatly filed in date order but it would do no harm to read through it all again. He'd just settled down to some serious study when the phone rang.

"Whitehead," he barked into the receiver.

"Good afternoon, Mr Whitehead, McDonald's the name, Charlie McDonald. I work for the 'News' and we're currently developing stories of local interest. I've been told you're having problems with the Town Hall."

"Well, you could say that. What did you have in mind?"

149

"It would probably be best if I came along and had a chat with you and talked over what's happening. Perhaps we could find a way to present the story in such a way that it will do you the maximum benefit while arousing public interest. When would it be convenient for me to call, how about sometime Wednesday afternoon or early Thursday?"

William paused only momentarily,

"Wednesday afternoon about three thirty suit you? Do you know where we are?"

"Roughly, I grew up round there myself but you'd better give me the exact address."

Arrangements concluded, William hung up with some satisfaction. Margaret had certainly not let the grass grow under her feet, things were moving now. He pulled the file towards him resolutely, careful planning and meticulous preparation were his plan of campaign. He intended to know the contents of the file inside out before his meeting with Charlie McDonald.

Chapter 11

Margaret looked quickly at her watch, five fifteen. She tossed the bundle of letters into her post tray for the boy to collect, pulled her wash bag and hand towel out of her bottom drawer and walked swiftly along the corridor to the ladies.

She stood back from the mirror and blotted her lipstick. Thank heavens the ladies toilet was empty at this time of night. She smoothed back her hair one last time, checking that all the ends were tidily tucked into the French pleat at the back, gave herself an uncharacteristic wink in the mirror, and turned smartly on her heel.

The skirt was tugged down, the blouse tucked neatly into the waistband and the shoulders of the jacket quickly brushed. She was just slipping the jacket onto her shoulders as Mr Robinson came out of his office.

"There you are, Margaret, I thought you'd gone. If you're finished, we'll walk down together."

There was nothing she could do. She felt she'd been caught red-handed like a naughty schoolgirl. She didn't know exactly why she didn't want Mr Robinson to know about her 'assignation' with Cyril Black but she didn't. She could feel the colour rising up the back of her neck. Actually, she felt a bit of a fool.

She looped her handbag over her arm and Mr Robinson opened the door for her. She could hardly concentrate on what he was saying and actually had her fingers crossed that Cyril Black would be late and not be waiting at the entrance to the building. She didn't know whether to hurry down the stairs in order to get it over with or to drag it out as long as possible to put off the evil day.

An evening just like any other, people were leaving the building and the commissionaire was at his desk as usual.

"Goodnight, Mr Robinson, Miss Hartley," he called out as they passed.

Margaret looked out into the street as they descended the last few steps outside the heavy double doors. No sign of Cyril Black, thank heavens.

"I'm meeting someone this evening,' she said as they reached the pavement, 'so you go ahead. I'll see you in the morning."

"Fine, see you in the morning."

Mr Robinson raised his hat and walked down towards the car park. He spotted a familiar figure coming towards him.

"Hello, Cyril. What brings you to this neck of the woods at this time of day?"

Cyril looked a little uncomfortable, shifty even, his eyes unable or unwilling to meet Norman Robinson's.

"I'm meeting a friend for a drink," he muttered.

"Well you'd better get on then. You don't want to be late. I'll see you soon, no doubt."

Cyril nodded, mumbled out a farewell and hurried on.

How peculiar, not at all like Cyril. He had a reputation as a bit of a ladies' man but had never been coy about his conquests. Norman Robinson had never encouraged any of his confidences about the women in his life. He found his tales of conquest rather unsavoury and knew there was a little wife tucked away somewhere. After all, he wasn't a close personal friend, just one of the boys, someone to have a drink with. Anyway, who was he to judge after what he'd put his own wife through over the last few months.

He shrugged and walked on and as he reached the corner looked back just in time to see Cyril stopping to talk to Margaret Hartley, still standing on the pavement outside the office.

Surely not, despite himself he was shocked. He'd always thought Margaret such an eminently sensible woman, what was she doing with such a 'bounder', the term springing involuntarily to mind? Perhaps there was a simple explanation, perhaps she was waiting for a woman friend and Cyril Black just happened to be passing. He tried to dismiss the picture of the two of them together from his mind but the nagging feeling of being somehow responsible refused to disappear.

***

He was still pre-occupied when he arrived home. As he opened the front door, his pyjama clad daughter came hurtling out of the kitchen to wrap her arms around his legs. He picked her up and walked through to where his wife was preparing dinner. He knew she was still unsure, still a little frightened, and it was apparent in the way she ran her eyes quickly over his face, looking for the slight redness in the eyes, belligerence or any of the other signs she must have been looking for every evening for the last few months.

He smiled at her and put his other arm around her shoulders, bending down to kiss her cheek.

"Everything OK?" he asked.

He could see her visibly relax, no smell of alcohol on his breath and his eyes were clear and bright. He underwent the same examination every evening but was so grateful not to have lost them both, he was prepared to suffer the same treatment every night for years if need be. Her constant need to reassure herself was an indication of how unsure she was, hoping that the improvement in their lives would be permanent but guarding against being too sure, just in case.

She smiled up at him, relieved.

"Fine, dinner will be on the table in fifteen minutes. Come and give me a kiss, darling, and perhaps your daddy will read you a story. But only one mind, dinner's nearly ready."

The child threw her arms around her mother's neck and gave her a big kiss, with sound effects. He took her hand and together they went into the hall and up the stairs.

"Go and pick your story while I take off my jacket, chicken. I'll be with you in no time."

Fifteen minutes later, he was on his way downstairs, his daughter safely tucked up for the night and well on her way to sleep.

Dinner was on the table as he entered the dining room and he took his seat while his wife served him.

"I can't tell you what a pleasure it is to have you home at a regular time again, to know that you'll let me know if you're going to be late and that it's worth my while cooking a decent meal."

"And a fine meal it is too,' he said, tucking into the food on his plate. 'I'll have to watch it, you'll have all my trousers too tight for me if I carry on eating like this."

He smiled across at his wife, trying to keep the mood light. He couldn't cope with an inquest tonight. A frown line appeared between his eyes as the thought of Margaret Hartley with Cyril Black crossed his mind.

"You look a little tired tonight or perhaps you have problems at work," she asked enquiringly.

"Not exactly, but I do have something on my mind. I'd like to talk it over with you after dinner. I'd value your opinion."

She positively glowed. It was a very long time since he'd asked her opinion about anything. They used to be so close, talking over day to day problems but that had all stopped once the heavy drinking started. Perhaps she could really allow herself to hope after all.

He rose to help her clear the table and carry the dishes through to the kitchen.

"Just put them in the sink, Norman. I'll see to them later. I'll just nip and check she's asleep and then I'll make some coffee. Why don't you go and sit down, the paper's in the sitting room."

As she brought the tray with the coffee into the sitting room, he put down his paper. She sat down on the settee, picked up her coffee and waited.

"It may be nothing at all and I may be over-reacting but I bumped into Cyril Black on my way to the car park. His office is miles away and he seemed a bit reluctant to say what he was doing so near my office. I saw him just a couple of minutes later talking to Margaret Hartley, it almost looked as though they'd arranged to meet. I know it's none of my business but he hasn't a wonderful reputation where the ladies are concerned and I wouldn't want her to get her fingers burned."

"Ah, Cyril Black. Well, you know my feelings on the subject. He's made a pass at every woman in the golf club, more or less. How his poor wife puts up with it I'll never know."

"I'm not sure there's anything going on at all, to be honest but if there is, I would feel partially to blame. I introduced them in the first place. She probably has no idea he's married. She's so straightforward herself it would never cross her mind and she's done so much for me these last few weeks, I'd hate to be responsible for her getting hurt or upset in any way. She has enough to worry about with this house business without Cyril Black."

He pushed his fingers through his hair and looked across at his wife expectantly.

"She's a grown woman and although she seems to have led a fairly sheltered life, she's eminently sensible. She'll soon see through him, I'm sure."

"You're probably right and I am reluctant to interfere in her private life. What she does out of office hours is really no concern of mine. Do you think I should drop a hint that he's married?"

"Why not? If he's told her the truth or if there's nothing going on, what will it matter? On the other hand, if she is seeing him and decides to carry on after she knows he's a married man, that's strictly her own business and you have no right to interfere. You

154

certainly don't owe Cyril anything and I know you don't care for his antics yourself."

"Right, I'll just mention it casually, if I can, and then I'll feel that my conscience is clear. Margaret must then do as she sees fit and it may be that I've got the wrong end of the stick anyway."

He put his coffee cup on the table and went over to sit next to her on the settee. She looked a little startled as he put his arm around her shoulders. She stiffened slightly and then relaxed as he gave her a friendly hug. Physical contact between them had been restricted to a peck on the cheek mornings and evenings for several months now.

"You always show such good sense and see things so clearly, that's one of the reasons I married you," he said, smiling down at her.

She put her hand tentatively on his knee and raised her head to meet his gaze.

"Oh, yes? What were the other reasons?" she teased.

"Because you're such a good cook, because I thought you'd make a wonderful mother, because you're so clever.' He reached over and put his hand over hers, his face suddenly serious. 'But the main reason I married you was that I loved you and wanted to spend the rest of my life with you, not to mention the fact that I fancied you like mad."

"Do you mean that?" she whispered.

"Yes, I mean every word and it's all still true. I know it will take you a while to trust me again and I know what I've put you through. I'll make it up to you, wait and see. Things will get better, we are at least really talking to each other again. I love you."

She turned towards him slightly and reached up and laid her hand against his cheek. She seemed suddenly stronger, more confident.

"How about showing me just how much?"

She kissed him lightly on the mouth, tugged him to his feet and led him slowly up the stairs. His hand was trembling and his knees felt weak.

"I feel like a bridegroom instead of an old married man," he whispered.

She felt powerful, in control, and turned on the landing to face him, putting her arms around his neck.

"Don't worry, Norman. Everything will be all right, you'll see," and she turned and, taking his hand again, walked with him into the bedroom.

William heard the knock on the front door and looked at his watch. That would be Charlie McDonald, right on time. He was keen on punctuality, a sign of good breeding.

Good breeding was not what sprang to mind as he opened the door to find Charlie McDonald standing on his front door step. Scruffy wasn't exactly the right word either but it wasn't far short. His shirt was clean enough, although his tie hung in a loop around his neck and the top button was undone. His suit looked as though it had cost a fortune a good few years earlier and was a little crumpled, to say the least. The battered trilby set on the back of his head was the finishing touch.

He stuck out his hand.

"McDonald, Mr Whitehead is it?"

"Yes, come in. It's good of you to come."

He led the way into the sitting room and gestured towards a chair.

"Can I get you something, a cup of tea perhaps?"

"No, thanks, not for the moment, I'd like to get cracking straight away."

He took out a notebook which had been jammed into his jacket pocket and fumbled in his inside pocket for a pen. He looked a bit slow and clumsy but William hadn't missed the shrewd gleam in his eye and was prepared to reserve judgement.

"I think it would be best if I ask the questions first and then we can talk about what we could do, if you're agreeable. Has the legal side been sorted out yet?"

"No, we have an appointment with a solicitor who we hope will act for us. We'll have a better idea of the time scale once we've seen him."

"OK, let's work round that. I've been thinking about how best to tackle this. I'll be quite honest with you. Although I believe that you have a case, and a good one, I'm in the business of selling newspapers. It's in both our interests to get the maximum publicity we can. It's an important local issue but we want to really stir things up. How far are you prepared to go?"

William looked at him appraisingly.

"I'm not prepared to break the law so what did you have in mind?"

"If we treat this as a campaign, plan our strategy to create interest and then build up public interest steadily, we could do your cause a lot of good. It may not be all plain sailing and there could be some unpleasantness. I would also want information from the rest of the tenants. With careful planning now, we can make everything that happens appear as though it's happening spontaneously. In fact, we can orchestrate events to slot in with the legal proceedings."

He paused, wondering how all this would go down with William.

"Before we start, I need to know that you have the full support of everybody involved and that they are prepared to back you one hundred percent. You need to make maximum possible impact and we need them all to get it. You've all got to be sure that you're willing to take my advice.

I'll handle the whole thing personally. It'll be a 'David and Goliath' story. You know the sort of thing, man in the street takes on the might of the Town Hall. The public loves those stories, they identify with the underdog and love to see the authorities beaten."

William nodded.

"Yes, I can see that sort of line might work. What sort of information would you want from the neighbours and how would they be involved? I'm not sure that they could cope with too much publicity. I think you know Margaret Hartley and her boss, so you know she's a lady, born and bred. As for the others, they are all pretty retiring types. We have a couple who fled Austria before war broke out and Mrs Goldman is painfully shy. Then there's young Mikey, who's lived on his own since his parents died and who's a little slow. Apart from Judy, who's about twenty three and lives with her young daughter, there's only me. I'm not sure how much help you can expect from them under the circumstances."

"It's up to you to convince them. We can still run a story without them but the impact will be a great deal smaller. With just you in the limelight, so to speak, the story will probably run for a day or two but it won't start any fires. I need something to raise on a daily basis so I can keep fanning the flames."

"We had talked about demonstrating outside the Town Hall as well to try to get some publicity. Would that help?"

"Brilliant, it would be the perfect start. Let me run this by you. Once we know the date for the appeal, start picketing the Town Hall the week before. How many adults are there?"

"Only five of us, and that includes Mikey."

"He can hold a placard, can't he?"

"I see what you mean."

"Strategy is everything. You need to plan it so that just about a week before the appeal, there are at least two of you outside the Town Hall every day, say from eleven until about six o'clock. You need banners with a slogan that catches the eye, 'Save our homes' or something of that sort. You should be there on the first day and I'll make sure that your picture, with a cover story, appears in the paper. Of course in the early stages, it will just be a bit of local news and will have to take its chances for space with whatever else happens that day."

The slow, clumsy manner was gone, replaced by sharp gestures and a crisp tone. William looked at him appraisingly. He could see the sense of what he was saying but felt reluctant to expose his friends to such measures. They had already agreed, in principle, to demonstrate outside the Town Hall but would they be able to carry this through.

Briskly, Charlie broke into William's train of thought, pausing only to light yet another Senior Service.

"At the same time, you could start a petition. Really go to town on it, stop people going in and out of the Town Hall and ask them to sign. In fact, you could start that already, the more signatures the better, start around here with the people you know, plenty of them will be on your side. Get them now before they move out and keep a careful tally of the number of signatures."

He really had the bit between his teeth now, ideas were coming thick and fast. He'd hardly finished with one idea when the next occurred.

"We can incorporate the number of supporting signatures into the story, keep a running total. We want it to build interest and this could be ideal. Appeal to the public to come along and sign up for you.

If we create enough interest initially, the story will capture the hearts of people all over the city. That's not all, I have another idea and this is where the tenants come in mainly. This could make or break the story."

Although William was becoming fired with enthusiasm almost despite himself and could see the sense of such a carefully planned campaign, he waited uneasily for the next suggestion, sensing in advance that he probably wouldn't altogether approve.

"Right, William. You don't mind me calling you William – or do you prefer Bill?"

"William will do fine."

"In the week before the appeal takes place, I want to run a story each day, starting on the Monday. Each day will feature one of the houses and its tenants, with pictures, and will be designed to tug the heart strings. We'll throw in everything that will raise sympathy, tragedy will be highlighted wherever we can find it, in fact I want the works."

William had never expected this. For once, he was lost for words. He sat with his chin in his hand, mulling things over.

"What do you think?"

"Quite honestly, I feel it's exploitation and I hate the thought of exposing them to this sort of thing. I'm not sure I could persuade them to go along with it. It's bad enough asking them to stand in the square outside the Town Hall waving placards, without this."

"It's up to you to convince them. If you want to save your homes you need to use every weapon available and I really believe that this kind of publicity can help. I've been in the newspaper business a long time and I know what works."

"I can only put it to them. I'm reluctant to try to talk them into something they really don't want to do and I won't consider this course of action without their consent. When do you need to know?"

"As soon as possible so that I can start working out story lines, I still have to convince the editor it's a 'live one' but I don't see too much trouble there. He knows as well as I do what will sell papers and I believe we have a gem here."

"I'll arrange to talk to them all together some time before the weekend and I'll ring you with their decision."

"Fine, well I'll be off then, I've taken up enough of your time already."

He stuck the battered old trilby on the back of his head, hurriedly pushed the notebook and Senior Service back into his jacket pocket and headed for the door. As he stepped onto the path he turned and stuck out his hand.

"I look forward to hearing from you. We can run the story anyway without them but why not give them a chance to make up their own minds. They might surprise you."

William couldn't see it somehow. He didn't think they'd agree to it and he didn't feel right about trying to persuade them if they showed reluctance.

Charlie McDonald shambled off down the street. His thoughts were rather more cynical and he knew that even the most dignified people could react in surprising ways at the prospect of getting their names and pictures in the paper.'

***

Margaret was already a little flustered before Cyril Black actually came to greet her. She had seen the exchange with Mr Robinson and what was worse, she had seen him turn and look at them as he took the next corner for the car park. She was beginning to feel uneasy about the whole thing. She couldn't help noticing Cyril's eyes shifting nervously to watch Mr Robinson turn the corner. What could be the problem, they were friends, weren't they?

Her cheeks were glowing pink for the second time in about ten minutes and she was already regretting the whole episode and wishing desperately that she could be on the bus on the way home. He raised his hat and came towards her.

"Good evening, Margaret, nice and punctual I see."

"Good evening, Mr Black."

"Tut, tut, Cyril, please. We don't need to be so formal, surely,"

His confidence seemed to have returned with the disappearance of Norman Robinson.

"Let's go and have a drink, shall we? We can try the Shakespeare on Fountain Street, it won't be too crowded at this time of night.'

"I'm sure that'll be fine," said Margaret, just wanting to be away from the doorway of the office in case anyone else came out and saw them.

Why on earth had she arranged to meet him outside her office anyway, she could have met him anywhere, five minutes' walk away.

Finally, they were settled in a corner in a small, dimly lit bar with drinks in front of them. Frank Sinatra's silky voice discreetly poured out of the speakers behind the bar. Cyril took out his cigarettes and offered them to Margaret. She shook her head and resumed turning the gin and tonic Cyril had insisted on ordering for her round and round on the table. She didn't really want it any way, she rarely drank spirits, they went straight to her head. Still, perhaps one wouldn't hurt.

Cyril exerted all his charm. He soothed her with his voice, speaking with authority of the history of this old pub and its black and white timbered facade. She hadn't known it had been moved piece by piece in 1926 from its original home in Chester. He sat close without being close enough to alarm her and led her on gently to talk about the latest developments with the houses, prompting her when she faltered.

He raised his hand and two more drinks appeared on the table. She felt a little safer now and it was flattering to be the focus of his attention, pleasant too, to be with someone who only had to raise their hand for service and be instantly obeyed.

She picked up the second drink.

"I really shouldn't, you know. I don't have much of a head for it."

"A little gin never did anyone any harm, Margaret. Now carry on, tell me all about yourself. What's it like, working for old Norman? Bit of a stickler, isn't he?"

Margaret rose rapidly to his defence and Cyril, seeing that this wasn't the most successful tactic, carefully turned the conversation to a more neutral topic, talking about films and the most recent production at the Palace, making her laugh with rather risqué stories about various members of the cast.

Imperceptibly, he drew closer, his hand was now lying upon hers and he looked into her eyes, hanging on her every word.

"Another drink?"

"Perhaps just one."

The first two drinks were beginning to have an effect, particularly on an empty stomach, and she was beginning to feel their warmth around her middle section. The third drink was placed in front of her and Cyril, she was calling him Cyril now without hesitation, looked into her eyes.

"You know I find you very attractive, don't you, Margaret?"

She blushed again, school girl blushes, would she never grow out of them?

"The blushes are charming, the colour in your cheeks makes your eyes look even brighter."

His hand now firmly grasped hers and his gaze was riveting. She felt as though she couldn't look away, like a frightened rabbit in the headlights of a car.

"Perhaps we could have a run out to the coast one weekend, spend some time together, get to know each other."

"I'm not sure. I'm pretty busy at the moment with one thing and another."

"Come, Margaret. You can't be so busy that you can't spare a couple of hours on a Saturday. You can work too hard, you know. The change would do you good. Think about walking along the promenade with the wind blowing in your face and all your worries thirty miles away."

He was very persuasive, leaning closer towards her now, smiling into her eyes, squeezing her hand.

"Come on, think of me. Put me out of my misery. I can't tell you how taken I am with you. There are so few ladies around these days that a man can really talk to. I feel as though we're on the same wave length. Don't you think so?"

Margaret suddenly realised that she needed to go the ladies' and gently pulling her hand away, whispered.

"I'll think about it. Perhaps you'll excuse me for a minute."

In the ladies', she quickly used the toilet and then looked at herself in the mirror. The cheeky look of earlier had disappeared. She didn't feel like winking at herself now, she felt out of her depth. Her eyes were far too bright, that must be the gin, and her nose was shiny. To her horror, she felt a little shaky on her feet. She didn't realise that the last two drinks had been doubles. She quickly splashed cold water on her face and tried to repair the damage as best she could.

"Ah, there you are. I was beginning to think you'd made a run for it. Another drink?"

His drinks were disappearing at an alarming rate. He could obviously take it and perhaps he didn't realise just how little experience of heavy drinking Margaret had.

"No, no thanks. I'll have to be going now.' She looked at her watch. 'My goodness, it's half past seven already."

She couldn't actually believe it was only half past seven, it felt like midnight.

"At least let me run you home."

She protested and he insisted until it just seemed easier to consent. Quite truthfully, she felt a little odd and didn't altogether fancy the bus journey. It seemed silly to insist on a taxi when he was offering her a lift.

She was a little concerned about the number of drinks he'd downed but to be honest, there were no obvious signs. His hands were steady, his voice unslurred and his walk across the bar straight as a die. He seemed to have himself under perfect control.

He opened the passenger door and saw her safely inside before closing it firmly. He walked around the bonnet and got into the driver's seat. He smiled at her.

"All right?"

She nodded, only too happy to be on her way home at last.

He realised he'd probably gone far enough for the first meeting. He didn't want to frighten her off. He was playing a private game of conquest, his very favourite game. Though he appeared to be concentrating on driving, in reality, he was thinking out strategy.

This was quite a different challenge, not like the shop girls he sometimes picked up in pubs or the acquiescent wives of one or two of his so-called pals at the golf club. She was a real lady, smart and clever, if a bit unworldly. This could prove to be his greatest challenge in the seduction stakes. He mustn't rush it though, softly softly was the way. He glanced across at her.

She still looked neat and composed, even after the gin. How he would love to see her looking a bit rumpled, hair loose, with sweat on her top lip, begging for him, if only with her eyes.'

"This is fine, you can drop me on the next corner."

"Of course not, I'll take you to your door, where is it?"

She indicated the brightly painted door.

"It's number seven."

It wasn't even eight o'clock yet it seemed like a week since she'd left the house this morning.

Cyril got out of the driver's seat and walked round to open the passenger door. She could see William coming along the row and he looked hard at her as he passed and nodded good evening.

"Thank you for bringing me home."

'It was my pleasure. Do think about the seaside and I'll ring you tomorrow.'

She stood at the gate until he'd got back in the car and driven away. She was just putting her key in the door when she heard Judy call from the doorway of number five.

"Margaret, can I have a quick word?' and she came down the path towards her. 'I've decided to go out with George Turner tomorrow, if you can sit for me."

"Yes, of course. I'll come round about seven thirty, if that's all right."

Her voice was sharper than she'd intended but she was beginning to feel rather strange.

"Thank you. I'll see you then."

163

Judy beat a hasty retreat. If she didn't know better, she would have thought Margaret had been drinking, her eyes were almost glazed and she looked a bit unsteady.

She carefully negotiated the stairs, hanging on to the banister rail and hoping she'd make the bathroom before she was violently ill. She lay in bed with her hands over her eyes, the room was spinning. She'd managed to get her clothes off but she hadn't cleaned her teeth and her mouth tasted awful.

She'd never do that again. Imagine Mr Robinson doing this to himself for enjoyment He must be crackers, her last thought before she slipped into oblivion.

Cyril's last thoughts were quite different. He couldn't understand what all the fuss was about. Yes, the little houses looked all right but the rest of the area was depressing, boarded up properties and rubble. He couldn't understand why they wanted to stay there, let alone put up a fight. Surely they'd all be better off with a nice, neat council house somewhere.

No doubt old Whitehead could buy himself something quite tidy with the proceeds of the sale but it was a pity about Margaret. She'd have no chance at all of buying property, even if she could afford it. Single women were rarely granted mortgages unless some man was prepared to stand guarantor and she did seem to be alone in the world. That was better for him anyway, he didn't want anyone interfering and giving her good advice before he got a chance to get her between the sheets and hoped it would be worth it when he did.

Chapter 12

About ten o'clock on Wednesday morning, Judy opened the door to find Mr Whitehead on her step, asking if everything was OK for Friday.

"Yes, Mrs Goldman has already promised to look after Nina and she's coming round about half past nine. That should give us plenty of time."

"Good, it might not be a bad idea to call a meeting on Friday evening, if everyone's available. There are one or two more developments I'd like to discuss but I think we might as well wait until after we've seen your Mr Hughes. Then we can kill two birds with one stone."

When was she ever not 'available' but then she remembered that she wouldn't be available tonight, she was going out with George Turner. She dismissed the thought quickly, that could wait until later.

She looked enquiringly at Mr Whitehead. He rarely lingered once he'd said what he'd come to say and he looked a little uncomfortable. He cleared his throat and looked down the street towards the main road.

"Hmm, did you happen to see Miss Hartley last night?"

"Why do you ask?"

"I saw her with a fellow in a flashy car and she looked a little strange, didn't you think?"

Good heavens, he was fishing. Judy wasn't about to say that she thought Margaret was tiddly and she jumped to her defence.

"She looked fine to me. In fact, she's sitting for me tonight, I'm going out for a couple of hours. With George Turner, do you remember, from the Town Hall."

"I just wondered. I was a little concerned about her, that's all."

He didn't seem to have registered the earth shattering news that Judy was going out, he was clearly distracted.

"That's nice," he mumbled. "I'll see you Friday, if not before."

Margaret felt as though her eyelids had been glued together. She forced her eyes open just a crack and saw the sun blazing through the familiar flowered curtains. She gave an involuntary groan, her head was pounding. It was already eight o'clock and she should have been up half an hour ago.

She pushed herself into a sitting position and her stomach rebelled. She just made it into the bathroom and knelt in front of the toilet bowl, resting her head on her arms and heaved and heaved although nothing much was coming up. She closed her eyes, she didn't think her legs would carry her to the bus stop, let alone all the way to work.

She hadn't taken a day off for over five years, turning in to work with streaming colds and hacking coughs. This was different, she felt too ill to stand. She managed a few sips of water and then got painfully back into bed, pulled up the covers and closed her eyes. Perhaps she could just die here and now and never have to face the world again.

Two hours later, she was roused by voices in the street outside and a tapping at the front door. She thought she felt a little better and struggled into her housecoat. She had to hold her head with one hand and the banister rail with the other to get down the stairs but she definitely felt better. She opened the door a crack to see Judy and Nina on the path.

"Come in, God forbid the neighbours should see me dressed like this at this time in the morning."

Judy slipped inside.

"I noticed your curtains were still drawn and wondered if you were all right. Are you ill?"

Margaret looked sheepish.

"You could say that. I think what I have is the mother and father of a hangover. I feel dreadful."

She smiled weakly and Judy had to bite her lip to stop the grin that was threatening to erupt. She cleared her throat.

"I'm sorry to hear that. Is there anything I can do or anything you want? I'm just on my way to the shops."

"I'd be grateful if you could call in at the chemist and ask for something to settle an upset stomach and if it's not too much trouble, could you 'phone my office and tell them I'm unwell. I've got some coppers for the 'phone and here's the number and extension,' she said, quickly scribbling on a piece of paper. 'Ask for Mr Robinson. He'll be wondering what on earth has happened to me. Tell him I'll be in tomorrow."

Judy pushed the coins and the paper into her pocket and, picking Nina up under her arm, went out quickly, pulling the door closed behind her.

By the time she returned, Margaret had bathed and dressed and had managed a cup of tea although she couldn't face even a slice of toast.

"Don't worry, I haven't forgotten you're going out tonight. I'll be fine by then. What time do you want me?"

"Quarter to eight all right?"

"I'll be there, don't worry."

She spent the rest of the day very quietly, her headache gradually subsiding. She almost wished it didn't, the cessation of pain left room for all sorts of other thoughts to cannon around her brain. She flushed at memory of Cyril's increasing familiarity, her hurried walk up the front path and William's shocked expression. Surely it couldn't have been that obvious that she was tipsy.

What would Mr Robinson say? She never had days off. She smiled wryly. It was certainly true that she had been too ill to work, self inflicted or not. She'd face that tomorrow, it would do no good to dwell on it.

By quarter to eight she was feeling much better and was shooing Judy out of her front door.

"Off you go. Have a good time and don't worry. No need to rush back, I can cope if Nina wakes up. Go on now."

***

It was a pleasant evening, the sun was still shining and a gentle breeze blew along the narrow streets. She noticed another house already boarded up and the family had only moved out that morning. She had seen the van when she went to the shops.

She waited at the bus stop for a few minutes and then boarded a number 92. This was quite different to travelling in the daytime. There were no housewives with bags of shopping, no mothers and young children, nobody in overalls. The passengers were mainly young people, dressed in their best, going into town for the evening, some to the cinema and a couple of girls in pretty dresses and high heels, obviously headed for the Plaza.

The hit records of the day were familiar and she was a regular listener to Radio Luxembourg. She sang along happily with Elvis and Cliff and the Everley Brothers but the two in front of her lived in another world.   They were raving about somebody called Jimmy Saville, who'd revolutionised the music played at the Plaza. She'd never heard of him.

She listened in unashamedly to their chatter. Apparently, the Plaza was all jiving to records with a couple of smoochy numbers at the end. The Ritz was too old fashioned and too straight-laced, they still had a band and played music for ballroom dancing. She was amazed at what she didn't know about her own city. They giggled and whispered to each other and Judy felt ancient watching them. She'd never been that carefree.

George was to meet her outside the Grand Hotel and to her relief, he was already there when she arrived, smiling and looking a little less stuffy in a pair of slacks and an open necked shirt.

"Hello, Judy. You do look nice. Look, I told my folks I'd met you and they'd love to see you. My dad let me have the car tonight so how would you feel about dropping in on them for half an hour? Then maybe we could go for a walk along the canal and stop for a drink somewhere."

"That would be lovely, it's so long since I've seen them and I know Mum and Dad were very fond of them."

They drove along the familiar roads into Didsbury, rows of semi-detached houses with neat front gardens and past familiar shops and landmarks. Judy's eyes filled with tears as they drove past the end of the road she had lived in so happily with her parents. George caught her eye,

"I'm sorry, I didn't think. Will you find this too upsetting?"

"No, I don't think so. Do you think we could drive past the house? I'd really like to have a look at it."

George stopped at the next corner, reversed and went back. He pulled up gently on the other side of the road and Judy gazed at number fifteen, her childhood home. It looked just the same, different curtains perhaps but the new owners had kept the smart black and white paint and the yellow roses in the front garden. There was an upturned tricycle abandoned in the middle of the path and a large red ball resting against the closed, wrought iron gates.

"I'm glad there's a family living here. Let's get off now and meet your Mum and Dad."

Harold and May Turner were in the front garden as they pulled up outside the house. Impulsively, May put her arms around Judy and, with tears in her eyes, said,

"I can't tell you how pleased I am to see you. We've wondered and wondered how you were. Come on in and let's have a cup of tea."

Harold put his hand on her shoulder and added gruffly,

"Yes, that's right, lass. Come on in and tell us what's been happening to you."

Judy sat balancing a cup of tea. It was years since she'd been inside this house and apart from new wallpaper and a new three piece suite, it looked pretty much the same. The same pictures still hung on the wall, the same photos of grandparents and George as a toddler stood in polished frames along the mantelpiece and the china cabinet displayed its gleaming contents of polished silver and porcelain knick knacks through shining glass doors. She gathered her wandering thoughts and turned to Auntie May.

"How did you come to be living in that run down area, Judy? It looks terrible when you drive past."

Judy remembered her Mum had remarked that May could be a bit of a snob, not that she'd ever said it to Judy, of course, but children sometimes pick these things up without knowing.

"It's not that bad, you know. The neighbours are really nice and they've been very helpful, especially with Nina."

"Nina, who's Nina?" asked Joyce a little sharply, exchanging a quick glance with Harold.

Judy's heart sank. She was going to have to launch into an explanation. Goodness knows, she wasn't ashamed of Nina but she had met disapproval in the past.

.... *such a young girl with a baby* .... *whatever were her parents thinking of* .... *no better than she should be* .... *notice she's not wearing a wedding ring.*

In fact, she'd taken it off and slung it in a drawer the day after John left. She'd been forced to put it back on within days though it was only a minor defence against such hurtful whispers.

Nina had been registered at birth as Nina Minshull, although she'd put John down as the father and their status as married so as not to embarrass Nina in later life. Unmarried mothers and illegitimate children didn't have an easy time.

She knew she'd have to deal with this every time she met someone new or someone from the past and hated the idea that they may think she was not quite respectable. She launched into the story, keeping it as brief as possible and watched Auntie Joyce's eyes narrow as she stumbled to the end.

169

Uncle Harold cleared his throat.

"You've obviously had a hard enough time of it, love. I would have thought your Dad would have left you enough to live on though and Mary's house must have been worth a few bob."

Perhaps they meant well but Judy could hear the underlying criticism, both of her situation and what was worse, of her darling father. Just because they were old friends didn't give them that sort of right. They hadn't seen her for years. She held her temper in check as best she could, dying to get away, out of the house and back home to Nina.

George stood up and took the teacup out of her trembling hands, looking pointedly at his parents.

"Come on, Judy. Let's go for that walk. It's a lovely evening and who knows how many more we'll get this summer. Let's make the most of it."

They all walked to the front gate together. Auntie May gave her a peck on the cheek and Uncle Harold patted her shoulder again, not unkindly.

"Now don't be a stranger. You must come over for tea one Sunday and bring Nina with you, mustn't she, Harold?"

"That's right, we'll see you soon."

They watched as George and Judy drove away.

"Well, that's that. Come down in the world a bit, hasn't she? There may well be some cash around but she still has a millstone round her neck," said May.

"It's a great pity. I always liked her and fancied that some day she and George might make a go of it. They always got on so well. But now, she's thrown her education away and I wouldn't like a lad of mine to start married life with another man's child underfoot. God knows, married life can be difficult enough without looking for trouble. Even a lump sum and Mary's semi in Didsbury won't outweigh that. I'll have a quiet word with him."

That was a long speech for Harold but his son was the apple of his eye. He did feel truly sorry for Judy but not sorry enough to encourage George to keep in touch. After all, he only had his best interests at heart. He looked at May's firmly set mouth.

That invite to Sunday tea would be a long time coming. He'd thought the world of Judy's dad, he'd been his best friend, but blood's thicker than water and he'd see his lad right before anybody else. He shook his head, pushing away the uncomfortable feeling that Judy's dad would have been more generous had the roles been reversed. Still

170

you had to face facts, a divorced woman with a child was hardly the ideal wife for a local government official and George was going to go far, he was sure.

The evening was spoiled. Although George talked to her about his work and they caught up with the news of recent years, the conversation was stilted. There seemed nothing else to say. George felt unable to talk about official business and Judy felt unable to talk to him about Nina, the only other topic of interest to her. Why would a twenty four year old single man be interested in the antics of a two year old?

"Fancy a drink?" he asked as they passed a pub on the way back to the car.

"I don't think so. It's so muggy this evening and that breeze has dropped completely. I've got a bit of a headache so I hope you don't mind if I get home?"

"As you wish," responded George a little stiffly.

The evening hadn't been a success, not what he'd hoped for at all but how could he have known about the marriage and the baby and even worse, the divorce? He'd walked straight into it, completely unprepared and had watched his parents' reaction.

Judy was very quiet all the way home and he insisted on running her to her door. Neither of them knew what to say, how to get themselves off the hook. They both just wanted to get away, for it to be over, almost too embarrassed to speak.

"I'd better go in. I want to check on Nina, it's the first time I've left her."

"Of course," said George quickly, leaning awkwardly over to open the passenger door.

"I'll no doubt see you next time you're at the Town Hall. Mum will be in touch about coming to tea soon."

"Fine, see you."

Judy slammed the car door and ran up the path, turning to wave as she opened the front door. Too late, he'd already pulled away.

"Good riddance," she muttered under her breath. 'Who needs you and your patronising parents? And you know what you can do with your mum's Sunday tea."

***

Margaret was in work almost an hour early the following morning. The main doors were open and she'd managed to slide by the commissionaire's window with just a brief wave.

By the time Mr Robinson arrived, she'd set her desk in order, had a look at the previous day's post and made a start on the new batch.

"Margaret, I'm glad to see you back. How are you feeling?"

"Much better, thank you. It was just some kind of a bug, I think."

She could feel her colour rising. She felt such a fraud. She couldn't look her boss in the eye but continued to shuffle papers around, hoping he'd just go away and leave her to it.

"Come in when you're ready then," he said going into his office and closing the door behind him.

Half an hour later, she squared her shoulders, picked up her folder and shorthand pad and knocked on the inner door. Mr Robinson was going through a heavy file on his desk.

"I need to do a report about this Atkinson job so we'll be tied up for most of the morning. But before we start, has Charlie McDonald been in touch yet?"

"Yes, he's been down to see Mr Whitehead and made some suggestions, I believe, and we're meeting to talk it over on Friday evening. Mr Whitehead seemed quite impressed and has one or two proposals to put to us."

"That's good. I know Cyril Black had some ideas too but perhaps it was a mistake to involve him. He's good at initial strategy but long term efforts are not necessarily his strong point."

Margaret continued looking down at her shorthand pad, gripping her pen.

"Anyway, I didn't know until early this week that his wife is expecting another baby within a couple of weeks and he'll probably be too busy to be much help."

Margaret, cheeks burning, looked up at last into Norman Robinson's kindly brown eyes.

"I'm sorry to have steered you in the wrong direction, really sorry."

Margaret felt her knees weaken with relief. She'd known there was something fishy about the man. He was too smooth, too familiar and she realised that Mr Robinson was trying to give her a gentle warning without actually saying anything.

"No, not at all. Mr McDonald seems to have been a great help and we're making progress. By the weekend we hope to have a proper plan of action. I'm sure I'm very grateful for all your help."

A great deal had been left unsaid although the meaning of the exchange was quite clear and she thanked heaven for Mr Robinson's diplomacy. She still felt like a fool and no doubt would do for quite some time but there was no harm done except to her fragile feelings and they would mend in time, no doubt.

Margaret staggered through the rest of the day, working steadily and trying to put the fiasco with Cyril Black out of her mind. She was grateful though when the hands on the clock finally reached five. She would be home in less than an hour, just the post to finish and she'd be on her way.

William was just coming out of his gate as she turned the corner into Tiverton Place.

"Ah, Margaret, just the person I wanted to see. Will you be at the meeting tomorrow night? I want to go over the latest developments and report on our meeting with the solicitor. I've got all the paperwork together and Judy and I are seeing him in the morning."

"Yes, of course. At Judy's at eight, as usual?"

"That's it. By the way, are you feeling better? I understand you weren't too well yesterday."

He looked at her keenly. Her eyes were clear and her gaze firm. He'd seen too many people 'under the influence' during the war not to recognise the condition when he saw it and suspected that Margaret's illness had been nothing more serious than a bad hangover.

Still, it was none of his business. Heaven knows she's old enough to know what she's doing and had had little enough in the way of fun in the last few years. He'd been surprised though and not too keen on the look of the chap that had brought her home. He'd looked a bit smarmy and the car was a bit too flash for his taste, not to mention that tie.

"William, I'm fine now. Nothing serious but I've had a busy day catching up and I'm ready to put my feet up."

William smiled and went on his way.

Margaret went wearily up her garden path. Judy had hardly spoken when she came in last night. It appeared all was not well on that front but she'd see if she wanted to talk about it after the meeting tomorrow.

173

She was feeling a little too bruised this evening to listen to someone else's problems. She'd just barely been saved from making a complete ass of herself and silently thanked Mr Robinson for his timely intervention.

Cyril Black would find out that the 'cold shoulder' from Margaret Hartley was not a pleasant proposition should he have the nerve to 'phone her about their trip to the coast. She hadn't really been taken in by him but finally admitted to herself that she'd been flattered and enjoyed being made a fuss of by a good looking chap, even if he had turned out to be a louse. Pity the poor woman who was married to him.

Chapter 13

Mr Whitehead stood, hands behind his back, facing the rest of the neighbours.

"Here's the strength of it. Judy's solicitor talked it over with us and made some suggestions.

The file's been passed on to Mr Jenkins, another solicitor in the practice, who specialises in property matters. They'll contact us again in about a week, once he's had a chance to work through all the papers. We were introduced to him while we were there and from what we were able to tell him, he seems optimistic that we have a reasonable case. The main factor is that he'll be able to confirm that plans for redevelopment of the whole site for housing have been shelved. That would strengthen our case enormously."

"That do seem pretty good then, Mr Whitehead. Small question – what's it gonna cost?" chirped in Mr Goldman.

"I don't want anyone to worry about the cost, at this stage. After all, it's my appeal and it's my property and ultimately, my income that will be affected so I'm prepared to foot the bill."

"But Uncle William," said Mikey half raising his hand. "What can we do? You and Judy are doing everything and you did say that I could help."

"Mikey, you're a good lad and no mistake and we're going to be finding you a job very soon now. Don't forget, Mrs Goldman has been helping by looking after Nina and Margaret has been helping make contacts through her boss. Your turn will come very soon, believe me. I have something to say to all of you."

He carefully outlined Charlie McDonald's proposal to do a series of features on the occupants of the houses, one a night for five nights.

"He thinks it will work better to build up a picture of what we're trying to do. Make the story like David and Goliath, ordinary people against the might of the Town Hall, you know the sort of thing. He also thinks it will help to get other people on our side, maybe people who have some influence."

He looked at them in turn. He'd caught them completely by surprise but Mikey caught on fast.

"Will we have our pictures in the paper then?"

"That's certainly the plan but I want you to think very carefully before you answer. Things are bad enough around here at present. If we go ahead with this, the publicity may mean that we lose our privacy as well and have all sorts of people poking their noses in our affairs.

I think the best thing is for you all to think about it over the weekend and let me know on Monday and then I can contact Mr McDonald. Please don't go ahead if it worries you at all, I don't want anyone to be pressured into doing something they don't want to do."

He looked at the Goldmans. Mrs Goldman was screwing a hanky round and round between her fingers and Mr Goldman, seated on the arm of her chair, had his arm around her shoulders, whispering into her ear. He looked up.

"We let you know Monday, OK?"

"That applies to the rest of you too. Margaret, Mikey, Judy."

"I don't mind at all, Uncle William. I think I might like being in the paper. The lads at work will love it."

"That's as may be, lad. We have to let everyone else make up their own mind. All right? Now, on to item two on the agenda."

"You mean there's more?" stuttered Mr Goldman.

"We want to get a petition organised. We need to get as many signatures as possible in support of our appeal and this is going to take some organising.

Margaret, if I can borrow a typewriter, will you be prepared to type up a stencil asking for support and putting in lines for signatures and names and addresses? I have a friend with a duplicating machine in his office who's prepared to let us run off as many copies as we need."

"Of course I'll type it up. Just show me the typewriter and the stencil and consider it done. We need to work on the wording though. Perhaps Judy and I can do that together and make a draft. We could look at that on Monday as well and as soon as we're all agreed, we can get on with the duplication."

"Right, things are hotting up a bit but we only have about six weeks before D-Day. It looks as though we need to meet again on Monday. Is that all right with you, Judy?"

"That'll be fine."

'Finally,' said Mr Whitehead.

"Cor Blimey and strike a light," interrupted Mr Goldman. "You mean there's even more?"

176

His accent became more pronounced the more excited he became and William could see that even Mrs Goldman was smiling and hiding her mirth behind her hankie.

"I want to organise some kind of demonstration outside the Town Hall during the week the articles appear in the paper. We'll need as much manpower as we can muster for that. It will be a case of the more the merrier and Mikey that's where you come in."

Mikey, looking very pleased, nodded vigorously.

"The plan is to make as much fuss as possible and at the same time, get as many signatures as we possibly can on our petition. Anybody got anything to add?

He looked around.

"We've all got plenty to think about for the time being. I'll go and put the kettle on, I think we deserve it,' said Judy.

"Come on Mikey, you're always asking for something to do, you can come and give me a lift. Even the little jobs count, you know."

Mikey grinned and followed her into the kitchen.

They sat around for another half an hour and then left for their own homes, each calling out in turn,

"See you Monday, goodnight."

Only Margaret lingered.

"Is everything all right, Judy?" she asked, a little concerned.

"It isn't actually. What a fiasco that was last night. George took me to see his parents. I used to be so fond of them but you could see from their faces how much they disapproved of me and what's more of Nina. I doubt I'll be hearing any more from them. Auntie May was really hatchet faced and Uncle Harold, who used to be so funny, was really cool with me. As if that wasn't enough, George drove me past the house I lived in as a child and that upset me too. We were so happy there.

All that on top of the letter from John........,"

She couldn't finish the sentence.

Her eyes brimmed with tears and Margaret could see she was struggling for control. Margaret, usually the least demonstrative of women, reached out in sympathy and put her arms around her sobbing young friend.

"Never mind, sweetheart. Let it out, let it out."

Judy gulped.

177

"It's not as though I care much about either of them, John or George, but I do feel let down and a bit sorry for myself."

"You have to laugh," said Margaret. "Nothing much happens in the street for twenty years and now it's like a melodrama. What can I say? I made a bit of a fool of myself with that chap you saw me with the other night and now I've found out he's married. There's no real harm done but I feel stupid for being taken in. At my age, I ought to know better."

Judy managed a watery grin.

"Men! They're just not worth the trouble, apart from Mikey, of course."

"Don't forget Mr Whitehead in that list and my boss at work is a good chap too, although he's had his moments."

'I tell you what, Judy. We women should stick together. How about going to the pictures tomorrow night? We've nothing to celebrate but the change would do us both good.'

"I'd love to. Do you think Mrs Goldman would sit with Nina? She's doing more than her share these days and I hardly like to ask again."

"We can only ask, in fact, I'll go round now."

Margaret popped along the row and was back in minutes.

"We're on. I think Nina moving here has made the world of difference to Mrs Goodman. She's brought her out of herself. I've heard her speak more in the last few weeks than in the previous ten years. She said she'd be happy to come. We won't be home late and all we have to decide is what we're going to see, there are a couple of good films on in town."

They discussed the pros and cons of the various films. 'Exodus' was ruled out as being a bit too serious and 'The Apartment' was struck off because they didn't need a love story just at the moment, thank you. They finally agreed that some real escapism was what they needed with 'Can Can', singing and dancing with Shirley McLaine, the handsome Louis Jourdan and the irrepressible Maurice Chevalier.

"There's something in it for everyone,' said Margaret, laughing. 'One of the girls at work said it was terrific and what's more it's on the Apollo just across the road."

"I haven't been to the pictures since long before Nina was born. I'm really looking forward to it. Out twice in one week, who would have believed it?"

178

The two woman, so different in their experiences and their outlook, came home the following evening from the cinema, arm in arm.

Margaret went along with Judy for a last cup of tea before bed. Mrs Goldman wouldn't stay for tea but said,

"Not one sound from the little one. I stay with her again if you want to go out. You should enjoy yourself, not always have all the cares of the world on such young shoulders. I come any time. Mr Goldman, he don't mind one bit. I think he glad to see me out of the house."

Judy thanked her and walked with her to the door, watching as she went along to her own house.

"Even with all the problems we've got now, Margaret, I thank my lucky stars that I moved down here. I was so alone and now I feel as though I have some real friends."

Her eyes started to fill again.

"Aunt Mary would say that my eyes are too near my bladder,' she whispered. 'She always had such a wonderful turn of phrase."

"Don't be silly. I think we're all glad you came. You've brought a bit of life to us all, shaken us up a bit. You've done us good. Even if we do have to move, Judy, we must keep in touch. I realise now that I've been a bit lonely myself over the past few years but it's easy to get into a rut, get out of the habit of going out. We must do it again soon."

She kissed Judy shyly on the cheek and went home. She'd sleep tonight, she thought, smiling.

***

Monday's meeting was duly convened, all parties present. William was in his usual place with his back to the fireplace, hands clasped behind his back.

"As we're all here, who wants to start?"

He looked around and Mr Goldman rose to his feet.

"Me and Mrs Goldman, we talk about it. We talk a lot and we decide. We do it. We see the man from the paper. I do all the talking so Luisa doesn't have to speak but we do it."

"That's wonderful, thank you both. I know that wasn't an easy decision for you. Margaret?"

179

"I'm no keener than anyone else to be in the public eye, except Mikey, of course. I've thought it over and I think it may work if we can get public opinion on our side. I'll do it."

"Me too," said Judy. "Nina won't care one way or the other but I'm game to try anything within our power."

"Me too,' spoke up Mikey, grinning from ear to ear. 'I'd like to have my picture in the paper. There will be pictures won't there, Uncle William?"

Mrs Goldman obviously hadn't thought of that and looked a little startled but she nodded resolutely.

"We still do it," she said.

"That only leaves me and I can hardly back out at this stage," said William. "That makes it unanimous. That's what I like to see. I'll ring Charlie McDonald in the morning."

He started to pass around copies of the petition which Margaret and Judy had drawn up.

"This is just a handwritten draft but if you all agree with the wording, we'll get some copies run off and set out getting signatures. I think they've done a good job."

Everybody studied the words of the petition and Mr Goodman was first to speak.

"I don't read English quite so good but it all look fine to me."

Mikey blushed a little. He didn't read that much better.

"I think it's wonderful. It sounds really official, like."

"That's it then, unanimous again. I'll pass around copies to everyone as soon as we've got them organised and I want everyone to get as many signatures as they can. It may mean making a nuisance of ourselves but this might be crucial."

He ran his eyes over the draft again.

We, the undersigned, support the residents of nos. 1-9 Tiverton Place, in their application to have the compulsory purchase order on these dwellings removed. We believe this is a fundamental breach of their civil rights. It is also wasting public funds to demolish properties which are in a good state of repair and which in no way impede further planned development of the area.

***

The next few weeks raced by. Each of the residents handed page after page of signatures over to William for him to count and file.

Mikey came home proudly from work.

180

"Look here, Uncle William, everyone in the firm has signed up. There's quite a few there. And I took the list to the chippie on Friday night and everyone there signed up too. I'm going to stand outside this week and catch everyone who goes in, if they haven't signed."

"That's marvellous, Mikey. Be careful though that nobody signs twice. That could spoil things for us."

William knew that once Mikey got an idea, he could get carried away.

"I'll be careful, Uncle William. I really will."

Judy had already filled several sheets with signatures. She took the petition to the park every day, talking to complete strangers and explaining the petition. Apart from one cantankerous old gentleman who called her 'a young hussy', her overtures were well received and few were unwilling to sign and many wished her luck.

Over the weeks, she'd made contact with two other young mothers and Nina now had someone to play with on fine days. Judy was making friends apart from her neighbours and it was reassuring for her to be able to talk things over with someone nearer her own age while their children played on the grass. Both young women were admiring of Judy's efforts to save her home and each of them offered to take a page home for their families and friends to sign.

"I can tell you, Judy," one of them said. "my auntie and uncle and their three kids have been shunted off to that new housing estate. Although they think the house is wonderful, miles more space than they had before, my uncle never stops cursing about the size of the garden. He's got no one to go for a pint with and it takes the kids so long to get into town they call the whole estate 'the land that God forgot.' Give me another page, they're coming down on Friday and I'll get them to take it back with them and get their neighbours to sign up."

The divorce was proceeding. She'd spoken to Mr Hughes who assured her that it was only a formality. John had agreed to admit adultery and as they had lived apart so long, he could foresee no problems. Custody of Nina would, of course, be granted to Judy and Mr Hughes seemed to think that something in the way of regular payments of maintenance might be achieved.

"You certainly won't be worse off than his current haphazard idea of maintenance and if there's a court order in place, he'll probably toe the line," he said.

"That would be handy. I'm very careful with money but Nina's growing so fast and needs so many things, it's hard to hang on to cash. I try to live within my budget but it can be difficult. If I can, I want to hang on to what capital there is for Nina's future. I know I'm looking years ahead but she may want to go to university. Aunt Mary told me often enough how much that all costs. I just don't want her to have the same restrictions as I did and have every penny spent on her pushed down her throat."

"Let's wait and see. Even a couple of extra pounds a week will make a lot of difference, I know. Things have a way of working out and once Nina starts school, which I know is still quite a way away, I hope you'll be able to start thinking about your own future too."

Judy rolled her eyes.

"We'll face that when we get to it. Let's get the roof over our head sorted out first."

***

Mr Robinson had made no objection to Margaret canvassing the staff at work. She caught visitors to her office on the top floor and most of the rest in the canteen at lunchtime. It wasn't easy for her to approach people on such a personal matter. Despite herself, she knew she had a very 'Miss Hartley' image but was pleasantly surprised to find that people were falling over themselves to sign.

She knew that some of them signed because they thought they could curry favour from the 'top floor' but many people were genuinely delighted to help. As word got round the building, people she knew only slightly were slipping into her office or coming over to her table in the canteen to put their names on the petition.

From Cyril Black she'd heard nothing. She wondered whether Mr Robinson had had a quiet word in his ear but didn't like to ask. She decided to let sleeping dogs lie, for the time being.

Mr Goldman had, in turn, collected his share of signatures. He'd also taken the petition into work. Despite his obvious foreignness, he was well liked for his cheerful manner, his sense of humour and his kindness.

He'd also taken pages over to the rabbi in the synagogue in North Manchester and these were steadily being filled. People took copies away to get them filled in the local shops and at social meetings and completed pages were slowly filtering their way back to him.

William took his pages into the local pub and along to the Territorial Army barracks and came back with more signatures.

He found himself constantly running off extra copies and now had a huge stack on his sideboard ready for collection or despatch. The filled pages were kept in a ring binder with a note of the running total kept on the front cover as each batch was filed. This was mounting faster than he could have believed possible.

He was feeling much better now that things were moving and there was actually something to do. It was almost like wartime again; everybody pulling together and helping each other out. Despite the disruption in the narrow streets around them, the mood was one of optimism amongst the neighbours. He resolutely pushed all thoughts of what they would do if they lost out of his mind.

They were taking the Corporation to court to appeal the compulsory purchase order, their solicitor had been instructed and all the legalities had been completed. The papers were to be served on Friday, 23rd September.

The first newspaper article would appear on Saturday, the 24th, with a follow up on each day of the following week.

The picketing outside the Town Hall was to start on Monday and continue every day until the weekend, rain or shine.

***

That morning, Judy was surprised to find yet another unexpected letter falling onto her doormat. She looked at the expensive envelope, the dark blue ink and the copperplate handwriting, irreverently thinking it looked like an invitation to Buckingham Palace. She took the envelope into the kitchen and carefully slit it open with a sharp knife. Somehow, she couldn't just rip this one open. She opened the pages and a five pound note fluttered out. She started to read the letter, scanning briefly to the end to see who'd sent it.

Dear Judy,
I know that you'll be surprised to hear from me after all this time. John has told us about the divorce and about his move.

183

I would dearly like to see you and Nina too. I haven't been well just recently and find it hard to get around so I can't come to see you.

I hope you can find it in your heart to grant my request and the enclosed money is so that you and Nina can come in a taxi. Next Wednesday at two o'clock would suit me very well, if it's convenient for you. Please let me know if you are unable to come but in the meantime, I'll keep my fingers crossed.

Please do come, I do so want to see you both.
Kindest regards
Christine Freeman

"Well I never,' said Judy under her breath. 'What a surprise, she's never shown any interest before."

Her first instinct was to put the letter, fiver and all, straight into the bin. She read it through thoughtfully again and decided to sleep on it. She slipped the letter back in its envelope and put it in the sideboard drawer. She wouldn't be hasty, she'd think about it.

After tossing and turning for a couple of hours she finally decided. She would go. After all, surely Nina should come first and Mr and Mrs Freeman were her only blood relatives, apart from John, who looked as though he was about to disappear forever.

Wednesday came around and Judy walked to the 'phone box at the end of the street and ordered a taxi to pick them up at one thirty. They might as well travel in style if funds were available and a bus journey would take over an hour and involve two changes.

The taxi drew up at the gate of a fine detached house in Bowdon and Judy noticed the net curtains at the bedroom window twitching. She paid the driver and walked up the drive and through the landscaped garden, holding Nina by the hand. She wasn't altogether sure she was doing the right thing but in for a penny, in for a pound, she thought as she rang the doorbell.

They were soon being ushered through a white painted hall and up the stairs to the bedroom at the front of the house.

Mrs Freeman, propped against a pile of pillows in the large double bed and dressed in a simple cotton nightie, lifted her hand in greeting. Judy was shocked, this was just a shadow of the smart, self-possessed woman she remembered from the wedding. She gestured to a chair by the side of the bed.

"Sit down, Judy. I can't tell you how pleased I am to see you both. This must be Nina. Hello Nina, aren't you a big girl now? Look there, in that box, you might find something you'd like to play with."

Nina looked a little unsure and Judy gently pushed the wooden toy box towards her.

"Have a look, darling."

Nina needed no further encouragement. She lifted the lid and tugged out all sorts of toys, all obviously brand new and bought for the occasion. Amongst the books and dollies, she found a car, which she proceeded to run all round the room, making appropriate noises as she went.

Mrs Freeman leaned back against her pillow, obviously struggling for breath.

"She's beautiful. You must be very proud of her."

"Yes, I am. Whatever mess John and I got ourselves into, she's been worth all the heartache."

"I can see that, although it can't have been easy for you these last couple of years and I know we've been no help at all."

"I hadn't expected any. I seem to have been on my own forever anyway and Nina and I manage although we may have to move again soon."

Judy chatted about Nina and the house they lived in now but she could see that Mrs Freeman was tiring fast and drew her story quickly to a close. It still seemed strange that she had wanted to see them so badly when she was obviously so ill.

"I can see you're tired now and it's time we were getting along anyway. Come on Nina, put all that stuff back in the box, there's a good girl," she said.

"Will you come again, Judy?" whispered Mrs Freeman.

Although Judy was still puzzled, she did feel sorry for her and nodded.

"Will the same time next week be OK?"

Mrs Freeman nodded weakly, tears in her eyes.

"Lovely, the housekeeper will get you a taxi home."

Judy had heard the front door close just a few minutes earlier and as she made her way down the stairs, holding Nina by the hand, she saw Mr Freeman waiting for them in the spacious entrance hall. Nina was tired now and grizzling a bit so Judy picked her up.

Mr Freeman, dressed in a smart three piece suit, had obviously come home early from work. He smiled at them both.

"So this is Nina. She's a big girl now isn't she but I can see she's tired."

Nina smiled back and put her thumb firmly into her mouth, resting her head on Judy's shoulder.

"I can't tell you what this means to Christine. She's been fretting about Nina for months now but didn't know what kind of reception she'd get if she contacted you. You can tell she isn't well and John is worse than useless. He hasn't been here for weeks and only telephones when the fancy takes him, which isn't all that often, I can tell you.

Now we hear that he's moving down south and hopes to get married again. It's breaking his mother's heart and if it weren't for upsetting her even more – I could kick his backside, I really could."

Judy squirmed a little, feeling embarrassed.

"Mrs Freeman asked me to come and see her again. Is that all right?"

"It's more than all right and it's more than we deserve after the way this family has treated you."

He looked at her sadly.

"She isn't going to get better and she knows that Nina's the only grandchild she'll ever see. She's had so much time to think and the guilt about John and our neglect of you both has been heavy on her mind. She'll maybe rest a bit easier now. If you can wait for a minute or two, I'll run you home. I'll just pop up and tell Christine where I'm going."

He took the stairs two at a time and was back in a few minutes.

"She's fast asleep, that's a good sign. Come on then, let's get you home."

In the car on the long ride home, Judy brought him up to date with her news.

"My goodness, you are a plucky little thing. When I first saw you, you looked as though you wouldn't say boo to a goose and now here you are, running campaigns and fighting the authorities. Good for you."

Judy was gladdened by the unexpected praise.

"By the way, here's the change from Mrs Freeman's fiver. We won't need the rest now you're taking us home."

"Good heavens, girl. Put it back in your purse, buy yourselves a treat with it."

They'd left the large houses and gardens behind them and were in fairly heavy traffic going into the city. She told him where to turn.

"This is it,' said Judy as they pulled into Tiverton Place, we're at number five."

"Well, I must say these few houses all look in excellent repair although the rest of the area is a shambles. Are you sure you'll be all right?"

Nina had fallen asleep on Judy's knee.

"Don't worry about next week. I'll send a taxi for you at the same time. I have an account with a taxi firm for business appointments and they can put it on my bill."

He could see that the exchange of money had stuck in Judy's craw.

"Look at it like this, Nina *is* our grandchild and we want to make it easier for her to come and see us. We've so much time to make up and we want to do something in return, a taxi ride now and again is little enough."

Judy nodded her assent.

"By the way, Judy, I know a couple of people at the Town Hall. I'll drop a word in a few ears. It can't do any harm and you never know."

Judy smiled and watched him as he drove away. She was truly sorry Mrs Freeman was so ill. She'd make the effort and visit again. She felt her own lack of family very keenly and felt it might help Nina in the future to know that she had loving grandparents at least.

Chapter 14

Thursday dawned bright and clear. Mid-September had brought clear skies although the heat of the sun was softer and the evenings cooler.

Margaret hoped the good spell would last a while yet, at least until the demonstrations were over. Everyone was enthusiastic enough but she didn't envy them collecting signatures outside the Town Hall in pouring rain and Charlie McDonald was coming round to take photographs on Saturday when everyone would be at home.

She took off her jacket and hung it on a hanger on the coat rack in her office. The post was already opened and sorted by the time Norman Robinson arrived and he smiled warmly.

"Leave that for a minute, Margaret. I'd like a quick word."

She followed him into his office and he waved her into a chair.

"Before we start the post, I've got something to tell you. I was at the golf club last night and Cyril Black was there and he's come up with one or two ideas."

Margaret looked at him a little sceptically. She was well acquainted with Cyril Black's ideas but waited for him to go on. Mr Robinson smiled gently.

"Now then, it's not quite as bad as that. For some reason, he seemed a little reluctant to 'phone you himself but he gave me this list of names and suggested you contact these people. That one there,' he said, pointing to the first one, 'is the head of the History Department at the university. Those two are involved in the management at the University Museum and the last one is with the National Trust.

He suggested you contact all of them and ask for their support. The tack he suggests you take is that the Town Hall are destroying local heritage. The houses are a perfect example of the back-to-back terrace built to house workers during the industrial expansion of the city.

If you contact them in advance, they may be prepared to give Charlie McDonald quotes to support his articles. He said 'any publicity was good publicity' and this would be exceptionally good publicity."

"It's a brilliant idea. I can do the letters in my lunch hour and get them in the post tonight."

"Why don't you knock up a draft and we'll look at it together straight after lunch. Two heads are sometimes better than one and the wording could be crucial."

"Thank you, I'd appreciate that. If you don't mind, I'll stay after work and type them up. I can drop them in the main post office on my way home and they should arrive in the morning. I think it's important we move fairly fast. I haven't time to consult everyone but I could 'phone Mr Whitehead and run the idea past him before I go ahead."

He smiled and nodded.

"Do that next. You can use your office 'phone while I have a look at the post and then bring your pad in. By the way, Cyril's other idea was that you ask Charlie to print a record each day, recording how many signatures are on the petition and showing how support is increasing."

"Another great idea but then again, Mr Black *is* pretty good in the ideas department, isn't he? I can't say he's completely redeemed himself and I really don't want to speak to him if I can help it. What do you think I should do?"

She looked at him enquiringly, still smarting a little from her run in with Cyril Black.

"Why not drop him a note thanking him for his help. I don't think he'll be in touch again. I wouldn't normally pass on gossip but the talk at the golf club is that his wife discovered something unsavoury and has threatened divorce if he doesn't toe the line. Funnily enough, he's passionately fond of his children and is willing to do almost anything not to rock the boat.

He's looking pretty sheepish at present, I can tell you. He's a plausible devil and has been getting away with murder for years but she's wise to him now and he's got the wind up."

"There's some justice in that, I suppose. I'll do as you suggest."

Back in her office, Margaret dialled William's number and waited impatiently while it rang out. Strictly speaking, private 'phone calls were not allowed from office 'phones but she had certain perks as a result of her position and this time, she had Mr Robinson's express permission.

She tapped the desk with her fingernails while the 'phone rang on and on. Surely, he couldn't be out, she needed to speak to him. She was just about to hang up when a breathless voice muttered,

"Ardwick 4569"

189

"William, is that you? I was just about to hang up. Margaret here."

"I was at the end of the garden fixing the back gate, is something wrong?"

In all the years they'd been neighbours, Margaret had never 'phoned him before. In fact, it was surprising if the 'phone rang two or three times a week.

"No, there's nothing wrong. I've just had one or two ideas put to me and wanted to tell you about them before I actually do anything. Strictly speaking, we ought to tell everybody first but if you agree, I really need to do something today."

She quickly outlined Cyril Black's proposals, diplomatically leaving out the source, and asked William what he thought.

He needed no time at all to consider.

"Go ahead, it's inspired. Can you manage to get the letters out today?"

"Yes, Mr Robinson's offered to go over the first draft with me and I'll stay after work tonight and get them off. If you like, I'll drop off a copy on my way home."

"On second thoughts, it might be better if the letters came from me as I have the major interest in the decision. Why don't you give me a ring here when you've finished. I'll come and meet you outside work and sign them and we can put them straight in the post tonight. You can put my telephone number on them so I can be contacted direct if they need more information."

"Better and better, will you trust me with the draft then?'

"Margaret, I'd trust you with anything.' William paused. 'And Margaret, as you'll be at work so late, why don't I take you for a meal as a thank you? You won't want to be cooking after an extra hour at work."

"What a lovely idea.' Margaret agreed without thinking. 'Thank you, William, I'll ring and let you know when I'll be finished."

She hung up, picked up her shorthand pad and went back into Mr Robinson's office. She had plenty of other work to do today and the sooner she got cracking the better.

At half past six, Margaret 'phoned again. The 'phone was snatched up on the second ring.

"Hello, William, it's Margaret. I'll be ready to leave in about fifteen minutes."

"That's fine, I'll be outside waiting for you."

"See you then, 'Bye."

William went out to the freshly polished car. Mrs Goldman watched him through her window and thought how smart he looked in his navy suit.

"Come look at Mr Whitehead, Jakob. He looks after himself well, that's for sure. Look how white his shirt and that tie with the blue stripes looks perfect. You can see the shine on his shoes from here."

Mr Goldman peered over her shoulder.

"He always do look smart but that is extra special smart. Must be something important. If it's something with the houses, we find out soon enough. Otherwise, not our business, eh?"

"You're right, as usual. Not our business."

Margaret looked at herself in the mirror. She couldn't believe she was feeling nervous. After all, she'd known William for years. Nevertheless, she took extra care with her appearance. She took down her hair and combed it through, twisting it neatly again into a French pleat. It was no longer the rich auburn of the past but still caught the light when she turned her head. She powdered her nose and touched up her lipstick and grinned at herself.

"You'll do, you hussy,' she whispered at her reflection. 'No men for years and then two in quick succession. At least I know I'll be safe with William, he knows how to treat a lady."

Back in the office, she quickly brushed the shoulders of her jacket and rubbed a duster over her shoes, interested to note that her heart seemed to be beating a little faster than normal. What was the fuss, after all it was only William she was meeting?

She picked up her handbag and the file of letters and closed the office door behind her. The lift took ages to arrive but she didn't want to get hot and bothered again. Waving goodnight to the commissionaire who was waiting to lock the building, she stepped out into the street.

There were few people around at this time of night. The streets looked strangely empty with the disappearance of the daytime crowd and it was still too early for people looking for an evening's entertainment.

William got out of the car as she came down the steps, opened the door for her and carefully closed it behind her, before walking around to get back in.

"Everything all finished?"

"Yes, the letters are here and I've made copies for your files. I hope you approve. They're all the same, just addressed to different people."

William sat and read through the first letter carefully.

"It seems perfect," he said, unscrewing the top of his fountain pen.

Balancing the file against the steering wheel, he quickly signed each letter and passed it to Margaret, who carefully blotted the signature and skilfully folded each letter and slipped it into its envelope. The stamps were already in place.

"Well prepared as usual I see, Margaret. I must admit, we seem to make a good team."

"Yes, we do," Margaret whispered and found herself blushing unexpectedly.

"We'll whip these straight up to Newton Street post office, shall we? There's a late collection from here. Is there anywhere special you'd like to eat?"

Margaret was inexplicably flustered.

"I don't know. What do you think?"

"I know a little place where we sometimes go after TA meetings. It should be quiet so early on. Shall we give it a try?"

Margaret nodded and a short time later found herself seated at a small table in a tiny restaurant. The checked cloth and small bunch of flowers looked bright and cheerful.

"Will this suit?" asked William, passing her the menu.

"Yes, it's lovely. I didn't even know this place was here."

The waiter came over and made an enormous fuss of William, straightening his knife and fork and leaning over him. He whipped up Margaret's serviette and draped it smoothly across her knee.

"How nice to see you again, Mr Whitehead. Will you have your usual?"

William nodded.

"And for the lady?"

William leaned towards Margaret.

"They do a wonderful chicken dish with a rich, spicy sauce. It's probably quite unlike anything you've ever eaten before but I acquired the taste when I was stationed in Italy and it brings back memories. They serve it with fresh vegetables and crunchy potatoes and it's always excellent. Or is there something else you'd like?"

Margaret was surprised. William so rarely referred to the past. She nodded.

"Sounds delicious, I'd like to try it."

"What about a bottle of wine. A glass or two won't do you any harm, particularly with a meal. It's drinking on an empty stomach that often leads to problems."

He smiled warmly, the memory of her tipsy stumble up the garden path still fresh in his mind.

Margaret nodded and smiled a little sheepishly, she could guess what he was thinking.

William beckoned the waiter.

"Bring us a bottle of the usual, please."

Margaret was seeing a side of him she'd forgotten. She remembered meeting him in town at the time of her engagement and he'd been confident and urbane. In recent years, she'd seen only a brisk demeanour and a sometimes gruff kindness although he was always the soul of politeness to everyone he dealt with. He was obviously well known and well liked here, treating the staff with easy familiarity and laughing at small jokes made by the waiter who'd just reappeared with a bottle wrapped in a napkin.

"Just pour it, Salvador. I'm sure it'll be fine."

He waited until both glasses were filled and lifted his glass.

"I think a toast is in order. To success in our endeavours."

"Success in our endeavours," echoed Margaret, sipping cautiously at her wine.

William studied her face, relaxed now. Her eyes were sparkling and her hair shone softly in the dim light. She was still lovely and it seemed such a waste that she'd never married and had children. She'd completely closed down after David died but this current crisis had shocked her back to life. Thoughts that had been pushed to the back of his mind for years were fighting to resurface.

They talked over the appeal and the effect it was having on the rest of the neighbours, their next course of action and the coming interviews with Charlie McDonald while the food steadily disappeared. Margaret hadn't realised how hungry she was and tucked in with a will, completely clearing her plate. She put down her knife and fork with a sigh and wiped her lips on the checked napkin.

"That was absolutely delicious. Thank you, I can't remember when I enjoyed a meal so much. It can be a bit of a fag to cook when you've been sitting at a desk all day and sometimes I can't be bothered with much more than a snack."

"I have the same problem myself. I sometimes ask Mikey round for tea and that forces me into making a proper job of it and the lad is no better than either of us, although he does get a decent meal at work. I suppose it's one of the disadvantages of living alone."

They were getting on so well, talking freely and easily and Margaret asked him something she had always wondered and never had the temerity or opportunity to ask.

"Did you never think of marrying, William?"

William sat back in his chair and looked at her.

"Yes, I did, once. I considered it very carefully. I've always been a cautious sort of a chap but there was a girl. I met her just before I was posted overseas. She was in the forces too and we just hit it off. I really thought the world of her but because of the war, I didn't want to tie her down. I knew I had a posting coming and to be honest, one never knew who would come back.

I didn't ask her to wait for me and I know that hurt her deeply but in my own mind, I was being sensible for her sake. She wrote to me a couple of times, chatty letters about the local news and what was happening in camp and then the letters just stopped. I tried to find her when I got my first leave until one of my friends took me on one side and told me she was married with a baby on the way.

I often wonder what would have happened if I'd been a little less sensible and thrown caution to the wind."

He took a sip of his wine and looked at her. She nodded encouragingly, fascinated.

"After that, I was moved around a fair bit and although there were one or two flirtations, I couldn't seem to settle for one person, couldn't make a commitment. Then I did meet someone, someone I liked a great deal, but unfortunately, she was involved with someone else. I never did anything about it but I still think about her. I suppose you could say I've been carrying a torch for years.

When the war was over, I was back on civvy street and up to my neck in houses and involved in the Territorial Army.

During the war, I'd enjoyed training young recruits and the TA was a natural follow on. Although we're training young men up and some of them do go on the forces, I like to think we're guiding

194

some fairly rough diamonds into a regular life and steering them away from potential trouble.

The other officers are a good crowd and, I suppose, the mainstay of my social life."

This was the longest speech on a personal level that Margaret had ever heard from William and she felt honoured by his honesty and his trust. She leaned over and gently touched the back of his hand.

"Thank you for telling me that, William," she said quietly.

"What about you? David's been gone a long time now. Did you never meet anyone else?"

"I never met anyone that measured up to him. I never really looked and just didn't think about it. I got involved in my job and built some kind of a life. I manage to keep busy but now that Judy and Nina are around, I realise that I've been quite lonely over recent years. We get locked into our own way of doing things and lose sight of the things that matter. I've always prided myself on being self-sufficient but just recently, I realise how much I've been missing. Do you know, despite all our current problems, I've laughed more in the last three months than I have for years."

"I think it's true that hardship brings out either the best or the worst in people. Look at the others. Mikey's having a wonderful time and the Goldmans, Mrs Goldman in particular. Nina's done wonders for her, brought her out from behind that closed door at long last."

Margaret was thankful that the conversation had turned to more neutral matters, enough confidences had been exchanged for one evening.

She let William choose dessert. He seemed to know his way around this menu and they sat for a while over coffee. The restaurant was almost full now and she hadn't even noticed. She looked at her watch.

"Good heavens, it's almost half past ten. We've been sitting here for hours. We really should make a move."

After settling the bill, William helped her on with her jacket.

"I'll have you home in no time."

Fifteen minutes later, they were pulling up outside Margaret's door. William opened the car door for her and walked with her to the end of the path. Uncharacteristically, he took her hand.

"I can't tell you how much I've enjoyed this evening. It's done me a world of good to get out for a change and forget the Town Hall and all that goes with it."

Margaret returned the pressure, saying warmly,

"I've enjoyed it too. I'm sure it's done us both a world of good."

William hesitated.

"Perhaps we could do it again sometime. You know, as a break from our problems."

"Yes, there's no reason why we shouldn't."

She turned and walked up the path and he watched as she put her key in the door. He stood for a minute or two, saw the lights go on and heard the bolts being shot.

"Hmm," he said reflectively, "Hmm"

William was far from inexperienced. After the disappointment of discovering that his girl friend had married while he was away, he'd played the field. There were, after all, many girls who were living life to the full, unsettled by the impermanence, by people leaving and arriving. They worked hard and played hard, subsisting on poor rations and cheap gin and many couples joined briefly, only to pass on to other partners when a new posting came through or their leave ended. The old morality of 'good girls' and chaps 'sowing wild oats' had largely disappeared. Young people took comfort where they could find it and William was no different.

He genuinely liked women, liked their company and the way they looked and smelled. He liked the feel of them in his arms and in return, they found him attentive and very attractive. He was never short of a girl to take for a drink, to a dance or even to bed for a couple of hours but was happy to leave them with a

"Catch you next time round," when his leave was over. Sometimes he did and sometimes he didn't.

He never asked for any commitment and never gave any and was happy with the way things were as were many of his generation. They didn't know if there would be a 'next time round' and which of them would never come back.

***

Charlie McDonald rapped sharply on the door of number 1 Tiverton Place. He heard footsteps coming along the hall and William opened the door.

"Good morning, Mr Whitehead. Are we all ready for the big day? By the way, this is our photographer, Tom Hedley. It might look as though he's just waving that thing around,' he said, gesturing at the young man standing beside him and at the camera round his neck, 'but I promise he'll do a good job."

"Everybody knows you're coming this morning. Come in for a minute. Care for a cup of tea before you start?"

Charlie shambled down the hall behind him, already patting his pockets, looking for his fags.

"You're a man after my own heart, William. Young Tom here can go out and weigh up the situation while the kettle's boiling."

Tom wandered outside, expertly familiarising himself with the lie of the row of terraces, the light and the other dingy streets. Fortunately, the sun was beginning to break through the early morning clouds, promising ideal conditions for his shots.

"It looks fine. I'll be taking several dozen photos and we'll pick out the best. I want to get cracking out here while the sunshine's on the front but can I have a quick look at the back?"

Tom was surprised to find a real garden out there, vegetables in neat rows, a bed of dahlias and a small lawn with a wooden bench.

"This is a surprise. Are all the gardens like this?"

"This is the biggest on the row but all the gardens are well tended, why?"

"I'm thinking we could add these to the publicity shots. What do you think, Charlie?"

Charlie had ambled out behind them and stood stroking his chin.

'I see what you mean. We do a feature each night, starting with number 9, its interior and a shot of the garden to illustrate their suitability for inner city living and follow it with a brief biopic and a photo of the people living in each house. We'll work down the row, finishing on Friday with you and your house.

We need the public to identify with you," he said, turning to William. "We need to raise sympathy and, if possible, outrage against the powers that be, paint them as destroyers not innovators. Stress the virtues of each person in each house, how hardworking, etc., etc. Get the public on our side."

"I can't say that I'm looking forward to any of this but I'm prepared to use any weapon at my disposal. I can hardly get cold feet now when everyone else has agreed to this kind of exposure. Let's get on with it, shall we?"

William and Charlie sat over their tea while Charlie explained the sequence of the articles. He welcomed William's suggestion of printing a daily total of signatures on the petition.

"We'll put it in a box each day. It's up to your lot to make sure the total rises dramatically."

"We'll do our best. We're all still working hard to add signatures and we start our demonstration outside the Town Hall a week on Monday, that should add a good few more."

"We'd better get on. We've a busy morning ahead of us. Who's next door?"

"That's Mikey Bradshaw. He's a good lad but a little slow although he keeps his place neat as a pin and works hard for his living. Just don't ask him anything too complicated."

William turned to Tom.

"He's really looking forward to getting his picture in the papers."

"Don't worry, I'll make every one look as good as possible. We want sympathy, we don't want to frighten people off."

They worked their way along the row, William introducing the two newspaper men. Charlie definitely knew his trade, even the Goldmans relaxed and opened up to his pleasant manner and gentle questioning. Tom put everyone at their ease, making jokes and jollying them along while he moved around, clicking and reloading film after film. He was a particular hit with Nina, tickling her and making her laugh. Judy caught him looking at her long and hard, approval obvious in his laughing green eyes, until she flushed gently and looked away.

Finally, they were all gathered in the street outside number 1 when Charlie said,
"I want to thank you all for your help this morning. I truly wish you luck in your campaign and hope that what we put in the paper will make a real difference. So now it's time I was back at the office. Thank you all again. Coming, Tom?"

"Yeah, I've done for now but I want to pop back this afternoon to take some shots of the gardens. Judy tells me the sun moves round to the back just after lunch and we want to show them at their best."

Charlie wasn't surprised to hear that Tom had homed in on Judy. He had a bit of a reputation with the girls in the office and Charlie McDonald didn't miss much. They got into Charlie's car and pulled away.

"I think it'll work. I've got a gut feeling that this will be something that sells newspapers."

"I hope so, for their sakes. They deserve it."

The rest of the journey back to the paper was spent in comparative silence, both of them deep in thought. Charlie decided to let sleeping dogs lie, Judy was probably well able to look after herself and Tom was a good lad at heart.

At three o'clock, Tom was tapping at Judy's front door. At twenty five, he was tall and wiry with a lock of dark brown hair constantly falling over his broad forehead. Dressed in slacks and a loose jacket, he nevertheless appeared carelessly elegant.

"I heard you next door with Mikey," she said. "I guessed we'd be next."

She laughed up at him.

"Come on through," she said and led the way out into the tiny back garden where Nina sat, her chubby brown arms and legs exposed to the September sun.

"We're taking advantage of the weather. Nina loves to be in the open air and if I can wear her out, it's easier to get her to sleep at night."

"I'll only be a minute or two. Can you sit there with Nina while I take a couple of shots."

Judy sat on one of the garden chairs and plonked Nina onto her knee.

"Watch the birdie, Nina," he chuckled as he waved the camera at them.

"Where birdie, Mummy? Where birdie?" Nina giggled and looked around.

"That's it, Judy. All done."

"Have you time for a drink? It won't take a minute."

"I'd love a coffee, I really am ready for one. I'll keep an eye on Nina. I left you until the last anyway although I do have to get back before the rush hour. I want to develop this little lot so we can start our selection."

Judy met his keen gaze and despite her good intentions, she was flattered. She had little experience with men of her own age but she recognised the open admiration in his eyes. She retreated to the kitchen, a little hot under the collar of her crisp white blouse and gave herself a talking to.

Come on, come on. Didn't you learn your lesson last week with George Turner. No young man is going to be interested in a girl who already has a child.

They sat in the sunshine drinking coffee and watching Nina, who brought a succession of items for Tom's examination. He oohed and aahed in the appropriate places and encouraged Nina to talk to him.

"How is it that you're so good with children? Have you any of your own?"

Tom was aware that she was doing a little gentle fishing.

"Good heavens, no. I'm footloose and fancy free, up to now. I've a name and a proper living to make before I think of settling down but I'm used to kids. I'm the eldest of five and one of my sisters has a couple so I'm sort of used to having them underfoot.

Thanks for the coffee. I'd better be on my way. Don't worry, I'll see myself out. 'Bye Nina."

He waved at Nina, who waved back and Judy rose, insisting on seeing him to the front door. He lingered for just a moment.

"I'll be seeing you outside the Town Hall the week after next, I hope."

"Of course, don't worry, I'll be there."

She watched as he walked the few steps to the front gate where he turned and lifted his hand. She smiled back and closed the front door. He really was very nice.

Chapter 15

The weekend passed quickly and by Monday, everybody had fallen back into their routines, going about their daily round, which now included carrying copies of the petition and picking up signatures wherever they could.

On Tuesday afternoon, Nina was upstairs taking a nap and Judy was making the most of the peace and quiet, trying to catch up with the ironing. The continued good weather was a blessing but it certainly increased the amount of washing and ironing that piled up as Nina's play in the park and in the garden invariably led to a couple of changes of clothing a day.

A knock on the front door interrupted her spinning thoughts, a memory of that lick of hair and green eyes making its presence felt despite her efforts to dismiss it.

She opened the door to see Mr Freeman standing on the step. His face was grey and his eyes haunted and red rimmed, his usually immaculate clothing a little dishevelled.

"Mr Freeman, what on earth's the matter? Do come in."

He stood in the small sitting room, shaking his head and visibly trying to pull himself together. Judy gently pressed him into a seat.

"Take your time, Mr Freeman."

He gulped.

"Mrs Freeman, Christine, that is, passed away yesterday morning. She's been fading for a couple of days but I hadn't expected this, not so soon, and when I went in with a cup of tea, she'd gone."

"Oh you poor man, how awful for you."

"I 'phoned the doctor and started the arrangements. I can't get hold of John. I never can when I want him," he said bitterly.

Judy sat beside him, her compassion overcoming her shyness and took his hand.

"Then I thought of you and Nina arriving at the house as arranged and walking into all that. I know you're not on the 'phone so I decided to get out of the house for an hour, clear my head and come down and let you know."

Judy sat and listened while he talked, his emotions were far from under control as the story of his wife's illness spilled out. He was bitterly disappointed with John and didn't know how he'd manage without Christine. Even ill as she was, she had been there. Gradually, he became calmer.

"There's one thing I'm grateful for. That she was able to see Nina before the end. John has never confided in us much and told the story of your separation in a way that reflected the least discredit on him. You know, you always want to think the best of your children so we went along with it. It was only when he was obviously so reluctant to disclose your whereabouts that we became suspicious.

We always thought he was making regular financial contributions for Nina but Christine was beginning to believe otherwise. The thought that her grandchild might be in need weighed heavily on her mind. When we saw you both last week, we realised we need have no fear about her welfare but could see that money was probably pretty tight."

"We manage, Mr Freeman. We don't go anything short," said Judy quietly.

"It should be better than just managing. That child is my grandchild and Christine's too. Despite the way we've behaved in the past, I want to assure you that things will be different in the future. I know the divorce is going through, I managed to get that much out of John and, believe me, I'll make sure that he makes an appropriate contribution to your little household in the future. I'm not above holding his inheritance over his head if he lets me and his mother down in this. I could easily take this over but it's time that young man faced his responsibilities instead of constantly running away. He couldn't bear to see his mother ill and so he didn't come, even though he knew it meant the world to her. He put his interests before hers, even at the end."

Judy felt no satisfaction that John had at last shown himself to his parents in his true colours, only a great sadness that Christine Freeman had received no comfort from her only child and that the man sitting here now felt so obviously alone and isolated.

"Staying power was never John's strong point," she murmured.

"You're right of course. Christine wanted a child so badly and waited so long, going through tests and then surgery, that when he was finally born, she was over the moon. She could deny him nothing, always took his side and made allowances for him, like most mothers, I suppose. I never stepped in and I blame myself, really, for not being firmer with him. But I didn't have it in my heart to go against his mother's wishes and in the end, we both paid the price for our indulgence.

She's gone now and I just don't know how I'll manage without her. The house feels so empty, like a shell, I don't know how I can carry on."

His body was racked with sobs and he'd buried his face in a large white handkerchief. She patted him on the shoulder and went into the kitchen to give him a chance to regain control, her eyes also brimming with tears. She heard the sobs subside and went back to stand beside him.

"I'm so sorry, my dear. Whatever will you think of me?"

"I think I'm looking at a man who loved his wife a great deal and has suffered a great loss."

"Bless you."

He wiped his face and stuffed the hankie back into his trouser pocket.

"When is the funeral?"

"Saturday morning but I truly don't expect you to come. I expect John will be there with his new girl friend and there's no need for you to go through that. It will be bad enough as it is. The main thing is that I've managed to stop you turning up at the house without knowing."

Judy was only too glad not to have to make the journey out to Southern Cemetery. There were only unhappy memories for her there.

"Thank you for that. I'm amazed you could even think of us with everything else that's going on."

Mr Freeman rose to his feet and put out his hand. Judy offered her hand and found it warmly clasped in both of his.

"Would it be all right if I came to see you and Nina again? I don't want to lose touch now. I know how much it would have meant to Christine."

"Of course you must keep in touch. After all, you're Nina's granddad aren't you?"

Mr Freeman managed a watery smile.

"That's true. Give me a couple of weeks to straighten our affairs out and I'll be in touch. There are a few things I want to discuss with you but nothing urgent, nothing that can't wait."

He walked towards the front door, with Judy following. He took his leave and leaned forward and kissed her gently on the cheek.

"Thank you, my dear. Thank you for your kindness. You'll never know what it meant to us."

***

On Friday morning, the papers arrived at the Town Hall and were sent up to the legal department. Chaos ensued. The chairman of the planning department was in deep consultation with the council solicitor. Action was obviously needed.

"Call a meeting for Wednesday of next week. No apologies will be accepted, I want full attendance and full reports. This can't get any worse."

Had he known what was to happen starting Monday, an uneasy weekend would have been made much worse.

***

On Saturday afternoon, all the neighbours were gathered in the street. The evening edition of the 'News' appeared in the shops about four o'clock and Mikey had been despatched to get half a dozen copies.

William and Mikey had spent the morning knocking up placards. As always, William wanted a 'proper job' and had toyed with several alternatives for materials. He'd finally decided to make them of thin plywood to keep the weight down, nailed on to a narrow timber support. Mikey had been given the job of rubbing down the handles to avoid splinters. He could put his hand to many tasks, if properly supervised. All that remained was the lettering. Margaret, having the neatest handwriting had been elected to pencil in the wording and William was to paint their message in bold letters. They had plumped for a simple message and were all keyed up with their efforts.

Even Mrs Goldman was at her gate, looking down the street, searching for Mikey.

"He comes," yelped Mr Goldman. "Here he is."

They could see Mikey galloping towards them, newspapers under his arm.

"Come on lad, let's have a look while you get your breath back," said William, relieving Mikey of his burden and passing a paper to each of them.

The papers were unfolded to reveal the banner headline;

204

"LOCAL HOUSEHOLDERS TAKE ON TOWN HALL"

And there they were, on the front page. A photograph of the whole terrace followed the headline, each of them standing at their front gate.

The story was briefly but succinctly told, outlining their efforts and the Town Hall decision but leaning heavily on phrases like, 'David and Goliath' and 'Might versus Right.'

The article closed with the words;

'No Town Hall representative was available for comment. Further photos on page 4.'

Mr and Mrs Goldman and Mikey were still struggling with the front page and Judy, William and Margaret were rattling the pages in a race to get to page 4.

"Wow," shouted Judy. "Just look at that."

In the right hand top corner of the page was a bordered box bearing the legend:

'Today's total
513 signatures'

There was a picture of a derelict house, a long shot of a street with half the houses boarded up and one of a furniture van being loaded and a woman in tears with two small children hanging on her skirts, with the caption:

"We don't want to go. I've lived in this house all my life."
The editorial continued:

'This is the story of a community being torn up by its roots. Progress is inevitable and many of these houses are in a poor state of repair. The authorities have, however, a responsibility to re-house these tenants in a sympathetic manner.

Many families welcome the new housing, with its extra space, indoor plumbing, bathrooms and gardens. There are many others who see this as the end of a way of life, breaking close family and community ties.

Most families will have to stretch already limited budgets to cover the travelling expenses involved in reaching the city centre and adding over an hour to each working day in travelling time.

Let us not forget, the rent revenue from these tenants will accrue to the Council for many years to come, not only now, but from future generations.

Hardly surprising then, that Mr William Whitehead and his tenants are vigorously resisting moves to demolish their homes. The whole terrace is in a superb state of repair and, what is more, is at the extreme edge of the demolition area.

Sources have revealed that initial plans for re-development of the site have been shelved indefinitely. No further funds are available due to the extraordinary expenditure involved in the new housing estate in Wythenshawe which is already running many thousands of pounds over budget.

Let them stay. It is certainly not in the public interest to subject these people to this kind of tyranny. It's bureaucracy gone mad.'

Mikey was ecstatic and shaking with excitement.

"Look at that, we're all in the paper. We'll be famous."

The impact of the inside pictures and editorial had passed completely over his head, his interest was only in the picture on the front page.

The Goldmans looked bemused.

"It certainly look very good. I think me and Luisa need to sit in quiet and read again but is very, very good."

William was grinning from ear to ear.

"They've done us proud. It's everything I could have hoped for."

Margaret and Judy hugged each other and pulled Mikey in to link arms and William watched indulgently while they waltzed around.

"Steady on now. We've still got a long way to go before we can celebrate. Let's not start counting chickens,' laughed William, amused at their antics. 'They'll have got the papers yesterday, I wonder how that went down."

"I would guess," responded Margaret tartly, "that the cat is now well and truly among the pigeons. I'll bet they're running around like headless chickens."

"Let's hope so, they need shaking up."

***

When Judy bumped into him on Sunday morning, he still looked chipper and confident.

"I had a 'phone call yesterday afternoon from the History Department at the University. They want to come along and have a look at the houses this afternoon. Later in the evening, somebody from the Museum 'phoned, said he'd been trying to get hold of me for a couple of days and he's coming today too. I must say, I'm impressed that they're all willing to give up an hour of their Sunday afternoon."

"That's wonderful. Does Margaret know?"

"I dropped in to tell her the news last night. She did seem pleased," he said, perhaps a little too casually. 'I'll mention it to Mikey and the Goldmans later on. I want to be sure they'll be in this afternoon in case these bods want to have a look at all the houses.'

Judy wondered if there could, perhaps, be a little romance in the air

"Hello, Nina, where are you off to?" he said to deflect the enquiring look in Judy's eyes.

"Park, come on Mummy," said Nina, tugging at Judy's hand. "Let's go now."

"She certainly knows her own mind," laughed William. "It's no bad thing in a lass."

"Yes, we'd better get off now anyway. We're meeting Mikey in half an hour and he's promised to push Nina on the swings. We'll be back by twelve."

"We all know the rota for the Town Hall, so I'll see you tomorrow."

Judy walked off towards the park, holding Nina's hand tightly, head bent to catch her chatter.

"Well I never," she thought to herself.

The visits from the University and the Museum went off smoothly enough. Many questions were asked, the houses evaluated in relation to the rest of the area and the actual houses examined in terms of their structure and whether they were representative of housing built for industrial workers.

Only Mr Hamilton from the university said he'd like to look at the other houses besides William's and he spent a few minutes in each, casting his keen eye over the state of repair, the decoration and furnishings and talking sympathetically with the occupants. They'd been impressed by the houses and by William and had promised their support. They would both write to the planning committee on Monday to register their objections to the demolition.

William caught Margaret on her way to evening service.

"They seemed quite impressed but we'll have to wait and see what comes of it."

"That's good, let's hope they can help," said Margaret. "I must dash now or I'll be late for church."

Inexplicably, she felt a little shy and touched the brim of her hat. For the first time, she seemed aware of the admiration in William's eyes and although she was flattered, she couldn't quite meet his steady gaze so she waved and set off down the street.

William stood with his hands in his pockets and watched until she was out of sight.

***

Monday was grey and threatening and they all prayed the rain would keep off.

Nina had been safely delivered to Mrs Goldman's care and the boards packed into the car. Judy and William were to take the first shift outside the Town Hall, intending to stay from around eleven thirty until about three when Mikey would come straight from work and relieve Judy.

William looked around the square, there were quite a few people walking through. Prince Albert's statue proudly faced the Town Hall and he wondered again why they'd chosen to put him here and Queen Victoria in Piccadilly. He supposed it was just another example of council bungling.

"This might be a bit harder than I thought,' muttered Judy. 'I feel a bit of a fool, standing here waving a clipboard around."

"It's not going to be easy for any of us. We've just got to bite the bullet."

He stepped forward and approached a grey haired gentleman in a navy suit. Judy watched William's approach carefully and was delighted to see him put out his hand for the clipboard and firmly place his signature, the first of the day on the new page.

"And the best of luck to you," he said, tipping his hat as he walked off across Albert Square.

"Come on Judy, you go next," encouraged William and she stepped forward to speak to a tired looking woman in a rather worn coat.

"'Course I'll sign up, love. I saw your picture in the 'News' on Saturday. I think it's wonderful, what you're doing."

They got into their stride as the day went on. Quite a few people just brushed past, not bothering to stop, but many more did take the time to write down their names and addresses.

There was a hectic period around lunch time when so many people were passing they hadn't the time to stop them all.

"Just keep going, Judy. We might get the ones we miss when they pass tomorrow. Quite a lot of these people seem to work around here."

Judy turned her head and saw, with some anxiety, Mr Moody approaching the Town Hall. Before she could speak, he'd marched up to Mr Hartley and aggressively leaned in towards him.

"What kind of tomfoolery is this now, Whitehead?" he seethed.

'The same kind of tom foolery I hope will save our homes, which as far as I can see, are being demolished for no good reason. You're not even going to use the land,' William responded cuttingly.

"Well, that's as may be. You know you can't take on the Town Hall and win, don't you?" he spluttered, pompous as ever.

"Now look here, Moody,' responded William icily, 'I can do what I damn well like, without reference to you. Now I suggest that you get on about your business and leave me to see to mine."

Councillor Moody stormed off up the Town Hall steps and Judy suppressed her smile as she watched William square his shoulders, a look of deep satisfaction on his face. She said it for him.

"Well that told him."

William nodded.

"Let's get on with it and show the beggar."

They carried on for a couple of hours, signatures mounting, and around two o'clock Tom Hedley appeared, camera at the ready.

"I'll just get a few shots and we'll possibly get them into tomorrow's edition. Now you stand there, Judy, and hold the placard straight and Mr Whitehead, you hold the clipboard as though you're going to approach the next person who passes."

"That's right, look natural. Smile, Judy, come on, give us a big smile."

He moved around them, clicking away, photographing them, the Town Hall, the passers-by, people signing up, until it seemed he'd taken a whole roll of film.

"That should do it for now. I'd better be getting along," he said but still he lingered.

"How's Nina?" he asked Judy. "Still as lively as ever?"

'You can say that again. She seems to be learning something new every day and is up to all sorts.'

"I expect she keeps you pretty busy, without all this going on. I was wondering whether you'd like to go out on Sunday for a couple of hours, you and Nina," he added, casually.

Judy could feel the blood rising to her cheeks and Mr Whitehead tactfully distanced himself from them a little. There was no mistake, she did like the look of Tom Hedley and she liked his attitude. He hadn't turned a hair when Nina appeared, hadn't asked any question but just accepted her. What's more, he'd talked to her and even played with her.

Judy had no feminine wiles. She'd led a secluded life with Aunt Mary, had married her only boyfriend and had never flirted in her life. She didn't know where it came from but she looked at him and half fluttered her eyelashes. With a little smile, she asked,

"What did you have in mind?"

"If the weather stays dry, we could go up to Belle Vue, it's not so crowded now the summer's all but over and Nina would love the zoo and the amusements. When I was little they used to do the chimps' tea party and one of the keepers used to walk around holding the hand of a chimp dressed in a suit and cap."

"That's right,' added Judy. I remember riding on an elephant and feeling like a queen. I don't think they do that kind of thing anymore and Nina's too young anyway."

Judy was delighted to see he wasn't quite as self assured as she had thought and the fiasco with George Turner completely forgotten, she smiled.

"That would be great, we'd both love it"

"That's a deal then, I'll drop by here on Friday and we can make some arrangements."

Judy watched him lope across the square and when she caught William's eye, they both burst out laughing.

"He'll do," said William. "He seems sound enough and I'm sure you'll come to no harm there."

They ploughed on steadily for the rest of the afternoon and were next interrupted by the appearance of Mikey, for once too excited to whistle. He was waving a copy of the 'News' and coming quickly towards them.

"We're in again," he gabbled. "At least, Mr and Mrs Goldman are – and that box thing with the number of votes is on the front page. Here, have a look at this." He thrust the paper under William's nose.

On the front page again, the box showing the number of signatures showed a rise to just over eight hundred and below;

'Signatures are being collected outside the Town Hall – give us your support.'
Local historian states:
'Our industrial heritage is being destroyed,' see page 3 for pictures.

William quickly turned the pages and found a picture of Mr and Mrs Goldman with the caption:

These are two of the people being victimised by the Town Hall. They escaped from the Nazis during the war – is this the land of freedom they hoped they had reached?'

It wasn't all that long since the Eichman trial in Jerusalem for atrocities during the Holocaust and public awareness of the horrors of the extermination camps was still fairly high. William looked relieved.

"I was afraid it might be too sensational,' he said, "but Mr McDonald has done us proud. Margaret's turn tomorrow; let's hope he's as kind to her."

***

Mr Moody's day was ruined within two minutes of his arrival in his office. He found a memo marked *very urgent,* on his desk, summoning him to a meeting a ten o'clock on Wednesday morning and instructing him to bring all records of correspondence and a full report of the situation at Tiverton Place. He was furious, and a little scared, and shouted for his assistant to bring in all files that touched the matter. The veins in his neck were bulging and his face almost puce. The young man dropped the files on his desk and made a break for it. It wouldn't do to hang around him at the moment, he was unpredictable at the best of times.

***

On Tuesday, Margaret had sniffed a bit at what she considered a rather patronising 'cameo' but people at work continued to stop her to wish her well. The younger girls in the offices were looking at her differently now, admiring rather than disdaining and she heard one of the head typists whisper to her colleague, 'I didn't know she had it in her.'

The response to their campaign for signatures outside the Town Hall continued to grow and people were stopping voluntarily, asking to sign the petition, even to the point of waiting if a queue had formed.

Councillor Moody had passed them several times on his way into and out of the Town Hall. He didn't speak but studiously ignored them. All in all, he looked a little cowed and averted his gaze as he passed. William was glad that the shoe was on the other foot again. Moody was reverting to type.

By Wednesday, their ranks had been swelled by a bunch of students, ever eager to confront authority and have a bit of fun at the same time. Their numbers rose and fell over the course of the day as they fitted in their protest around their college hours but one or two of them were willing to give a hand collecting signatures. The rest of them were happy to stand and chant every time someone left or entered the Town Hall.

'Please save Tiverton Place – pulling down is a disgrace'

It wasn't the most elegant of slogans but it got the message across and what's more, when they were at full strength, their voices could be heard inside the hallowed corridors of the Town Hall.

***

The Chairman of the Planning Committee opened the meeting, looking extremely grim.

212

"How on earth did it come to this? Half the city is up in arms and we can't afford this kind of publicity. We need to take some swift action to contain the problem. You all know Mr Jones from the legal department. He's going to outline our position."

Mr Jones stood and shuffled his papers.

"Under section 99 of the Public Health Act 1936, compulsory purchase can be instated in regard to nuisance rendering premises unfit for habitation. Section 92 defines as 'statutory nuisance' a number of factors, one of which is that the premises are in such a state as to be prejudicial to health and unfit for human habitation.

We need to establish whether the houses in question are unfit for human habitation. Mr Moody, it's appropriate we have your report at this point."

"We don't actually have a report on the status of the houses and their condition. They were included in the compulsory purchase as they border on an area which is planned for clearance. Should certain properties not comply with the criteria that demand demolition, they can still be demolished as part of the greater plan. We couldn't leave one or two buildings standing in the middle of a clearance site, they would have to be removed to allow re-development of the whole site."

"And are these houses in the middle of the clearance site?"

"No, actually they are on the edge,"

"Are they part of the site?"

"No they're separated from the site by a street."

"As I understand it, there are now no plans to redevelop the site due to lack of funds, is that correct?"

Moody was faltering now.

"No sir, all development plans have been shelved for the foreseeable future. It would, however, make sense to clear the whole area so that when funds become available, the land is already in our possession."

"That's as may be. It doesn't help our current situation. Have you seen the 'News'? Those articles are pounding us into the ground, making us look like villains and have you seen that shower outside the Town Hall? I have some contacts and have heard a whisper that the whole story will go national within a day or two, with television and radio coverage too. We need to nip this in the bud.

In addition to that, I've had letters from the Museum and the History Department at the University objecting strenuously to the demolition of these houses which are, they say, 'an integral part of our local heritage'. Representatives both of the Museum and the History Department have satisfied themselves as to their condition. It would seem that they're better informed than you are, Mr Moody. Quite apart from the university, there's been pressure from the commercial community, several people in fairly high places are 'having a quiet word'.

Has anybody met this Whitehead fellow? What's he like?"

"As stubborn as hell, he's been in here making a fuss several times just recently and made an application for exclusion and won't take no for an answer."

"What? You mean you had a chance to play this down and you blocked him without consulting anyone else."

Moody could see which way the wind was blowing. Somebody would be blamed and it looked as though he was elected. A suitable scapegoat had already been found.

"Mr Jones, what's our legal position? What's likely to happen if the case goes to court?"

He huffed a bit, took his glasses off and put them back on, and cleared his throat.

"We don't have our own report as to the condition of the properties but I think we can assume that the letter from the History Department presents the case accurately, i.e. that the houses are in extremely good condition and that they are, in fact, fit for human habitation.

In a previous court case in Nottingham, the court made it perfectly clear that justices may decide to make a nuisance order requiring the houses be demolished or brought up to standard. However, it was pointed out by this court that, although bound to make a nuisance order, *they had considerable tolerance in deciding precisely how many of the complaints required to be remedied.* This court made it perfectly clear that justices faced with this situation *can use their common sense* and are entitled to take into account all the circumstances, and thus avoid the expenditure of public money unnecessarily."

"Where does that leave us?"

"There is no clear way to know how the court will decide. On the one hand, the houses are in a clearance area on the other hand, they are more than fit for human habitation and there are no plans to re-develop the site in the foreseeable future."

"Answer the question, man."

"There is no guarantee we could win. I'd say no better than fifty fifty, if that."

Moody had gathered himself a little.

"Surely, we can't let a single individual get the better of Manchester City Council. We have our reputation to think of."

The long suffering Chairman looked at him disdainfully,

"At the moment, our reputation is in tatters. There's a public outcry going on outside and we're being accused of bullying innocent citizens. In short, our name is mud throughout the City."

The solicitor spoke up again,

"We could approach Mr Whitehead in an effort to come to some arrangement. Test the water, see how he feels. His solicitor has advised me he'll be delivering that blasted petition at three o'clock on Monday. We could talk to him then."

"I think that's our best course. We can't retrieve the situation but we can, perhaps, limit the damage."

Moody was furious and not a little frightened to think that Whitehead had got the better of him again.

"And by the way, Mr Moody, you can leave the files here. Are they complete?"

Moody nodded, now it really would hit the fan.

"I'll look through them thoroughly myself and the legal department can check them. We need to know exactly where we stand."

***

That evening, Mikey's story appeared in the paper with a clear photograph of the house and garden. His story was sympathetically told, a young man bravely coping alone after the death of his parents. He was over the moon and was off to the 'News' office to get copies of the pictures. These would eventually be framed and hung on his sitting room wall.

The box in the paper showed an enormous increase in the number of signatures, it had been steadily climbing since the start of the week.

Judy felt a bit uncomfortable to see her picture in the 'News' on Thursday, especially as people were now recognising them in the street but she just put her head down on got on with it. Apart from a few ill wishers, the great majority of people she spoke to were only too glad to give their support. A short version of the story had appeared on the inside pages of two national newspapers but it was obvious that the story was going to run, maybe even get bigger by the weekend.

On Friday, the going was tough. There were more people on the streets and they were grateful for the students who helped out with the signatures. The rest of them stood and chanted. It must have been driving the folk in the Town Hall crazy.

Mikey arrived at lunch time to relieve Judy and she was able to get home early. She found a note pushed through the door. It was from Mr Freeman congratulating her on her efforts and wishing them luck. He promised to be in touch soon and sent his love to both of them. She was touched that he could think of them at such a time.

She was now beginning to feel the pressure. She was glad to collect Nina from Mrs Goldman and spent the afternoon playing with her in the garden. It was a relief to get off her feet and do something normal for a change.

The 'News' article that evening was a bit of a bombshell. Nobody had known that William had been highly decorated for bravery, he'd kept that under his hat. Great emphasis had been laid on

'local war hero fighting for his home'

As well as the current picture, someone had ransacked the archives and found a picture of William in uniform, complete with medals. That went down a storm with the neighbours and Margaret thought how handsome he'd looked in uniform when she first met him in 1942. Come to think of it, he looked pretty good even all these years later.

On Saturday, the final day, William, Margaret and Mikey were outside the Town Hall from ten thirty until the shoppers started to thin out about four o'clock. There were fewer people about on a Saturday and although they added to their total, it was a bit of an anti-climax.

The week had been hard on William. Although he was basically a fit man, standing around for several hours every day had taken its toll and he was tired. He consoled himself with the thought that it was nearly over. There was now little else he could do. The court case was set for late October and he'd be delivering the petition on Monday. After that all they could do was wait.

"We might as well pack up now, I don't think we can do any more. It's in the lap of the gods now. Tell you what, let's call it a day and go home. I think we deserve it."

***

On Sunday, after a cloudy start, the sun broke through as Tom Hedley knocked on Judy's door.

"Looks like we've got a decent day for it,' he said to Judy and bent to talk to Nina. 'What about you, young lady, are you ready to go and see the lions and tigers?"

Nina nodded, clinging to her Mum. She wasn't quite sure about him yet.

Judy had packed a picnic and she dumped this, with Nina's pushchair, into the back of Tom's car. It wasn't more than fifteen minutes' ride to the zoo and they were soon walking round the animal enclosures. Tom showed infinite patience with Nina, pointing to the animals and telling her about them as Judy watched. She hadn't been to the zoo since she was a child, the last time with her mum and dad. How long ago that seemed.

They found a patch of grass where they could eat their picnic and Nina could run round for half an hour before settling into her push chair and nodding off. Judy watched as Tom gently covered her with a thin blanket. What a difference to the reactions of George Turner at the mere mention of a child.

They sat in the autumn sunshine, idly chatting and watching families walk by, some of them squabbling, and one or two with screaming children but for the most part, just enjoying the day out in the open air.

By four o'clock, the sun had disappeared and there was a definite chill in the air so they packed up the bags and walked off back to the car park. Nina had wakened and was grizzling a bit but she soon recovered when she was back in the car on her mum's knee, watching the traffic whizz by.

They were home in fifteen minutes and Tom helped Judy into the house with the pushchair and the bags.

"I can't thank you enough, we've had a lovely time and Nina will be talking about the animals all week."

"It really was my pleasure." He took her hand in his. "I'd love to do it again sometime, I've enjoyed the day and the company and I'd like to see more of you. I don't want to push you but perhaps we could go out one night, just the two of us, if you can get a sitter."

"I'd like that, maybe we could fix something up for next weekend."

"I'll drop in towards the end of the week and we'll see how you feel then."

She stood on her doorstop and watched him get into his car and drive away, waving until he turned the corner. She did like him. She liked everything about him, the way he looked and the way he talked, easily and honestly, no airs and graces there, just a thoroughly nice chap.

***

On Monday morning, cages were being rattled all round the Town Hall. The Chairman of the Planning Committee and the solicitor had been huddled in conference since just after nine and they were mad as hornets. The Chairman was white faced with anger, livid almost to the point of speechlessness.

"Get Moody up here," he clipped out, "*now!*"

Summoned by a peremptory 'phone call, Mr Moody sat behind his desk, hands clamped over his eyes, wishing he could disappear into thin air, that the Town Hall would burn down, that the Chairman would drop dead; anything rather than face what was coming. Putting his hands flat on the desk, he pushed himself to his feet and pointed himself unwillingly down the corridor towards the lift. His feet seemed to move of their own volition, he certainly wasn't consciously putting one foot in front of the other. He decided to take the stairs, anything to put off what he guessed was coming.

Taking a deep breath and almost choking on his own saliva, he pushed open the door to the secretary's office. She looked rattled too, she'd never seen the Chairman so mad and the raised voices and the bad language escaping through his closed door had made her blush. The Chairman was such a gentleman, she hadn't supposed such words were in his vocabulary.

Things were certainly far from normal in the Town Hall, Mr Moody was ashen and his hands were shaking.

"He said you're to go straight in," she whispered. "He's waiting for you and he really is not in a good mood."

She'd always had a gift for understatement and although she'd never cared much for Mr Moody and his blustering, self important manner, she actually felt sorry for him, he looked so crumpled.

He crossed uncertainly to the door and knocked and entered. The Chairman looked at him disparagingly and gestured toward a seat. He went straight for the jugular.

"Can you tell me why the compulsory purchase order for these properties was raised almost eight months after the rest? I could kick myself for not realising there was something fishy going on. The rest of the houses are already being vacated and the tenants rehoused and yet these tenants are sitting tight."

"Well, sir, when I looked at the site and the plans again, it seemed a sensible move to clear the whole of the site from Hyde Road to Stockport Road without leaving anything standing. To give us full scope for redevelopment, you see."

His voice was shaking and he looked increasingly nervous. He could hardly admit that he'd included Tiverton Place only after he'd discovered that William Whitehead owned the whole block. It had seemed the perfect opportunity to pay him back, both for the stand-off in the mess and for the later and much more serious crime of having a hand in his demotion. That had really stung and he'd sworn to 'get him' no matter how long it took. What he had thought his masterstroke had now backfired and bitten him on the bum.

"Why weren't the properties included in the original compulsory purchase orders then?"

"They seem to have been overlooked, sir, I'll have to check with the clerks and see what happened. Someone's head will roll."

"Yes, it will! That's all for now Moody. You can go back to your office and start your 'investigation'".

He'd been dismissed and although he couldn't get out fast enough, he knew that the matter was far from over. Better get back to the office and look for somewhere to lay the blame.

The Chairman turned to the solicitor, grimacing in distaste.

"I'll deal with him later. He's got us into this mess but there's no way he can get us out. What do we do now?"

"We can still go with the compulsory purchase, we can present a case for this when we go to court but it all looks pretty unsavoury, particularly in view of the public outcry and the publicity that's been generated and it does seem that there is something not quite above board going on."

"Go on."

"My suggestion would be to finish this off as quickly as possible. Get it out of the way. The sooner it's sorted out, the sooner the dust will settle. Whitehead's coming in today to present his petition, let's make him an offer."

"What kind of an offer?"

"We'll rescind the compulsory purchase order, offer to pay his legal costs so far and perhaps make nominal compensation, apologise, and then apologise again. In short, grovel. He does seem a reasonable type and to be honest, I do have a sneaking sympathy with him."

"Much as it hurts to say so, I think you're right. Let's work out what we can offer him. He's due at three. Meet him on the Town Hall steps and ask him in for a quick discussion. Let's see if we can't wind this up today. It will all die down quickly enough and we could turn ourselves into 'reasonable' people, sympathetic to the needs of the public. Bring him up to my office, I'll get Barbara to lay on tea and cakes, soften him up and put our case to him.

We'll do what we can to make this go away. My guess is that he'll be spot on time so be ready for him. Nab him and bring him straight up here. The press will probably have been alerted and we don't want to give him time to make a statement. With a bit of luck, he'll be able to make a statement on his way out and we'll be turned into heroes instead of villains."

They called for tea, lit up again in the already smoke wreathed room, and set about calculating just what they could offer, that is to say, what they could get away with. After all, it was public money they were considering giving away.

Chapter 16

William had pottered all morning, unable to settle properly to any particular job. It was unlike him and he had to admit he was unsettled. Instead of feeling elated that they were now in the home straight, he felt jittery and although there could be no comparison, the last time he'd felt this way had been waiting to go into action. Ridiculous, he dismissed the thought, this was just another trip to the Town Hall.

By half past two he was dressed in his smartest, shoes buffed to a military shine, and was backing the car out of the garage. It was no more than fifteen minutes drive into town, even at rush hour and he had plenty of time to park and get across to the Town Hall.

The students, bless their hearts, were out again in force. They knew this would be their last chance to take on the establishment, make some noise and generally make a legitimate nuisance of themselves.

Tom Hedley was in Albert Square, perched casually on the steps of the Albert Memorial and he greeted William.

"Charlie's not here yet but I'm expecting him any minute. He'll want to have a word when you come out, get your views on their reaction to the petition and put together some kind of a statement."

"That's fine, I'll see you later."

"I'll just get a couple of shots of you on the steps, holding the petition. We never know what we'll have space for but we might be lucky, the story's been so well received."

William posed stiffly on the steps, the publicity really was getting to him. He'd be glad when that was over, they'd been in the limelight far too long. After today there'd be a bit of a lull, time to recoup, but no doubt it would all start up again when the court case started.

Mr Jones, the solicitor, was waiting for him just inside the main doors.

"Ah, there you are Mr Whitehead, complete with petition, I see. The Chairman would like a word, if you can spare half an hour."

"Of course, I'll be glad to take the time."

William was a little wary, he knew he'd been ambushed and although caught unawares, was quick to see there may be some advantage here. They climbed the stairs to the first floor and into the

Chairman's office. There was nobody in the outer office and they went straight through.

This was a far cry from George Turner's little cubby hole. The arched windows overlooked the square and even the panelled walls waited with bated breath.

The Chairman rose to his feet and came from behind his desk, hand outstretched.

"Good afternoon, Mr Whitehead, I'm glad you could spare us the time. Please take a seat."

William placed the petition on the desk and sat, waiting, giving nothing away. A knock on the door and in came a very smart secretary, holding a tray with a china tea set and a plate of very expensive biscuits.

"Leave it there Miss Jones. That'll be all, no calls and no interruptions until we've finished here."

William still sat, waiting. The ball was in their court and he'd let them play their hand but he knew, of course, that in some way, they'd been caught wrong footed and were trying to soften him up.

"Mr Whitehead, I won't beat around the bush, I'll come straight to the point. We're rescinding the compulsory purchase order as of today. You'll get confirmation in the post."

Although William was 'gobsmacked', he kept his face straight. This was no time to grovel in gratitude, there was probably something else to be gained.

"That's good news."

He waited again, he knew the value of a silence, of making the other person speak first.

"We're also prepared to pay your legal costs up to the present time. Ask your solicitor to send his final bill to me here and I'll have it passed for payment immediately."

"That's good news too."

He didn't ask for clarification, didn't show any emotion, just continued to wait, poker faced.

"It may be possible for us to make an ex gratia payment as compensation for the distress and inconvenience you've suffered."

At last, William spoke, now he needed information.

"I'd be interested to hear why you've taken this sudden about-face. Has there been some irregularity?"

The Chairman flushed and picked up his teacup, playing for time, wondering how to handle this. This Whitehead character was a cool customer. He'd half expected him to throw his hat in the air with joy when he heard the news and that would have been the end of that. No such luck, he'd been outmanoeuvred. He decided to take a chance.

'May I speak frankly and in confidence?'

"Of course, I wish you would."

"There has been some irregularity. Apparently, the purchase order for your properties was made eight months after the order on the rest of the site. It's been difficult to establish how this happened and we're still investigating. However, it makes the whole scenario look suspect and in view of the publicity and the bad feeling among the general public, we don't want to have the added fuel of a court case."

"If we're speaking frankly and in confidence, I think you already know that these events were set in progress by your planning office. I'm not naming any names but I've crossed swords with someone down there on more than one occasion and come off best. I wouldn't be surprised to find an element of revenge in all this."

"My God, I had no idea. I thought it was just incompetence."

Now he was really rattled and looked across at the solicitor who looked studiously at the floor.

"Imagine what the press would do with this. Mr Whitehead, what can we do to make this go away?"

"You mentioned compensation."

"How does three hundred pounds sound?"

"Five hundred sounds better. There'd be a hundred for everybody who's been through the mill and I think you'll agree, it's little enough for hush money. Additionally, I don't wish to pursue personal revenge, but I do think that the ethics of the Town Hall should be above such underhand dealings. Closer checks need to be kept on these planning matters. Who knows what else has gone on? Most people just buckle, thinking they can't possibly take on the authorities and win."

"Five hundred it is. This conversation has taken place in the strictest confidence and I can see you're a man of your word and this will go no farther."

"You have my assurance of that."

"In return, I can assure you that the planning department will be subjected to the severest investigation and, if necessary, clear out. Every single case will be gone over with a fine tooth comb. No public authority can allow individuals to make decisions which endanger the rights of the public."

There was nothing further to be gained and William rose to his feet. The Chairman also rose and put out his hand, yet again.

"I can't say this was a pleasure but I am pleased to have met you. You can get on with your life and we can all put this behind us. Goodbye, Mr Whitehead, you'll be hearing from us."

"Goodbye. I'll look forward to that. I'll find my own way out" and William made a dignified exit.

They may have been surprised if they'd seen him doing samba steps along the corridor and skipping down the curved grand staircase.

His first thought that he must tell Margaret.

The students were still outside, raising hell, chanting and waving placards in the air. William raised his hands for silence and eventually, the noise subsided.

"The compulsory purchase order has been removed. We can keep our homes."

A great roar erupted which echoed through the Town Hall and then a clamour of questions.

"What happened? What did they say? 'Well done.' 'What a beauty."

"I'll be making a statement to the press but in the meantime, I want to thank you all for your support. We couldn't have done it without you. Now I think it's time for us all to go home. Thank you again, all of you."

He showed no sign of saying anything else and crossed the square to speak to Charlie McDonald. He'd seen Tom Hedley clicking away at him and the crowd but he'd now disappeared. The crowd, a bit let down now it was all over, was beginning to disperse.

"I didn't expect that," said Charlie laconically.

"Let's just say that they saw the light and reconsidered their decision. I'm not at liberty to say any more."

"Fair enough, I won't push you although I know there's more to it than that. I need to 'phone my editor, it will take about ten minutes and then why don't I buy you a pint?"

"Where will we get a pint at this time, the pubs closed half an hour ago."

"Newspaper men always know where to get a drink. Let's go."

He led the way to an unobtrusive door in one of the side streets off the square, knocked, and identified himself. They went in, down the steps and into a long, narrow bar, buzzing with conversation and dense with cigarette smoke. The barman obviously knew him and nodded.

"What'll it be, William."

"I think a scotch might be in order."

"Right, two large ones, Alec, I'll be right back" and he disappeared to make his 'phone call.

A couple of drinks later and William had had enough. He was still euphoric but had had enough of the smoky bar.

"Where's that 'phone you used. I need to make a quick call."

Charlie nodded towards the back of the club and William checked for change and went into the booth. He got through straight away.

"Mr Robinson's office."

"Margaret, it's William. I've got some news. Can you meet me after work?"

"Yes, of course. Is everything all right?"

"Yes, there's nothing to worry about. I'll tell you later. Can you meet me at that Italian place we went to before, about six o'clock?"

He obviously wasn't going to tell her anything over the 'phone.

"OK, I'll meet you there at six. Bye now."

Margaret was intrigued but put it out of her mind. She'd her work to finish, especially if she wanted to get away on time.

In the meantime, William had gone home. A quick cup of tea and a snooze in the armchair soon put him right. Although he had a good head for drink, a couple of doubles that early in the day didn't altogether suit him. He didn't want to be driving again today, he definitely intended to have another couple of drinks tonight so he washed his hands and face, changed his shirt and went off to the bus stop at the end of the road.

The buses coming out of town were crammed to the platforms but going into town, were almost empty. He was in no hurry and took his time walking through Piccadilly in the evening sunshine and down to Luigi's.

When Margaret arrived, he already had a glass of wine in front of him. He rose to his feet and went to meet her. He looked at her, although she looked anxious, she looked lovely.

"We've won. They've dropped everything and withdrawn the compulsory purchase order."

At first, his words didn't sink in and then he saw the light of understanding in her eyes. She gasped and threw her arms around him.

"How wonderful, how absolutely wonderful."

Happy as he was to have her arms around him, and he couldn't deny that it gave him a great deal of pleasure, they were in a public place and were a bit conspicuous even though there was no one else in the restaurant apart from the staff.

"Let's sit down," he whispered in her ear. She smelt marvellous.

She now looked a bit embarrassed and although she waited for William to pull out her chair, she was glad to be seated and presenting a lower profile. She'd seen one of the waiters smiling, whatever would he think? Could it really be all over?

He gave her a very edited version of what had happened in the Town Hall, as he'd promised, and she hung on his every word. They managed to eat a meal and finished the bottle of wine while he filled her in on the details.

"Does anyone else know yet, Judy and the others?"

"No, I felt I wanted to tell you first. I'll tell you what, it's only half past seven. I suggest we have one last drink, a nice little liqueur for you, I know just the thing, and a brandy for me and we'll have a pot of coffee. Then I'll get someone to call us a taxi and we'll go home and call an emergency meeting. I can't wait to see their faces."

They raised their glasses in a toast,

"To the future," they said almost in unison.

Margaret knocked on Judy's door. It was only nine o'clock but still late for a social call. Judy cautiously opened the door and looked at her enquiringly.

"Judy, there's some news. Would it be all right if I asked everyone round."

"Of course, what's it all about."

Margaret nodded to William who was waiting at the end of the path and he went along knocking on doors and asking people round to Judy's.

226

"Just wait a few minutes, until we're all here. William wants to tell you something."

Margaret's eyes were shining, her hair a little mussed but she looked so happy, what could have happened?

The neighbours all came piling through Judy's front door. Mikey looked worried and Mrs Goldman was wringing her hands while Judy waited calmly, she had a gut feeling that this was good news. They all started talking at once, asking questions, looking anxiously at William.

"If we're all settled, I have some news for you, good news. The compulsory purchase order has been withdrawn, our homes are safe."

For a moment, nobody spoke and then the questions burst out again. William answered them one at a time until they were all reassured that it was true, their homes were safe.

"There's more,' he said. 'The Town Hall have agreed to pay all our legal expenses, so no one need to worry about that."

"I don't know for sure I get it all right but I guess they should pay for the worry they cause us. Seems fair to me," spluttered Mr Goldman.

Mrs Goldman was weeping quietly with relief.

"*And* they've agreed some compensation. It could be a little while until I get the cheque but they've offered me five hundred pounds. That would a hundred each."

"Just a minute,' interrupted Margaret. 'Surely that's *your* compensation not ours. After all, you own the houses."

"That's as may be but I doubt we would have got this result if each and every one of you hadn't thrown in your lot with me, put in the time and effort, and given me your support. I want to share my good fortune with my friends. Surely, there's nobody here who couldn't make good use of a hundred pounds."

A hundred pounds was a fortune to all of them. They looked at each other, smiles lighting their faces.

"I have another suggestion. Let's have a party, Saturday night. What do you think? Judy, I know it's a lot to ask but I don't want you to miss it. Any chance we could have it here? There'd only be the six of us and I thought I'd ask Charlie McDonald if he could spare us half an hour and that young photographer and maybe a couple of other people who've been particularly helpful."

Judy smiled and nodded.

"Of course, I'd love it and if Nina wakes up, for once I'll bring her down and let her join us. What do I need to get."

"I'll pay for everything as my thanks to you all, now what do we need."

They set to making plans, who'd drink what, how much they should buy, what about food, everybody volunteering for something, getting themselves organised for a 'blow out.'

The meeting finally broke up, people going along to their own houses, shouting cheery goodnights to their neighbours.

William stood with Margaret at the end of her path, watching the front doors close. He took her hand gently.

"That was terrific. I felt like the conquering hero. I'm only just realising what this means to us."

"William, you *are* the conquering hero. I don't know and don't want to know what went on today in the Town Hall but I do know that there's more than you're letting on. I suspect you ran rings round them. Well that can be your secret, but I'm proud of you."

She leaned across and kissed him gently on the cheek before starting smartly up to her front door.

He watched as she turned the key in the lock and went in and muttered a quiet, 'bless you, Margaret,' under his breath.

***

On Saturday, the row was buzzing with excitement, lots of coming and going, William ferrying Margaret and Mikey back and forwards to the shops, Judy giving her house a last minute 'wash and brush up' and Mrs Goldman in her kitchen, baking pies and strudels.

At last seven o'clock came and Judy was on pins. William had brought down his decorating table, which was now set up in Judy's kitchen, covered with a fancy cloth and loaded down with food, while drinks and glasses were laid out on the kitchen table. Margaret had brought her record player and that was set up on the sideboard with a stack of records and Judy decided to put a record on while she waited.

The music had just started with the first knock of the door. Of course it had to be Mikey. His hair was slicked back and his face shone as if it had been scrubbed and polished and his wide smile almost cracked his face in half.

Then came the Goldman's, bearing a bunch of flowers for Judy, immediately followed by Margaret, looking lovely in a

228

matching blouse and skirt, hair down and a beaming smile that echoed Mikey's. William arrived a few minutes later and there was a bottle neck in the kitchen while William, who'd appointed himself bartender, rushed to get everybody a drink.

Although they were all so happy, standing together and chatting about their good luck, the party atmosphere hadn't yet swung into motion, it needed a push to get it going. William found a record of 'sing-along' songs in the pile and they were soon singing their heads off, swaying in time to the music and lifting their glasses.

A knock at the door brought in Tom Hedley and Charlie McDonald and they, too, soon had glasses in their hands, Charlie leaning against the wall and Tom perched on the arm of Judy's chair. The final arrival was Nina's granddad, who Judy had invited at the last minute. He still looked pale and had lost weight but he had a smile on his face and two bottles of champagne, "for toasts, later."

Tom, with a quick, "may I?" rummaged through the pile of records and found some dance music, Ted Heath and Dickie Valentine. It was a bit behind the times but it would do. He put the record on and stood, clicking his fingers.

William looked at Margaret,

"What do you reckon? Think we can still do it?"

"Of course we can," she responded rising to her feet and putting out her hand.

The style was a little different than the current jive but after a couple of false starts, they picked up each other's rhythms. Margaret was soon spinning around the floor, her outstretched hand being caught by William, only to be spun off again in another turn and then caught again, William's arm around her waist whilst they moved around the front room. Their steps matched perfectly, they might have been dancing together for years. Judy looked across at Tom, who would have thought these two had it in them, prim and proper Miss Hartley and the very formal Mr Whitehead but could they move? A burst of applause saluted their efforts although they were both puffing a bit.

The record changed and Mr and Mrs Goldman got up and started to dance. It looked a bit like a quick step with faster footwork but they held each other differently, elbows tucked in, and the turns were tighter, very accomplished and very, very European. Tom gestured to Judy,

"Want to have a go?"

229

She coloured up. "I haven't danced since I was at school. I have never had time to learn properly."

"Come on girl, it's like riding a bike and I'll soon have you jiving, I'm a terrific teacher, did I ever tell you that?"

Mikey had momentarily disappeared and he came back with Nina in his arms. He'd heard her yelling above the sound of the music and brought her downstairs. She was now happily jigging away in Mikey's arms, hanging on while he dipped and whirled. Charlie McDonald and Mr Freeman stood in a corner, drinking scotch and watching the others dance.

"It all turned out well in the end then. I'm so glad they won their fight. They still have a fair amount of disruption to get through but I think they'll be all right now. A lot of this is down to your efforts with the paper, I'm sure."

"Without their co-operation and their fight, it would never have taken off the way it did. In the end, it looked as though the petition had been for nothing as the Town Hall had already decided to buckle. All the goings on in Albert Square and the publicity highlighting the petition had a big part in the final result."

"I'd love to know what happened in the Town Hall on Monday but William is close mouthed about it so I guess we'll never know but he's a man it wouldn't pay to underestimate."

Nina had been brought a drink and was now on her granddad's knee while Mikey danced with Judy and Tom danced with Margaret and William had actually persuaded Mrs Goldman up for a dance. Everyone was having a great time and the party was in full swing. They had no need to worry about the neighbours, they were all there.

At ten o'clock, William gave Mikey the nod into the kitchen.

'I think there'll enough glasses. Put them on a tray and hand them out and I'll get this champagne open. It's a while since I popped a bottle but no doubt I'll manage.'

Mikey circulated with fresh glasses and Tom turned off the music. William came in with the champagne wrapped in a tea towel. He popped the cork with the minimum of spillage and circulated until everyone's glass was charged.

He tapped his glass for silence and everyone stopped talking and looked towards him.

"I'm not going to make a speech, as such. I just want to thank you all for everything you've contributed. We would never have got here without everybody's efforts so thank you again. Now let's have a toast, *to Tiverton Place"* and he raised his glass.

"Tiverton Place" they echoed and lifted their glasses and drank. The women all looked a bit weepy but the men too, all of them, looked a little damp around the eyes.

"Three cheers for Uncle William," chirped up Mikey, "hip, hip hurray."

"Hip, hip hurray," shouted everyone, including Nina.

"Right, that's enough of that. Let's get on with the party!"

William stood in contemplative mood, glass in hand, looking at his friends. Although they had come so close to losing their homes, they had all gained something from the experience.

Mikey had been so proud to be a part of this, his self esteem had risen and he'd decided to spend some of the coming money on a week on the Costa Brava with some friends from work.

He had no doubt that a large part of the money coming to the Goldmans would find its way to help young people making a new life in Israel but the real revelation was change that had been wrought in Mrs Goldman. She was out from behind those lace curtains at last.

Margaret had come to life again, the prim spinster had to some extent turned back the clock and he could see the slim, vivacious girl he had known so long ago. Her cash was to go in the bank until she made her mind up but she and Judy were talking about a trip across the channel for a week on a French beach.

Judy had blossomed from the quiet little mouse he'd met just those few short months ago into a self assured young woman, ready to grasp life with both hands. She'd always put Nina first but had come to realise that it was her life too and she should make the most of it.

He watched Tom dancing with Judy, Nina held between them. He seemed like a nice chap – maybe something would come of it. He'd accepted Nina with open arms and that was a sure way into Judy's affections.

Margaret caught his eye and as she smiled warmly, his hopes rose. After all these years, could there a future for them too? He felt a flicker of desire and thought,

I can wait. I've waited this long but she's looking at me differently now, as though she really sees me – and likes what she sees. I can build on that but I'll have to give her time.

He'd learned something else too. He'd been jolted out of complacency and forced into action again and although he recognised he'd had moments of despair, it had felt good to be actively involved in planning and carrying through strategies. He realised that this was just a quick stop along the way, they all still had to carry on living and get through whatever joys and sorrows that may bring but just at this moment, life felt good with a great achievement under their respective belts.

"That's enough of that,' he muttered and called across the room, 'Come on Margaret, let's show them how it's done! This is a party, isn't it?"

***

Within a matter of months, the rest of the property across the site had been demolished, the streets eradicated, grass had been laid and trees planted. The houses now looked across an open aspect to the road beyond. Locals had taken to calling them 'the houses on the Green.'

THE END